W9-BCU-772

THE STRATFORD-UPON-AVON LIBRARY 3

★

General Editors
JOHN RUSSELL BROWN
& BERNARD HARRIS

THE STRATFORD-UPON-AVON LIBRARY 3

★

ELIZABETHAN NARRATIVE VERSE

edited by
NIGEL ALEXANDER

HARVARD UNIVERSITY PRESS
Cambridge, Massachusetts
1968

First published 1968

First published in
the United States of America in 1968

First published in Great Britain by
Edward Arnold (Publishers) Ltd

Printed in Great Britain by
Butler & Tanner Ltd, Frome and London

General Preface

THIS Library has been formed for the student, teacher, and general reader who is interested in Elizabethan and Jacobean life and literature. It does not provide further editions of Shakespeare's Works, or *The Faerie Queene*, or Jonson's *Works*, nor will it duplicate readily available editions of any poet or dramatist. We hope to reprint what is generally unavailable outside the great libraries and microfilm and photostat collections.

Already published in the Stratford Library are a selected works of Nashe (providing more than half his total writings and including four works in their entirety), and *The Elizabethans' America* (reprinting letters, reports and pamphlets about the New World). These are now joined by selected non-dramatic works of Dekker, including the first full version of *Lantern and Candlelight* and *Pound Wise and Penny Foolish*, and by this volume of *Elizabethan Narrative Verse*.

The next volume to appear in the Library will be devoted to material illustrating Elizabethan and Jacobean concern with witchcraft, a selection of critical writings on Elizabethan rhetoric, and a volume of selected sermons by the Cambridge Platonists.

The texts are presented in modernized form. Editors have been asked to reparagraph, repunctuate, substitute italic type for roman, or *vice versa*, wherever they consider that such changes will avoid unnecessary confusions or obscurities. Modernization of spelling is sometimes difficult because of our slender knowledge of the spelling habits of authors and compositors, and our total ignorance of the many accidental decisions made during writing and printing: generally editors have retained archaic forms only where rhyme or metre requires, or where a modernized form does not give the required primary sense. *Elizabethan Narrative Verse* has been presented in accordance with these special requirements. Exceptions will sometimes be made where an author clearly distinguishes between two forms, for works surviving in autograph manuscript or for verse carefully printed from authorial manuscripts. Textual notes will define the editorial procedures for each volume. We believe that this presentation, in

v

banishing the clumsiness of original editions and hyperconservative reprints, will often reveal liveliness and sometimes an added elegance.

Editors have provided brief annotations, a glossary or a glossarial index, whichever seems appropriate, and also textual notes, collating substantive changes to the copy-text and briefly discussing its textual authority. Each volume has an introduction dealing with any topics that will enhance the reading of the texts. We have not aimed at minute consistency between each volume, or even between each item in a single volume; editors have been encouraged to present these texts in the clearest practicable manner and with due consideration of the fact that many of the works reprinted have hitherto been 'known about' rather than known, more honoured or dishonoured in scholarly works than read and enjoyed as substantial achievements and records of Shakespeare's age.

JOHN RUSSELL BROWN
BERNARD HARRIS

Contents

Acknowledgements

I AM grateful to the Bodleian Library and the British Museum for their kind permission to make use of their copies for this edition. The Oxford University Press very generously allowed me to make use of their photo-copy of the 1598 edition of Marlowe's *Hero and Leander* now in the Folger Shakespeare Library. I am grateful for Mr Horseman's courtesy at the Press. My debts to previous editors are legion and are recorded in the notes but E. S. Donno's *Elizabethan Minor Epics*, London 1963, requires a special mention. I owe a great deal to the help of the library staff at the Bodleian, British Museum, Edinburgh, Glasgow and St Andrews University Libraries. I am most grateful to my colleagues in St Andrews and Glasgow who have answered so many of my questions, particularly Dr D. Davidson, whose advice on botanical problems was invaluable, Mr T. E. Kinsey, who helped to unravel Chapman's Latin, Professor M. F. M. Meiklejohn and Professor M. L. Samuels. The general editors have been extremely patient and have provided many valuable suggestions but any errors or omissions remain my own.

I have to thank the University Court of St Andrews and the University of Glasgow for generous travel grants in the preparation of this volume.

Note on the Text

THIS edition provides a critical old spelling text with i/j, long s and u/v modernized. Accidentals of spelling and punctuation are taken from the earliest editions except that some obvious misprints have been corrected silently. In cases where authors have revised their work, as in *The Complaint of Rosamond* and *Englands Heroicall Epistles*, I have preferred to print the earliest version to permit comparison with other poems of the period.

Abbreviations

C.J.	*Classical Journal*
E.L.H.	*English Literary History*
J.E.G.P.	*Journal of English and Germanic Philology*
M.L.N.	*Modern Language Notes*
M.P.	*Modern Philology*
P.Q.	*Philological Quarterly*
R.E.S.	*Review of English Studies*
S.P.	*Studies in Philology*
T.A.Ph.A.	*Transactions of the American Philological Association*

Introduction

NARRATIVE verse is not a separate kind of poetry in its own right but a technique used by many poets for an infinite variety of effects. This technique is most closely associated with the classical epic and attempts to translate it or rival it in some modern European language. Consequently some other term, such as epyllion or minor epic,[1] is frequently used to describe narrative verse whose immediate methods are derived from Ovid rather than from Homer and Virgil. Such a term is obviously convenient but, in insisting on the exclusive nature of the Ovidian genre, it tends to obscure the fact that the Ovidian poems of Marlowe, Shakespeare, Chapman and other poets were not minor and unimportant poetic exercises but a distinctive contribution to a European movement of thought and feeling. The poets of the late sixteenth and early seventeenth century were almost all engaged, as working dramatists, translators or writers of narrative verse, in the creation of various forms of poetry and almost all use the experience they have gained in one form in their efforts to subdue another. This selection of narrative poems, from the years 1560 to 1610, is designed to emphasize that continuity of poetic effort and artistic endeavour in the age most conveniently described as 'Elizabethan'.

Spenser and Milton, in their attempts to give their country and language its own great epic poem, mark the beginning and the end of one of the most definite periods of English poetry. Within this period many poets attempted to grapple with the problem which lay behind the immense European debate about the nature and form of epic poetry. Their problem was one which: 'had beset European artists in all branches of art since the fall of Rome. They had to consider how to reconcile the strong heritage from Greece and Rome with native traditions and ... other influences.'[2] In choosing Ovid as their master the Elizabethan poets were drawing upon a tradition that was already some centuries old. Ovid had been 'Venus clerke' to Chaucer, and to others he had appeared as the stern guardian of morals. The *Metamorphoses*, in particular, was one of the great source books of classical myth and legend for the Middle Ages and the Renaissance. The myths had already been subjected to a long process of interpretation and commentary and Ovid's poetry in general was widely used for Latin instruction in schools.[3] But, in becoming the text-book of Europe, Ovid's poetry had not yet lost the power to excite the imagination. The Elizabethans knew that they were continuing a tradition but the new contributions of individual talents not only changed this tradition but had a vital effect on dramatic and epic poetry. This relationship must be stressed because the critical revolution of the seventeenth century has long prevented an effective examination of this kind of poetry.

The most melancholy prophecy that Thomas Carew could make over the grave of John Donne was that his death might mean the revival of Ovidian poetry in England. His prophecy appeared fulfilled in 1634 when a year after Carew's *Elegie upon the death of Dr John Donne*, Milton's masque of *Comus* was presented at Ludlow castle. Its lines are certainly full of the gods, goddesses and tales from the *Metamorphoses* which Carew dreaded; but Milton's work ends their influence for a time. Donne's metaphysical successors had no need of Ovid and the Augustans used his poetry for very different purposes. Their criticism helped to reinforce Carew's disparaging view of the older poetry and confirmed his adverse judgement. Carew's witty and pointed attack deserves consideration here, despite its familiarity, since his objections are the foundation of the critical arguments which have caused the neglect of this kind of poetry.

> But thou art gone, and thy strict lawes will be
> Too hard for Libertines in Poetrie.
> They will repeale the goodly exil'd traine
> Of gods and goddesses, which in thy just raigne
> Were banish'd nobler Poems, now, with these
> The silenc'd tales o'th'Metamorphoses
> Shall stuffe their lines, and swell the windy Page,
> Till Verse refin'd by thee, in this last Age
> Turne ballad rime, Or those old Idolls bee
> Ador'd againe, with new apostasie;[4]

The *Elegie* ends with a comparison between two aspects of Donne:

> Apollo's first, at last, the true God's priest.

and such a definite contrast warns the reader to take seriously the opposition between Apollo and the true God. Consequently Carew's references to libertines and idols have a double significance. The libertines refuse to obey the new laws of poetry and continue to adore the old idols. Such idols are, in one sense, false principles of poetry which are bound to have a bad effect on the metre and matter of the Libertines' verses, but they are also the graven images of pagan idolatry and it is suggested that the licence allowed by the tales of the *Metamorphoses* is not merely poetic. The new poetry of Donne is contrasted with poetry which is not only immoral and pagan but, a much more damaging suggestion, clumsy, long-winded and extremely dull. It is a brilliant attack and it contains enough truth for it still to pass as the standard reaction to mythological poetry.

Five centuries of European art and literature, however, have demonstrated that the myths still have power to affect the imagination while the psychologists have now rivalled the mediaeval scholiasts in their comments and interpretations of this revelation of human nature, 'often hidden; sometimes overcome; seldom extinguished'. Once again we are convinced that myths are: 'symbolic stories which have meaning beyond their value as narratives, and call for interpretation in some "spiritual sense", as myths or symbols embodying some kind of inner truth.'[5] Ovid can now, with safety, again be regarded as one of the great classical poets and the tales of the *Metamorphoses* need not remain silenced on moral or aesthetic grounds. The case is altered when we come to examine the work of the Elizabethan poets whom Ovid inspired to imitation and emulation. If *Hero and Leander* or *Venus and Adonis* may be granted sensuous appeal they do not seem to have any readily identifiable spiritual significance. And in the case of some of Chapman's poetry or in Tourneur's *The Transformed Metamorphosis*[6] the modern reader may well feel that the poet has taken elaborate precautions to hide its significance altogether. It is easy to see why Carew's view has prevailed and why Elizabethan mythological poetry has been dismissed as a minor and unimportant genre.

The Elizabethan interest in Ovid, however, is neither minor nor insignificant.[7] If it is true that Ovid's elegy at *Amores* I. 13, the lover's address to the dawn, gave rise to a whole genre of European poetry then the Elizabethan use of this tradition is particularly interesting. Ovid's elegy is an attempt to prolong the night by the force of rhetoric, an attempt which is doomed but which manages, in comparing love to a number of other human activities which will start with day and finding them wanting, to convey the full force of the parting. The parting of lovers at dawn is a fairly common occurrence and one might be unwilling to ascribe all examples of the Provencal alba, the French aubade, or the German tagelied to the literary influence of Ovid. In a number of Elizabethan instances, however, the influence of Ovid is apparent and the effect is startling. In *Hero and Leander*, which is indebted to the *Heroides*, Marlowe's lovers part at dawn with echoes of the horses of the dawn from the *Amores*, but in the last soliloquy of *Dr Faustus* Marlowe actually refers to line 40 of the elegy:

Clamares, lente currite noctis equi

which he has adapted for his own purposes as

O lente, lente currite noctis equi

The love which this night would prolong is not the beauty even of Helen but the love of God. In giving Ovid's lines a Christian context Marlowe is working within a European tradition but the stark contrast of this situation is unique. Throughout the play Faustus has been demanding the love of woman, a demand finally gratified by the demon Helen, and the insertion of the lines from the *Amores* into the final speech when Faustus is facing damnation gives to Ovid's emotion a new tragic dimension.

The irony that the coming of daylight should be a cause of grief rather than rejoicing is not necessarily Ovidian and it is hardly possible to ascribe Shakespeare's aubade in *Romeo and Juliet* Act III sc. 5 to the influence of Ovid. But the words of the lovers at this crisis of the action:

Jul. O now be gone: more light and light it growes
Rom. More light and light: more darke and darke our woes

refer back to Juliet's speech in III. 2 where her longing for night and Romeo starts the whole climax of the love story:

Gallop apace, you fiery footed steedes
Towards Phoebus lodging, such a Wagoner
As Phaeton would whip you to the west
And bring in Cloudie night immediately

These lines are an echo of Ovid *Metamorphoses* II. 392 and Shakespeare has clearly read them in Golding's translation which uses 'firiefooted' and describes Phaeton as a 'Wagoner'. The Ovidian night which Juliet longs for here is the same wedding night which the lovers hope in vain to prolong in scene 5 and the lines in between are full of echoes of Marlowe's *Hero and Leander*, itself Ovidian in inspiration. The emotion at these crises of tragic action owes something to the Renaissance interpretation of Ovid as well as bearing the stamp of the individual talent. The Elizabethan Ovid casts a long shadow.

What is true of crises in the drama is true also of the mythological poetry which was frequently written by men who were also dramatists. The goodly train of gods and goddesses are there for a purpose other than swelling pages. They help to create the emotions they are used to describe. In the formal atmosphere of narrative poetry it is perhaps easier to trace this movement than elsewhere but the formal atmosphere should not blind us to the dramatic range and possibilities of this poetry.

The influence of Ovid on European literature is a remarkable phenomenon. Latin learning had been valued throughout Europe as the symbol of civilization and, more important, salvation. But the survival of Latin as the language of the Church also involved the survival of pagan literature. Ovid's popularity in the Middle Ages was perhaps greater than his prestige in the Roman world for a number of complex reasons. His work was regarded as a storehouse of wisdom which had the double advantage of appealing to the Church and to those who found the Church's disapproval of passion an intolerable burden. Like many great works of art Ovid's poems are concerned with such fractures and dividing points in the human psyche that it is perhaps unreasonable to expect any general agreement about their nature. Different interpretations of Ovid frequently involve different and indeed opposed ways of looking at the world; and to some extent an account of English Ovidian poetry is bound to be an account of how first one and then another interpretation of Ovid's works influenced his successors. Even in Imperial Rome the *Amores* and the *Ars Amatoria* were provocative titles and Ovid's plea that he was a libertine only in poetry was not sufficient to save him from banishment, although the actual reason for this remains obscure. The moral argument has gone on ever since and is unlikely to be resolved, but the Middle Ages were able to profit from this convenient ambiguity. As 'Venus clerke' Ovid was the great authority on the religion of love which had emerged, or re-emerged, no one seems quite clear how, in twelfth-century Provence. This religion might often be condemned by the Christian church and many of those who paid it poetic service showed, by retraction or recantation, that they were aware it stood within danger of damnation, but it permitted the expression of emotions and passions which even the threat of damnation cannot totally suppress. The Church, however, was fortunate in possessing, in the fourfold interpretation of the Old Testament in terms of the New, one of the most perfect instruments ever devised for the re-direction of inconvenient emotions. Since Ovid was part of the great Latin tradition it was usually agreed that his poems must contain many important truths. It only remained to show how these truths corresponded to the great and important truths of the Christian religion. The work was so well done that in 1497 a Parisian monk was able to dedicate his edition of the *Ars Amatoria* to the praise and glory of the Virgin Mary.[8] The allegorical interpretation of Ovid was a long and enduring process and it would be a mistake to regard the reasons and emotions which produced such an interpretation as either feigned or necessarily foolish.

John of Garland's *Integumenta* (c. 1234) is one of the first instances of Ovid moralized and the manuscript in which his poem is preserved also contains prose passages from the earlier allegories of Arnolphe d'Orleans. It seems probable that their work influenced or was referred to by the compilers of the enormous thirteenth-century French poem the *Ovide Moralisé*. Petrus Berchorius continued this tradition in his Latin work *Ovidius Moralizatus* and completed what might be described as the formal aspect of moralizing Ovid. The characters of the *Metamorphoses* and the fate which overtakes them have now become examples of sin overtaken by a just retribution. Narcissus and Niobe are clear types of pride, Hermaphroditus is a warning against the lusts of the flesh, Phaeton falls like Lucifer and Deucalion survives a flood which, like the one which overtook Noah, is caused by man's sinful nature.[9]

This theme of sin and retribution is also found in works which are intended more as collections of mythological stories than as direct moral exposition. The huge compilations of Giovanni Boccaccio (1313–1375) are probably the most important of these collections. *De Genealogia Deorum*, *De Claris Mulieribus*, and *De Casibus Virorum Illustrium* continued to exercise great influence on European literature throughout the Renaissance. Other frequently consulted compilations were the *De Deis Gentium Varia et Multiplex Historia* of Lilius Giraldus, published at Basle in 1548, and *Mythologiae sive Explicationum Fabularum* by Natalis Comes, published at Venice in 1551. Chaucer had imitated Boccaccio in *The Legend of Good Women* but the most influential of the attempts to turn Boccaccio into English literature was *The Fall of Princes* by John Lydgate. Here we find the history of Oedipus and Lucrece, Alcibiades and Scipio all interpreted in terms of the Christian concept of sin and its punishment. The heroes and heroines of ancient myth and history are thus presented, in the same way as the moralizers of Ovid had presented the characters of the *Metamorphoses*, as types and symbols of pride and the other deadly sins. *The Fall of Princes* was composed between 1431 and 1438. It was still in print a century later and proved so popular that various authors attempted a collaborative continuation using characters from English instead of ancient history. This work, called *The Mirror for Magistrates*,[10] appears to have been published in 1555 as the second part of Wayland's Lydgate but was at first suppressed by the authorities presumably for political reasons. Re-published four years later in the second year of Elizabeth's reign it became one of the most improving and influential works of the age. Frequently re-published and often added to, it influenced the drama as well as acting as a model for many later poets. Daniel's *Complaint of Rosamond*, Lodge's *Elstride* and even Shakespeare's *Lucrece* are indebted to the tradition of the *Mirror*. In some way this traditional influence of the compilations may have had more effect than direct consultation—though it is clear that Chapman at least had studied the *Mythologiae* of Natalis Comes.[11]

A third class of mythological compilations also influenced the literature of the period. The Renaissance classical dictionaries[12] not only provided suitable equivalents or translations for individual words but frequently lists of proper names and explanations. The first of these dictionaries had been produced by a Dutchman, Herman Torrentius; revised by Robert Stephanus and his brother Charles it became one of the standard reference works of Europe. In 1538 Sir Thomas Elyot had used it and the dictionary of Friar Ambrosius Calepine (1502) in the preparation of his Latin–English Dictionary. This in its turn was revised by Thomas Cooper and his *Thesaurus Linguae Romanae & Brittanicae* of 1565 was to go through four further editions and become the standard reference work for the last quarter of the sixteenth century, familiar to pupils at the grammar schools and students at the universities.

The Elizabethans not only inherited Ovid as part of the Latin tradition and a text used for illustration in grammar books, they also inherited a tradition of interpretation. This traditional interpretation they now changed and adapted to their new needs. It was not a change accomplished all at once or by deliberate policy and the history of narrative verse in this period is in part an account of the clash of rival interpretations of Ovid.

Translation of the *Metamorphoses* into English begins with William Caxton. He claimed to have produced a translation by 1480 but, if this was a printed book, no copies have survived. What has survived is a unique manuscript with unfinished illumination. Books 10 to 15 of this manuscript were bought by Samuel Pepys at auction and are now in

Magdalene College, Cambridge, but books 1 to 9 were lost until 1966. Discovered among wastepaper in the Sir Thomas Phillipps' collection they are now also, fortunately, at Magdalene. Caxton follows the prose version of the *Ovide Moralisé* of the printing house of Colard Mansion with the addition of material from Berchorius. The first printed translation of Ovid is an anonymous version of book III of the *Metamorphoses* published in 1560 and titled *The Fable of Ovid treting of Narcissus*. 'In England', writes Professor Pevsner of Elizabethan architecture, 'the Gothic past is the Gothic present.'[13] On the evidence of this translation one could take this view of the literature as well. The story of Narcissus is recounted in 'poulter's measure' competent enough for Arthur Golding to borrow details for his later complete translation. But the story of Narcissus is followed by 128 seven-line stanzas of moral commentary. Here one finds the complete doctrine of Ovid moralized:

> I meane to shewe, accordying to my wytte
> That Ovyd by this tale no follye mente
> But soughte to shewe, the doynges far unfytte
> Of soundrye folke, whome natuer gyftes hath lente,
> In dyvers wyse to use, wyth good in tente
> And howe the bownty torneth to theyr payne
> That lacke the knowledge, of so good a gayne.

> Whiche Ovid now this Poete sure devine
> Doth collour in so wonderfull a sorte
> That suche as twyse, refuse to reade a lyne
> Wyth good advice, to make there wytte resorte
> To reasons schole; their Lessons to reporte
> Shall never gather Ovids meanyng straunge
> That wysdome hydeth, wyth some pleasaunt chaunge.

Narcissus is treated as an example of the deadly sin of pride and Croesus, Samson, Sennacherib, Darius, Helen and Cleopatra are cited as supporting cases. The poet conducts an examination of the sin in all its aspects; Narcissus himself is compared to Lucifer while Eccho represents the Satanic element of flattery. Solemn warnings are issued 'to suche as speke without advisemente' and 'to suche as geve themselves over to pleasur of vanites'. The prophet Tiresias is invested with the authority of the Old Testament but this authority is supported by references to Boccaccio, Ficino and 'Walles', since the work of Berchorius appeared under the name of Thomas Waleys.

Similar in form is the *Hermaphroditus and Salmacis* by Thomas Peend published in 1565. Hermaphroditus is the type of Youth tempted by the pleasures of the world who receives the wages of such a sin. Peend had apparently projected a complete translation of the *Metamorphoses* but had been anticipated by Arthur Golding's version of 1565/7. Other Ovidian poems were written in the 1560's, Thomas Underdowne's *Theseus and Ariadne* (1566), Thomas Howell's *Cephalus and Procris* (c. 1568) and William Hubbard's *Ceyx and Alcione* (1569), but Golding is more adequate as an interpreter of Ovid than his contemporaries because his verse does greater justice to Ovid's poetic effects.

In his introduction Golding sufficiently marks out the area that lies between the 'Gothic present' of Ovid moralized and the new poetry. He does regard the *Metamorphoses* as a storehouse of notable moral examples but he does not contemplate producing an Ovid moralized after the French fashion. His reasons are that it would require a book of many quires and that such a labour would be tedious for the author and his readers. A critic, looking before and after Golding, might reasonably conclude that here is clear evidence of a shift in sensibility. If literature for Golding is still a moral activity it need no longer be a moralized one. The poet is assumed to be a moral philosopher without having to expound his doctrine at tedious length. The way is open for Sidney's defence that the poet is the actual creator of the golden or ideal world and for Spenser's attempt to give England a poem at once heroic and philosophical. Golding's merits as poet and translator are considerable and unquestionably helped to make Ovid's poetry once again the gateway to a new age.

Sensibility, however, changes slowly. *The most famous and tragicall historie of Pelops and Hippodamia* (1587) by Matthew Grove can hardly be described as a great advance from the lamentable history of Hubbard. In 1589, however, Thomas Lodge published *Scillaes Metamorphosis* and this poem, although it can be called 'not so much the first poem in a new genre as one of the last in an old one',[14] has certain significant features. The story of Glaucus and Scilla in the *Metamorphoses* involves Circe. Glaucus confesses his love for Scilla to Circe and asks for her help; instead of help she offers her own love and, enraged at its rejection, transforms Scilla in revenge. Lodge transposes this whole scene to the banks of the Isis (which has led some commentators to suggest that he wrote the poem while an undergraduate at Oxford) and Glaucus confesses his love to the poet who is himself wandering love-lorn by the river-bank. Circe does not appear. This changes the whole balance of the poem, for the entire action is now seen through the eyes of the poet. From the beginning of the poem he has been conducting a dialogue with Glaucus on the nature of love; the action is to some extent a demonstration for his benefit, and although the poem is not expounded in moralistic terms it does have a lesson which the poet expects some, at least, of his readers to understand. The only person, according to the poem, really competent to give an account of 'the course of all our plainings' would be 'he that hath seen' the history of Venus and Adonis, Cephalus and Procris, the pangs of Lucina and Angelica the fair. Lodge's ideal spectator is one familiar not only with Ovid but also with Italian epic. The assumption is that the poet is a lover appealing to those who are also in love. The poet comes to understand his own case through his appreciation of the story of Glaucus, and other lovers and their ladies, who are addressed in the Envoy, are offered an increase in self-knowledge. Lodge's mythological parallels and details are there to show this love in all its aspects and 'Furie and Rage, Wan-hope, Dispaire and Woe' exist in this poem for the same reason that they exist in *The Romance of the Rose* and other mediaeval allegorical love-visions. They raise love from a physical to a psychic act. Lodge calls this world of mythology into being because the whole central debate on love can only be understood in its terms. If the actors in the poem, Venus, Glaucus and Scilla herself, are definite in their attitudes and decisive in their actions the poet cannot expect such a final solution in his own case:

> Our talke midway was nought but still of wonder,
> Of change, of chaunce, of sorrow, and her ending;
> I wept for want: he said, time bringes men under,
> And secret want can finde but small befrending.
> And as he said, in that before I tried it,
> I blamde my wit forewarnd, yet never spied it.

Lodge's central concern is with the poet rather than the transformation of Scilla and the ironical warning to the ladies. Unlike their moralizing predecessors the Elizabethan Ovidian poets did not claim to know all the answers.

Lodge's new world of mythology was inherited by his successors. A word of caution, however, is necessary. In accounting for a genre of poetry the literary historian is always tempted to treat it as an organic growth with clearly defined origins, flowering and decline. The form is seen as living and dying in the same way as the poets. This is probably a misleading analogy. Every poem is in itself a fresh assault upon the problems of experience and if Lodge's successors were aware of using a form which he had fashioned they also created it new.

For this reason it is not vital to decide whether Shakespeare was 'imitating' Marlowe or Marlowe 'emulating' Shakespeare in their Ovidian poems. It is clear that both poets were capable of learning from each other and both gain from the experience. The date of *Venus and Adonis* is not in doubt. Published in 1593 as 'the first heire of my invention' it was probably composed in 1592/3 when the theatres were closed by plague. *Hero and Leander* is more problematic. Entered in the Stationers' Register on 28 September 1593 it does not seem to have been published until 1598. Henry Petowe, in the dedication to his continuation of the poem, states quite clearly that the poem was interrupted by Marlowe's death. On the other hand many parallels between this poem and the early translation of Ovid's *Amores* have caused some scholars to propose an early date. Certainly Marlowe was thinking of the *Amores* when he wrote the poem as well as consulting his more immediate sources—the Greek poem of the Alexandrian poet Musaeus and Ovid's *Heroides* XVIII and XIX. Whenever it was composed *Hero and Leander* is concerned with subjects which occupied Marlowe all his working life. Leander uses the arguments against virginity from the *Amores* like a bold sharp sophister, and Gaveston in *Edward II*, an even sharper sophister, determines to use the whole apparatus of Ovidian mythology, sylvan nymphs, satyrs grazing on the lawns, a lovely boy in Dian's shape and 'One like Acteon peeping through the grove', to keep King Edward's interest. Gaveston even compares himself to Leander. Love as the exercise of power is one of Marlowe's most constant themes.

From the moment that the two cities 'in view and opposit' are introduced *Hero and Leander* appears to be full of opposites and contradictions. The cities are opposed, will and fate are opposed even in the councils of the gods, the lovers are contrasted and, most important of all, contradictions in character and purpose are emphasized. Hero, whose hair could make her the consort of the sun-god, is actually introduced as Venus' Nun and, although 'nun' is the usual translation for 'priestess', Marlowe makes full use of the ambiguities involved in such a title. Her dress has wide green sleeves, which may themselves be significant, and is bordered by Venus's vain wooing of Adonis, while the bloodstains on her blue kirtle emphasize the sacrifice that may be required of followers of the goddess. The dress reveals that the rites of the goddess Venus may be rather different from the ones that Hero appears to be practising and introduces the theme of love's sacrifice—a sacrifice that will be required of both Hero and Leander. Hero is at once the fairest part of Nature and, in her power over bees, sparrows and Cupid, a force which challenges comparison with Nature. She is both temptress, provoking love, and victim, since she herself will become one of the sacrifices. This contrast is insisted on throughout the poem as she alternately provokes and resists Leander's sophistries. In the temple she admits to herself:

> Were I the saint hee worships, I would heare him,
> And as shee spake those words, came somewhat nere him.

When Leander begins his attack on her virginity she yields, although neither yet realizes that she has:

> These arguments he us'de, and many more,
> Wherewith she yeelded, that was woon before.
> Heroes lookes yeelded, but her words made warre,
> Women are woon when they begin to jarre.

The first evidence of her yielding is the revealing slip of the tongue which invites Leander to her tower and initiates the next stage of the action.

The second Sestyad opens with Hero's faint and Leander's reviving kiss. She leaves him, but drops her fan

> Thinking to traine Leander therewithall

but in vain. When these mutual manœuvres do eventually end with both lovers in one bed Hero is both a helpless bird cruelly seized for prey and a willing victim:

> Treason was in her thought,
> And cunningly to yeeld her selfe she sought.
> Seeming not woon, yet woon she was at length,
> In such warres women use but halfe their strength.

Hero's contradictory attitudes, intelligible in themselves, become extremely sympathetic when united to the equal series of contradictions which form the character of Leander in the poem. In contrast to the first description of Hero the introduction of Leander seems un-ambiguous. He is amorous Leander with smooth breast, white belly and the heavenly path imprinted by immortal fingers along his back in the act of creation, perhaps, or the act of love. By general consent he is 'made for amorous play' and the first time that he sees Hero is in the context of the temple of Venus:

> There might you see the gods in sundrie shapes,
> Committing headdie ryots, incest, rapes.

The whole tone of the poem leads the reader to expect similar conduct from Leander. These expectations appear fulfilled when Leander accosts Hero like a bold sharp sophister with Ovid's arguments against virginity. Unfortunately, when these arguments provoke the invitation to the tower, the faint and the dropped fan, it turns out that:

> He being a novice, knew not what she meant

At a later stage when Hero, moved to action:

> offers up her selfe a sacrifice

Leander toys 'as a brother with his sister' and:

> yet he suspected
> Some amorous rites or other were neglected.

The contrast would be ridiculous if Leander did not also possess the force to swim the Hellespont for love. The contradictory qualities of both lovers are necessary to lead them, and the reader, to the orchard of the Hesperides and display Hero naked to Leander's sight.

Marlowe's two digressions make his view of these contrasting emotions completely clear. The inset story was a favourite device of Ovid but the stories of Mercury and the country maid and Neptune's attempted seduction of Leander are not conventional flourishes. Both are completely in keeping with the mock-heroic tone of the poem. The first disgression occurs between Hero's slip of the tongue and dropping her fan. It is clear that if these events succeeded each other directly they might have suggested a rather harsher interpretation of the lady's conduct. Marlowe has provided for this interpretation in the story of the country maid who knew her own price and demanded from Mercury a draught of nectar in exchange for her chastity. The ludicrous situation in which Mercury and Cupid find themselves as a result allows the poet to make some observations about the nature of passionate love which are essential if his readers are not to conclude that he is naive. Yet, if he allowed such thoughts at the expense of his heroine, he would alienate all sympathy.

Neptune provides the same commentary on Leander that the country maid gives on Hero. Neptune's ambivalent advances show the poet aware of a number of unadmitted attitudes and motives which might well be present in the wooing of a bold sharp sophister. Neptune does not command the reader's sympathy and so his wooing appears crude and ridiculous. By his satire on Neptune Marlowe both criticizes Leander and, at the same time, provides protection from him. It is perfectly possible that the homosexual theme held a personal attraction for Marlowe, but homosexual love was forced upon the poem here for dramatic rather than personal considerations. Leander could hardly again be shown as unaware of the advances of another woman, and the ironic effect of the episode requires that he should be unaware of Neptune's design.

The effect of both digressions is not entirely comic. In both the Fates are present and this recalls the tragic theme which runs through the whole poem. The will of the lovers is overruled by fate and if it throws them into each other's arms it is also leading them to death in the same capricious style that it frustrates Mercury and Neptune. The whole action of the poem is formed of these concentric rings of irony; and this irony, created by the Ovidian mythology, is the most effectual and tender way of treating the passions involved. In the story and in the digressions it is clear that love is a dangerous emotion and the action is complete—there was no need for pious continuations. By the end of the poem more has been revealed than Hero all naked to Leander's sight. Their passionate love in all its cruel, comic and finally tragic aspects has been revealed to the reader. It is not surprising that the author of *Romeo and Juliet* read *Hero and Leander* with attention.

Venus and Adonis, Shakespeare's contribution to the Ovidian genre, is equally a sensuous poem treating in mock-heroic terms a deeply felt tragic conclusion. The true comparison for such poetry is not the mock-heroic of the later Augustan poets—though the methods are to some extent those of Pope whose later poetry is full of metamorphoses—but Elizabethan tragedy itself where precisely these mock-heroic ironies are used to produce the most tragic effects. It is no objection to Shakespeare's poem to protest that this is not the all-conquering golden Aphrodite of classical legend. This is Aphrodite faced with a revolt in the natural order and a failure of even the arts of love. Seduction, at least in Ovid, depends upon the creation of an atmosphere in which the beloved will enter into love without inconvenient second thoughts. Here the atmosphere is created with infinite labour in the ornate terms of goddess as deer park:

> Graze on my lips, and if those hils be drie,
> Stray lower, where the pleasant fountaines lie.

But the atmosphere fails to achieve its purpose although the episode of the stallion and the jennet suggests that 'naturally' it should. Venus is deprived of the banquet of sense which she had proposed for herself:

> But oh what banquet wert thou to the tast,
> Being nourse, and feeder of the other foure,
> Would they not wish the feast might ever last,
> And bid suspition double locke the dore;

Instead of feasting her own senses and providing grazing for Adonis there is only the vain struggle through the undergrowth of the forest to the place where Adonis lies dead.

Both of these poems had an immense success in the 1590's. But such unashamed sensuality was bound to provoke a reaction. In 1594 there was published a poem called *Willobie His Avisa*. This claims to give the true picture of a modest maid and a chaste and constant wife. It recounts the many attempts made on the chastity of Avisa, an innkeeper's daughter, before and after her marriage. She is shown as resisting the obvious appeal of rank and wealth and the insidious charms of foreign styles of wooing. A Nobleman, a man only identified as Caveleiro, D. B. a Frenchman, Dydimus Harco Anglo-Germanicus, and H. W. who uses the Italian or Spanish style of wooing, all fall victims to her beauty and all are rejected with many proper sentiments. Since an edition of the poem was called in by the authorities in 1599 it is reasonable to suppose that the Elizabethans could detect personal references in it. It is now, however, a little difficult to provide the exact key. A reference to Austin's monkish tent has led to the identification of Avisa's village as Cerne Abbas since the abbey nearby had been founded by St Augustine. This should make the brothers who bought and sold the castle to the east of it Sir Walter Raleigh and his brother Carew. In March 1594 a commission appointed by Archbishop Whitgift was sitting at Cerne Abbas inquiring into allegations of heresy and it has been supposed that this poem contains scandalous suggestions about the Raleigh circle. Also the last suitor H. W. is given good advice by his friend W. S. who is fairly clearly identified as an actor. If these initials are then identified as Henry Wriothesley, Earl of Southampton, and William Shakespeare an attempt can be made to link Avisa to the story of Shakespeare's sonnets. The biographical puzzle, if there is one, which surrounds these poems has not been solved and those who find the exercise of the imagination the most vital part of historical investigations are free to indulge in speculation. The danger is that in searching for the 'real story' the literary problems may be lost sight of. In this case they are both more interesting and more important.

As C. S. Lewis has pointed out[15] the author of *Willobie His Avisa* is using a style of poetry earlier than the Italianate style fashionable in the 1590's. This style is used, not because the author is unaware of the new fashion, but because he regards foreign forms in poetry as inextricably linked with foreign forms in manners—the 'continental' method of wooing employed by Avisa's suitors—and he considers that both have turned England into Sodom's sink. If the Ovidian poets have called into being a world of myth to gloss over sin then this poet is engaged in the deliberate process of demythologizing to expose the corrupt reality which lies behind the fine posturing. The arts of love displayed by her suitors break against the rampart of Avisa's Christian virtue. It may be an attempt to expose particular persons but its importance is its attack on all the values and attitudes implied in the Ovidian poems. It shows already the clash in religious outlook which was to become so bitter in the next century and is, in its way, a tribute to the power of the mythological poetry. Obviously the author of *Willobie His Avisa* considered such poetry dangerous and his attitude should serve to remind modern readers that they are dealing with more than fine writing.

The clash in attitudes can be seen clearly by a comparison with Chapman's *Ovid's Banquet of Sence* published in 1595. In this vision of Corynna in her garden Ovid employs the four senses of Auditus, Olfactus, Visus and Gustus and is interrupted as he moves to Tactus. But it is with Visus, 'he venters to see her in the pride of her nakednesse', that the poem is most intimately concerned. It needs no certain identification of Cerne Abbas and the Raleigh circle to make it plain that the heroine of one poem, the 'unseen' Avisa, is poetically opposed to the so shamelessly seen Corynna of Ovid's banquet.

But Chapman's poem also differs markedly from *Venus and Adonis* and *Hero and Leander*. Chapman saw poetry as the servant of a higher truth as his dedication 'To the Trulie Learned, and my worthy Friende, Master Mathew Royden', makes clear. There the poet's use of the most simple and unaffected phrase is compared to a painter's use of perspective and: 'Obscuritie in affection of words, and indigested concets, is pedanticall and childish; but where it shroudeth it selfe in the hart of his subject, utterd with fitnes of figure, and expressive Epethites; with that darknes wil I still labour to be shaddowed.'

Chapman, like Lodge, also insists that the reader will require special insight before he can expect to understand the true significance of the poem. Only those fortunate few: 'that before-hand have a radiant and light-bearing intellect, will say they can passe through Corynna's garden without the help of a Lanterne.' Unfortunately, even if the modern reader is prepared to concede his lack of light-bearing intellect, a lantern is rather difficult to provide. Corynna's garden is the garden of the Emperor's court where Ovid has hidden in order to watch Julia bathing, playing upon her lute and singing. She is beside a fountain which contains statues of Niobe and her children and these, as Professor Kermode has pointed out,[16] are types and symbols of pride. He suggests that Ovid's progression through the senses is a process of degradation which reduces him to the level of a beast. Other commentators have emphasized Chapman's debt to Renaissance Platonism and interpret the poem as the rise of the soul through the senses to the contemplation of ideal beauty. The way may become clearer if one does not attempt to interpret the poem in isolation but considers it as Chapman's distinctive contribution to the Ovidian debate.

A banquet of sense is certainly a feature of *Venus and Adonis* and Venus displays herself to Adonis on a bank of flowers, in this case of primroses, and describes him as a stone statue. Corynna's appearance on a bank of flowers surrounding a fountain which contains a stone statue is not a decisive parallel but the resemblance is perhaps sufficient to persuade the reader that the arrangement of the figures is not entirely fortuitous. The bank of flowers round the fountain is described in such a way:

Of Chloris ensignes, an abstracted field

and in such detail that it seems to offer a challenge to the light-bearing intellect. The passage begins and ends with pollination and has many suggestions of embraces, caresses, marriage and impregnation. Bees swarm to drink nectar from cup-like plants and pollinate them. Flowers cling to Corynna to taste her sweets. As the bees are associated with the sweetness of their honey and the sharpness of their stings so the flowers may yield balm or poison. Corynna naked is sweet but in tasting her Ovid himself may be pricked. Even if it is not possible to identify all of Chapman's plants with complete accuracy it seems clear that there is a general pattern in his description. The flowers are at first sweet-smelling and yielding precious balm. Then they are connected with love, pansies for nuptials, Diana's arrow and Cupid's crimson shield. The next group of plants can probably all be identified as in some way poisonous—deadly nightshade certainly is and the others are possibly bindweed and pennywort. The stanza is completed by a reference to violets, also a plant connected with love, and Calaminth which is again sweet-smelling. In his careful description of the bank of flowers following immediately upon the vision of Corynna naked, Chapman gives us the theme of his poem. Love is sweet, certainly, but also dangerous in the same way as the poisonous plants are found in the midst of the sweet-smelling and medicinal ones. Its wounds may require all the purgatives of care which can be obtained from *Rumex*, the common dock, also used for bee-stings. Chapman takes up the comparison of Corynna to a landscape in stanzas 57–62, her body resembles Elisium or Paradise, and the metaphor of gathering sweet flowers is again insisted upon. But so is the fact that this can only be a flawed paradise. Elisium can only be reached by the practice of virtue and virtue can yield no joy where Corynna is concerned since she is 'a sweet Elisium for the sence'. She is a paradise where poison lurks. Chapman was not a prude and the ending of his poem with its Latin motto, 'Intention, the action of the mind', leaves the reader in little doubt that Ovid's banquet was completed. The course of the poem should also leave him in no doubt that he is

> disputing still
> For Sence, gainst Reason, with a sencelesse will.

The claims of passion are recognized in every line of the poem but the claim of Reason must still be regarded as paramount. Beautiful as Corynna is she is still, like the natural order which surrounds her, capable of yielding precious balm or deadly poison; and only reason can distinguish between these conflicting powers.

Reason and order are again contrasted with the passions of Ovidian love in Chapman's continuation of *Hero and Leander* (1598). The continuation does not simply bring Marlowe's story to its unhappy conclusion; it changes the mythological structure of the poem. Marlowe's union of opposites and conjunction of contradictions ensured that the commitment of the lovers to each other should be total. Chapman's poem is designed to show that their true loyalties should have been to the divine order. Nothing in Marlowe's poem had prepared for:

> Sweet Hero left upon her bed alone,
> Her maidenhead, her vowes, Leander gone,

And nothing with her but a violent crew
Of new come thoughts that yet she never knew.

In preparation for this new theme of guilt, remorse and tragic death
Chapman therefore introduces the goddess Ceremonie. She comes to
convince Leander and the reader that he has sinned in omitting the
sacrament of marriage. She clearly represents the true vision of love but
creates for the poet an extremely difficult technical problem. Since her
intervention at this stage of the story is too late to save the lovers her
role must be a negative one. To reinforce his vision of what love should
be Chapman makes use of the tale of Teras—the story of Hymen, the
spirit of marriage, and his bride. This tale, with the Epithalamion
at its end, is one of the most perfect poems Chapman ever wrote. It
expresses exactly the value which he wished to add to the Ovidian love
poem and is essential to his view of the story. As in Marlowe's poem
the digressions are there to demonstrate the real dramatic value of the
action. Obviously Marlowe and Chapman took very different views
of the action and the complete poem of *Hero and Leander* represents the
examination of Ovidian love which was carried on in the poetry and the
drama of the 1590's. It is a debate not yet resolved and consequently
one need not expect much critical agreement between those who find
Marlowe's poem a tragic action complete in itself and those who feel,
with C. S. Lewis,[17] that completing *Hero and Leander* was the work
Chapman was born to do.

Henry Petowe who also published a continuation of *Hero and Lean-
der* in 1598 says in his preface that Marlowe was killed before he could
finish *Hero and Leander*. This doubtful piece of information is usually
regarded as Petowe's only contribution to English literature. In its way
his strange poem is instructive because it links Marlowe's lovers with
Spenser's wayfaring Christian knights. Petowe treats the story (fol-
lowing, he says, 'the true Italian discourse') as a high chivalric romance.
He metamorphoses Hero into the chaste victim of a wicked Duke while
Leander is the true knight who appears at the blast of the trumpet to be
her victorious champion. There was never a more unlikely union of
classical mythology with chivalric Christianity and the result is im-
probably sentimental. But the synthesis which eludes Petowe was
eventually achieved by the artists of the Renaissance. His work reveals
the struggles and aspirations of an age more clearly than the work
of better poets. It would be a mistake to dismiss his work as simply
absurd.

The innovations of Lodge and the success of Marlowe and Shakespeare encouraged many poets to follow their example. Thomas Heywood's *Oenone and Paris* (1594), Thomas Edwards's *Cephalus and Procris* (1595), and Michael Drayton's *Endimion and Phoebe* (1595), are all variations on the Ovidian themes and attempts to catch the style. Chapman tried to alter the pattern while John Marston seems to have been in doubt whether his *Pigmalions Image* (1598) was a piece of calculated eroticism or a parody of the whole genre. If it was meant, as he claims, to expose:

> The Salaminian titillations,
> Which tickle up our leud Priapians

then he must have misunderstood the deliberate self-mockery and parody which is as much a part of the best poems in the Ovidian tradition as it is of the Elizabethan drama.

The combination of wit and passion which distinguishes this poetry at its best is caught exactly by the author of *Salmacis and Hermaphroditus* first published in 1602 and attributed in the edition of 1640 to Francis Beaumont. The story, from *Metamorphoses* book IV, had already been used by Shakespeare for details of Venus's wooing. It might be expected that another variation on this theme, however clever, would be tedious. But the details are used for a different effect which is in itself a new contribution to the Ovidian debate. The poem's purpose is most clearly revealed in the supporting digressions. Jove's journey to Astraea's palace in search of justice and the jealous combat of wits waged by the other gods round the body of Salmacis provide an ironic commentary on the nymph's own wooing of Hermaphroditus. All the arts and stratagems of love deployed with such care by both gods and nymph fail for a variety of absurd and ludicrous reasons. But where art fails passion and prayer can still produce the desired result in the strange union of the pool. Unfortunately the answer to that final passionate prayer has produced a result, or indeed a catastrophe, very different from all the original intentions of the actors in the drama. This too is a story of purposes mistook which fall upon the inventors' heads. If Beaumont's comic irony is not used for such obviously tragic effects as Shakespeare's or Marlowe's his lack of solemnity need not imply a lack of seriousness.

Comedy of this kind has always to contend with the constant demand that art should be grave, moral and most profitable. When William Basse used the central situation of *Salmacis and Hermaphroditus* for his poem *Urania, The Woman in the Moone,* he added to his parody a satirical moral account of its meaning. This ancient duty was soon again being performed in earnest. In 1632 George Sandys republished his earlier translation of the *Metamorphoses* with a new, but familiar, moral commentary. *Ovid's Metamorphosis, Englished Mythologiz'd and Represented in Figures* is an answer to popular demand which marks the end of the Elizabethan Ovid even more definitely than Carew's elegy.

These serious inclinations had never been satisfied simply by Ovid moralized. The conventional wisdom concerning sin and its punishment had found its expression in the tragedies of Lydgate and the English history of the *Mirror for Magistrates.* Its popularity and sobriety made it still an obvious model.[18] Samuel Daniel's *Complaint of Rosamond* (1592) has clearly been influenced by Thomas Churchyard's tragedy of Shore's wife in the 1563 edition of the *Mirror.* The ghost of Rosamond, mistress of Henry II, appeals to Daniel to tell her story so that the sighs of lovers may free her soul to cross Charon's ferry. The story of her seduction, concealment at Woodstock and murder by Eleanor of Aquitaine is told in straightforward fashion clearly designed to arouse pity for Rosamond at the same time as it presents her as a warning of the unwisdom of adultery. Its moral ambiguity is very similar to Ovid moralized and it has the great advantage that, despite references to Charon and the classical pantheon, it is not as overtly pagan as even the most moral of Ovidian poems. It provides a suitable counterpart to the lighter tone of the sonnets to *Delia* with which it was published.[19]

Daniel's poem proved so popular that the ageing Churchyard brought out a new edition of his tragedy, 'much augmented with divers new additions', in 1593. In the same year Thomas Lodge based his *The Tragicall complaynt of Elstred* upon various tragedies contained in John Higgins's additions to the *Mirror* of 1574. Michael Drayton published two complaints in the same style in 1594, *Peirs Gaveston, Earle of Cornwall* and *Matilda.* In the second poem Drayton's heroine pleads that her story is more worthy of attention than Rosamond, Shore's wife or Elstred since her tragedy was the result of her refusal to become a king's mistress. Shakespeare also uses the theme of chastity in *The Rape of Lucrece* published in the same year. This poem is no doubt the counterpart of his own earlier erotic poetry but he has returned to Ovid for his inspiration. Many of the sympathies which were later to find expression in his tragic drama are already contained in this poem. *The Rape of Lucrece* has the dramatic force which the other verse tragedies so conspicuously lack—but this lack should not be allowed to obscure the influence which they did have on the Elizabethan drama. It was more than convenience which caused Daniel to publish his closet drama *Cleopatra* (a companion to the Countess of Pembrokes' translation of *Antonius* of 1592) in the same volume as the augmented *Rosamond* of 1594. They are comparable works and it could be argued that his tragic play is an attempt to achieve the dramatic effect which is missing in the poem. These dramatic defects in *Rosamond* he tries to remedy by extending the scene between the wronged queen and Rosamond and allowing the reader to hear Rosamond's dying and penitent thoughts. This resource may have increased the poem's popularity but, as Professor Sprague has argued, it destroys its balance.

Drayton had also contrived to supply the popular demand for this kind of poetry at the same time as he sought to improve his own work. Revised versions of *Matilda* and *Peirs Gaveston* were published in 1596 together with a new tragical legend, *Robert, Duke of Normandy*. In the next year, however, Drayton solved the problem of presenting this material dramatically: this solution he found in the poetry of Ovid. One of the most popular of Ovid's works was the *Heroides*, love poetry which takes the form of letters written by famous lovers of legend at some crisis of their fortunes. In revising the poem Ovid had included some of the replies. This idea Drayton extends to English history and calls the result *England's Heroicall Epistles*. Since Henry and Rosamond are his first pair of lovers it seems reasonable to conclude that Daniel's *Complaint* and his own attempts at verse tragedy provided him with his opportunity. However he came by it, the idea is employed with magnificent effect. So far as one can judge, his moral attitude to such a situation cannot have been very different from Daniel's. But the form he has adopted compels him to leave all such judgements to the reader. What is portrayed and dramatized is the mutual agony of lovers in a situation which both feel, for very different reasons, to be intolerable. While the natural recoil of the human spirit from the hell of its own making is carefully presented, the reader is also invited to understand, and therefore to sympathize with, those so lapsed in time and passion. It could be argued that *England's Heroicall Epistles* is not only Drayton's most popular poem but his most decisive contribution towards that epic history of England which he and Daniel laboured all their lives to write. Nor is its importance merely parochial for it challenges comparison with such later examples of the genre as Donne's *Sapho to Philænis* or Pope's *Eloisa to Abelard*.

The logical result of the defence of poetry as a moral activity was the attempt to present the story of man's creation, fall and redemption. Since presentation of biblical scenes on the stage had been banned for religious reasons the story had to be told in epic or narrative verse. This inevitably involved the use of classical concepts so that even the Bible was liable to be corrupted by the old idols. Christian doctrine had long been influenced and interpreted by Renaissance philosophers who remained undismayed by amalgamations of Platonic thought, Hermetic doctrine and Pythagorean concepts of number. Spenser produced poetic order from this chaos by concentrating his poem round the figure of Arthur. This allowed him to translate doctrine into personal terms without losing the artistic freedom of action which the presence of Christ so often inhibits. The careful use of the Arthurian cycle absolved Spenser from any charge of profanity and eliminated the difficulties of amplifying or adding to biblical narrative.

Spenser's method is probably wise but artists who profess Christianity are bound to feel attracted by biblical subjects—more especially if there is some aspect of doctrine which they wish to emphasize. Giles Fletcher begins his preface to *Christs Victorie and Triumph* by attempting to satisfy those who feel it 'halfe sacrilege for prophane Poetrie to deale with divine and heavenly matters', and also those who would 'banish it with Plato out of all well-ordered Commonwealths'. St Paul, the example of the Church fathers, the classical poets and Mr Edmund Spenser are all used to provide reasons for: 'recommending theas my idle howers, not idly spent, to good schollers, and good Christians, that have overcome their ignorance with reason, and their reason, with religion'. These reasons, however, do not quite prepare the reader for the presentation of Divine Mercy accompanied by all the mythological attributes of Ovidian love. Her dress clearly owes a good deal to Marlowe's invention and the whole idea of a debate between Justice and Mercy in heaven is more classical than Christian in inspiration. These elements may appear so incongruous that the poem can only be treated as a literary curiosity and Fletcher, like Petowe, dismissed as a poet who has attempted to create an improbable fiction. The final synthesis of faiths and cultures eluded Fletcher and Petowe, as it has eluded so many of their successors, but the effort which they and their fellows made allowed other poets to find a new starting point. After attempting to justify the ways of his peculiar god to mankind Milton turned back and, in a work which created the spirit of the Old Testament in classical form, brought the English tragic drama to its superb conclusion. While Milton's tragedy is unquestionably the product of his individual talent it could scarcely have taken shape without the pressure of a long tradition. It would be absurd to trace a definite and complete pattern in the long series of poems which stretch between Spenser and Milton, but it would be equally obtuse to regard Fletcher's poem merely as a literary curiosity. If Milton read Fletcher with the same kind of attention that he gave to Spenser it was because he recognized that both had important contributions to make to a debate which still continues and which is liable still to leave the reader in the same situation as Chapman's Ovid in Corynna's garden—an involved and far from ideal spectator.

Fletcher has not advanced beyond Marlowe but he does reveal new perspectives. His use of Ovidian imagery for the debate between Mercy and Justice in heaven and the careful re-creation of Spenser's Bower of Bliss as the temptations of the world offered to Christ in the wilderness, permits him to explore the ambiguities and ironies of the Christian position with a new understanding. Instead of detracting from the solemnity associated with such events the Ovidian mythology sharpens an image which custom or repetition might have staled. This poem concentrates, as its title had promised, on victory and the triumph won by the forces of love even in face of death and dissolution. To link this triumph of love with the one insisted on by the Ovidian poets is an emphatic rejection of the sin and punishment morality which had for so long dominated the conventional thought of the age.[20]

Fletcher joins the tragedians in perceiving a quality of mercy in the Ovidian tradition which he felt to be a fitting accompaniment to the Christian story and which the allegorizing moralists had overlooked. In Elizabethan narrative verse between Spenser and Milton the old idols of classical mythology and the tales of the *Metamorphoses* became, as they had for Ovid, instruments which could express not love only, but compassion.

Notes for Introduction

[1] For a discussion of the problem of the epyllion see: M. M. Crump, *The Epyllion from Theocritus to Ovid*, London 1931; W. Allen, Jr, 'The Epyllion', *T.A.Ph.A.* lxxi 1940; J. F. Reilly, 'Origins of the word Epyllion', *C.J.* xlix 1953–4; P. W. Miller, 'The Elizabethan Minor Epic', *S.P.* lv 1958; W. Allen, 'The non-existent Classical Epyllion', *S.P.* lv 1958.

[2] H. T. Price, 'Shakespeare and his Young Contemporaries', *P.Q.* xli Jan. 1962.

[3] See T. W. Baldwin, *William Shakspere's Small Latine and Lesse Greeke*, Urbana 1944.

[4] Helen Gardner (ed.), *The Metaphysical Poets*, Penguin 1957, p. 141.

[5] Helen Gardner, *The Business of Criticism*, Oxford 1959, p. 90.

[6] But see A. C. Hamilton, 'Spenser and Tourneur's *Transformed Metamorphosis*', *R.E.S.* viii no.30. May 1957, for an interpretation of this poem.

[7] For the Elizabethan Ovid see:

L. F. Ball, 'Background of Minor English Renaissance Epics', *E.L.H.* i 1934.

F. S. Boas, *Ovid and the Elizabethans*, London 1947.

D. Bush, *Mythology and the Renaissance Tradition in English Poetry*, Minneapolis 1932.

E. K. Rand, *Ovid and his Influence*, New York 1928.

F. L. Schoell, *Etudes sur L'Humanisme Continental en Angleterre*, Paris 1926.

L. P. Wilkinson, *Ovid Recalled*, Cambridge 1955.

I am also indebted to John Forrest's unpublished thesis *The Elizabethan Ovid*, Edinburgh 1945.

For general critical accounts of the poetry see:

M. C. Bradbrook, *Shakespeare and Elizabethan Poetry*, London 1951.

D. Bush, *English Literature in the Earlier Seventeenth Century*, Oxford 1945.

E. S. Donno, Introduction to *Elizabethan Minor Epics*, London 1963.

C. S. Lewis, *English Literature in the Sixteenth Century excluding Drama*, Oxford 1954.

Hallet Smith, *Elizabethan Poetry*, Cambridge 1952.

[8] Franz Funck-Bretano, *The Renaissance*, London 1936.

[9] L. K. Born, 'Ovid and Allegory', *Speculum* ix 1934. J. Engels, *Etudes sur L'Ovide Moralisé*, Groningen 1945. P. Bercheur, *L'Ovidius Moralizatus di Pierre Bersuire* (ed. F. Ghisalberti), Rome 1933.

[10] Lily B. Campbell (ed.), *The Mirror for Magistrates*, Cambridge 1938, and *Parts Added to the Mirror for Magistrates*, 1946.

[11] See F. L. Schoell, op. cit.

[12] D. T. Staines and E. W. Talbert, *Classical Myth and Legend in Renaissance Dictionaries*, Chapel Hill 1955.

[13] Nikolaus Pevsner, 'Mannerism and Elizabethan Architecture. II', the *Listener*, March 5th 1964.

[14] D. Bush, *Mythology*, p. 83.

[15] C. S. Lewis, *English Literature in the Sixteenth Century excluding Drama*, Oxford 1954.

[16] J. F. Kermode, 'The Banquet of Sence', *Bulletin of the John Rylands Library* xliv Sept. 1961.

[17] C. S. Lewis, op. cit., and *Hero and Leander* (British Academy Lecture 1952).

[18] W. T. Farnham, 'The Progeny of *A Mirror for Magistrates*', *M.P.* xxix 1931–2.

[19] It is clear that the author of *Willobie His Avisa* had read it with attention since he borrowed some of his nobleman's arguments from it.

[20] A. Holoday, 'Giles Fletcher and the Puritans', *J.E.G.P.* liv 1955.

The Fable of Ovid treting of Narcissus

ANONYMOUS (1560)

The Argument of the fable

Lireope had a Sonne by Cephicious named Narcissius, whose conty-
nuaunce of lyfe Tyricias a prophete, affyrmyd to be longe, yf the
knowledge of hym selfe, procuryd not the contrary, whose sentence
here nowe Ecco the callynge Impe, frome whome Juno had berefte the
ryght use of spechc, so loved this Narcyssus, that throughe the thought
and care that she sustayned, for the gettynge hys good wyl that ever
despysed her, she consumed the relykes, of whiche consumed Carcas
were torned into Stones. The greate dysdayne of Narcyssus, herein
Ramusia Straungely revenged, for he heated through huntinge by the
drynkynge of a well, supposynge to quence hys thurste espyed therin
the shadowe, of hys face, wherewyth he was so ravyshed that havynge
no power to leve hys blynde desyre for the attaynyng of an impose-
belytye, there he starved. For the preperacion, whose buryall the
Nimphes, had ordyned souch furnituer as ther unto apperteyned &
had. Retornyd to the Solemne, Erthynge and buryall of suche a
carcase, they founde in sted of the ded Corpis a yelow floure which
with us beareth the name of a daffadylly.

Lireope whome once Ciphicious, dyd embrace,
And ravshe in his crokid floudes wher she was shut from grace
Dyd travell and brynge forth, when tyme of berth befel
A chyld even then whom love had lyked well,
And hym Narcissus named of whome the lot to learne,   5
Yf he shoulde number manye yeares, and perfecte age discerne
Thc reder of hys fate Tiricious yea dyd saye
If that the knowledge of hym selfe, his lyfe dyd not decaye,
Ful longe a vayne pronounce, this semed tyll hys death,
By furye quaynte dyd make it good, and unsene lose of brethe   10
For twentye yeares and one, Narcissus death escaped

27

What tyme no chylde was seene so fayre, nor yong man better shapyd,
A nomber bothe of men and maydes, did hym desyre,
But bewtye bente wyth proude dysdayne, had set hym so on fyre
That nether those whome youthe in yeares, had made his make　15
Nor pleasaunte damsels freshe of heue, coulde wyth him pleasure take
This man the fearfull hartes, inforcynge to hys nettes
The caulyng nimphe one daye, behelde that nether ever lettes
To talke to those that spake, nor yet hathe power of speche
Before by Ecco this I mene, the dobbeler of skreeche　20
A body and no voyce, was Ecco yet but howe
The blabbe had then none other use of speach, then she hath now
The later ende to geve of every sence or clause,
Wherof the wyfe of Jupiter, was fyrst and chyfe the cause
For that when she dyd seke, the syllye Imphes to take　25
That ofte she knewe wythin the hylles, had lodged wyth her make
This Ecco wyth a tale, the goddes kepte so longe
That well the Imphes myght her escape, but when she sawe this wrong
This tonge quod she where wyth, so ofte thou dydeste dysceave
The goddes Juno lyttyll use of speche, shall erste receave　30
And so her thretininges prove, yet Ecco endyth speche
Wyth dobling sound the wordes she heareth, and sendeth againe with
　　screch
Thus when Cyphicious Sonne, the desartes walkinge faste
Wyth wandrynge pace she had espyed, her love and on hym caste
Wyth stealyng steppes, she foloweth fast her hote desyre　35
And styl the nerer that she comes, the hotter is her fyre
None other wyse then as the nerer fyre dothe lye
To brimstone matters mete to borne to flayme doth more applye,
Howe ofte oh wolde she fayne, wyth plesaunte wordes him glad
And faune on hym wyth prayers swete, but nature it forbad,　40
And letteth her to begynne, but that she doth permytte
Full preste is Ecco to perfourme accordyng to her wytte,
In lystynge for to heare, some sounde hys mouth escape
Whereto her wordes she myghte applye, and him an answere shape.
By chaunce Narcissus, led from companye alone　45
Dyd saye is anye here to whome, she answereth here a none,
He musyth and amasyd, doth loke on everye syde
And caulyng loude come nere he sayth, whom she byds yeke abyde,
Agayne he looketh aboute, and seynge none that came,
Why flyst thou me quod he, who harde her answere even the same　50

He stayeth and not knowyng, whose this sounde should be
Come hether let us mete he sayde, and let us mete quod she
Then with so good a wyll, as thoughe she never harde
A sound that lyked her halfe so well, to answere afterwarde
And to perfourme her wordes, the woodes she soone forsooke   55
And to imbrace that she desyred, aboute the necke hym tooke
He flyeth faste awaye, her foulded armes that sprede
Aboute hys necke he caste awaye, and ever as he flede
Death would I chuse, ere thou hast power of me quod he
Whom she none other answere made, but thou hast power of me   60
And after that wyth leves, she hid her shamefast face
Wythin the woodes in hollow caves, maketh her dwellynge place,
Yet love dothe no whyt more decrese, but wyth her smarte
Agmentith styll and watchynge cares, consumyth her wretched harte,
By lenenes eke her skyne is drycd, and to eare   65
Her bloude consumeth, so hath she nought, but voyce and bones to
    spare,
Whereof is nothinge lefte, but voyce for all her bones
They saye as to her lykeste shape, were tourned into stones,
And sence the woodes hath bene, her home her selfe to hyde
From everye hyll and nought, but sounde in her dothe nowe abyde, 70
Thus here they other nymphes, of wooddes and waters borne
Had he dysceaved, and youngmen yeke, a nomber had in skorne,
At last wyth handes lyfte up, some to the goddes dyd playne
That so hys hap myght be, to love and not be loved agayne,
Wherto it semed wel, Ramusya gave eare   75
And sought to graunte this juste request, it after dyd appeare
A sprynge there was so fayre, that stremes like sylver had
Whiche nether shepardes happe to fynde, nor gotes that upwarde gad
Uppon the rocky hyls, nor other kynde of beste,
Wyth flashyng feete to foule the same, or troble at the leste, 80
Wherin them selves to bathe, no byrdes had made repare,
Nor leffe had fallen from any tree, the water to appeare,
About the which the grounde had made some herbes to growe
And eke the trees had kept the sunne, from commynge doune so lowe
Narcyssus theare through heate, and wery hunters game   85
Glad to take rest dyd lye hym downe, and fast beheld the same,
And as he thought to drynke, hys fervent thurste to slake
A dryer far desyre hym toke, by lokyng in the lake
For seynge as he dranke, the image of hys grace

Therewyth he rapt, fell streyght in love, wyth shadowe of his face 90
And museth at hym selfe, wyth whych astonyed cheare,
As image made of marble whyte, his countenance dyd apeare,
Lyke starres he seyth hys eyes, and Bacchus fyngeres swete
He thoughte he had on goulden heares, for Phebus not unmete
A necke lyke yvery whyte, a mouth wyth favoure good   95
A face wyth skynne as whyte as snowe, well coleryd wyth bloud
All whych he wonders at, and that he lyketh well
Is even him selfe that wonder makes, with small advice to dwell
He sees that he doeth aske, agayne doth hym desyre
Together he doeth burne him selfe, and kyndel eke the fyre   100
The well that him dysceaved, how ofte kyst he in vayne
Howe ofte there in his armes he dround, in hope for to attayne
The necke, that he desyred so muche to imbrace,
And yet himselfe he could not catche, in that unhappye place
Not knowyng what he seeth, therewith he is in love   105
And those same eyes that, erroure blindes, to errour dothe him move
Ah foole, why doest thou seke, the shape that wyll not byde
Nor beyng hathe, for turne thy face, away and it wyll slyde
The shadowe of thy selfe, it is that thou doest see
And hath no substaunce of it selfe, but comes and bydes with thee 110
Yf thou canste go awaye, with thee it wyll departe
Yet nether care for meate or slepe, could make him thence astarte
But in that shadowe place, besyde the well he lyes
Where he behelde his fayned shape, with uncontented eyes
And lyfting up those eyes, that his, destruction made   115
Unto the trees that stode aboute, he raught his armes and saide
Hath ever love, oh woodes delte crueller with man
You knowe that hyding place, hath bene to lovers now and than
Now can you call to mynde, you that suche worldes have laste
That ever anye pyned so, by love in ages paste.   120
I see and lyke it well, but that I lyke and see
Yet fynde I not suche errour loe, this love doth bring to mee
And to increase my grefe, no say nor yrkesome waye
No hylles nor waleys, with closyd, gates, dothe saye our meting nay
A lytle water here, dothe sever us in twayne,   125
He seketh I see, that I desyre, to be imbraced as fayne,
For looke how ofte my lippes, I move to kysse the lake
So oft he sheweth his mouthe, content, full well the same to take
To touche thee, mighte full well, a man wolde thinke be done

It is the leste of other thinges, that lovers oughte to shone 130
What so thou be come forthe, why doste thou me disseyve
Why flyest thou hym, that the so muche, desyreth to receyve
My bewtie and mine age, truely me thynkes I se
It is not that thou doste mislyke, for Nimphes have loved me
Thou promyste to me a hope, I wotnot howe 135
With frendly cheare, and to mine armes the same thou dost unbowe
Thou smylest when I laughe, and eke thy trekeling teares
When I doe weepe I ofte espy, with sines thy countenaunce steares
By moving of thy lyppes, and as I ges I lerne
Thou speakest words, the sence whereof, myne eares can not deserne
Even this I am I se, my proper shape I knowe 141
Wyth loving of my selfe, I borne I mone, and beare the gloue
What shall I doe, and if I aske what shall I crave
Aboundaunce brings me want, with me, it is that I would crave
Oh wolde to God I myght, departe my body fro 145
In hym that loves this wyshe is strang, hys lyking to forgo
But nowe my strength, throughe payne is fled, and my yeares
Full sone ar lyke to ende, thus dethe away my youth it beares
Yet dethe that endeth my wooes, to me it is not so sure
He whom I love ryght fayne, I wold myght lyve alenger houre 150
Nowe two to one quod he, together let us dye
In evell estate and to his shape, returneth by and by
And wyth his gusshynge tearys, so up the water starte
Hys shape that ther by darkened was, whiche when he sawe departe
Nowe whether doste thou go, abyde he cryed faste 155
Forsake not hym so cruelly, hys love that on the cast
Thoughe thee I may not touche, my sorowes to asswage
Yet maye I looke, relefe to geve unto my wretched rage
And whylest he thus tormentes, he barred all his cheste
Before the well with stonye fystes, and beates his naked breste 160
Wyth a carnacion hue, by strockes thereon dyd leave
None other wyse then apples whyte, wyth ruddy sydes receave,
Or as the growyng grapes, on sundry clusters strepe
A purpyll coler as we se, or ever they be rype,
Whyche as he dyd espye, wythin the water clere 165
No lenger coulde he duere the payne, he sawe he suffred there.
But as by fyre, to waxe ameltyng doth insue
And as by hete the rysing sunne, consumeth the mornynge due,
So feblyd by love, to waste he doth begynne

At length and quyte consumeth, by heate of hydyng fyre wythin, 170
And nether hath he nowe, hewe of red and whyte
No lyvelynes nor lusty strength, that earst dyd eyes delyte
Nor yet the corpys remaynes, that Ecco once had loved
Whiche tho wyth angry mynd she vewed, to sorow she was moved,
And loke howe ofte alas, out of hys mouth dyd passe   175
So ofte agayne wyth boundyng wordes, she cryed alas alas,
And when that he hys sydes, wyth rechles handes dyd stryke
She also then was hard to make, a sounde lamentynge lyke
Thus lokyng in the well, the last he spake was thys
Alas thou ladde to much in vayne, beloved of me amys,   180
Whych selfe same wordes agayne, this Ecco streight dyd yell
And as Narcissus toke hys leve, she bad hym eke fayre well
Hys hed that hym abused, under the grasse he thraste
And deth shut up those eyes, that on there master mused faste
And when he was receyved, into that hellye place   185
He yeke wythin the ogly Styxe, behelde hys wretched face
The wood and wattrye nimphes, that all hys susterne were
Bewayles hys lot as is ther wonte, wyth cuttynge of theyr heare
Whose waylinge Eccoes sounde dyd mournyng lyke declare
For grave pompe, a bayre wyth lyghtes and fyre they dyd prepare 190
Then body was ther none, but growing on the ground
A yelowe flower wyth lylly leaves, in sted therof they founde.

FINIS. FABULE

Scillaes Metamorphosis

The most pithie and pleasant
Historie of Glaucus and Silla

THOMAS LODGE (1589)

Walking alone (all onely full of griefe)
Within a thicket nere to *Isis* floud,
Weeping my wants, and wailing scant reliefe,
Wringing mine armes (as one with sorrowe wood);
    The piteous streames relenting at my mone   5
    Withdrew their tides, and staid to heare me grone.

From foorth the channell, with a sorrowing crie
The Sea-god *Glaucus* (with his hallowed heares
Wet in the teares of his sad mothers dye)
With piteous lookes before my face appeares;   10
    For whome the Nimphes a mossie coate did frame,
    Embroadered with his *Sillas* heavenly name.

And as I sat under a Willow tree,
The lovelie honour of faire *Thetis* bower;
Reposd his head upon my faintfull knee: 15
And when my teares had ceast their stormie shower
    He dried my cheekes, and then bespake him so,
    As when he waild I straight forgot my woe.

Infortunate, why wandreth thy content
From forth his scope as wearied of it selfe;   20
Thy bookes have schoold thee from this fond repent,
And thou canst talke by proofe of wavering pelfe:
    Unto the world such is inconstancie,
    As sapp to tree, as apple to the eye.

33

Marke how the morne in roseat colour shines,   25
And straight with cloudes the Sunnie tract is clad;
Then see how pomp through waxe and waine declines,
From high to lowe, from better to the bad:
    Take moist from Sea, take colour from his kinde,
    Before the world devoid of change thou finde.   30

With secret eye looke on the earth a while,
Regard the changes Nature forceth there;
Behold the heavens, whose course all sence beguile;
Respect thy selfe, and thou shalt find it cleere,
    That infantlike thou art become a youth,   35
    And youth forespent a wretched age ensu'th.

In searching then the schoolemens cunning noates,
Of heaven, of earth, of flowers, of springing trees,
Of hearbs, of mettall, and of *Thetis* floates,
Of lawes and nurture kept among the Bees: 40
    Conclude and knowe times change by course of fate,
    Then mourne no more, but moane my haples state.

Here gan he pause and shake his heavie head,
And fould his armes, and then unfould them straight;
Faine would he speake, but tongue was charm'd by dread, 45
Whil'st I that sawe what woes did him awaight,
    Comparing his mishaps and moane with mine,
    Gan smile for joy and drie his drooping eyne.

But (loe) a wonder; from the channels glide
A sweet melodious noyse of musicke rose,   50
That made the streame to dance a pleasant tide,
The weedes and sallowes neere the bancke that groes
    Gan sing, as when the calmest windes accorde
    To greete with balmie breath the fleeting forde.

Upon the silver bosome of the streame   55
First gan faire *Themis* shake her amber locks,
Whom all the Nimphs that waight on *Neptunes* realme
Attended from the hollowe of the rocks.
    In briefe, while these rare parragons assemble,
    The watrie world to touch their teates doo tremble. 60

Footing it featlie on the grassie ground,
These Damsels circling with their brightsome faires
The love-sicke God and I, about us wound
Like starres that *Ariadnes* crowne repaires:
    Who once hath seene or pride of morne, or day,   65
    Would deeme all pompe within their cheekes did play.

Nais faire Nimph with *Bacchus* ivorie touch,
Gan tune a passion with such sweete reports,
And everie word, noate, sigh, and pause was such,
And everie Cadence fed with such consorts,   70
    As were the *Delian* Harper bent to heare,
    Her statelie straines might tempt his curious eare.

Of love (God wot) the lovelie Nimph complained:
But so of love as forced Love to love her;
And even in Love such furious love remained,   75
As searching out his powrefull shaft to prove her,
    He found his quiver emptied of the best,
    And felt the arrowe sticking in his breast.

Under a Popler *Themis* did repose her,
And from a brier a sweetfull branch did plucke: 80
When midst the brier ere she could scarce suppose her
A Nightingale gan sing: but woe the lucke;
    The branch so neere her breast, while she did quicke her
    To turne her head, on sodaine gan to pricke her.

Whil'st smiling *Clore* midst her envious blushes,   85
Gan blame her feare and pretilie said thus;
Worse prickes than these are found among these bushes,
And yet such prickes are scarcelie feard of us.
    Nay soft (said *Chelis*) prickes doo make birds sing,
    But prickes in Ladies bosomes often sting.   90

Thus jest they on the Nightingales report,
And on the prickle of the Eglantine
On *Nais* song, and all the whole consort
In publique this sweete sentence did assigne;
    That while some smile, some sigh through change of time; 95
    Some smart, some sport amidst their youthlie prime.

Such wreathes as bound the *Thebans* ivorie brow;
Such gay trickt garlands pleit these jollie Dames;
The flowres themselves when as the Nimphes gan bowe,
Gan vaile their crestes in honour of their names:　　　100
　　And smilde their sweete and woed with so much glee,
　　As if they said, sweet Nimph come gather mee.

But pencive *Glaucus* passionate with painings,
Amidst their revell thus began his ruth;
Nimphes, flie these Groves late blasted with my plainings, 105
For cruell *Silla* nill regard my truth:
　　And leave us two consorted in our gronings,
　　To register with teares our bitter monings.

The flouds doo faile their course to see our crosse,
The fields forsake their greene to heare our griefe,　　110
The rockes will weepe whole springs to marke our losse,
The hills relent to store our scant reliefe,
　　The aire repines, the pencive birds are heavie,
　　The trees to see us paind no more are leavie.

Ay me, the Shepheards let their flockes want feeding,　115
And flockes to see their palie face are sorie,
The Nimphes to spie the flockes and shepheards needing
Prepare their teares to heare our tragicke storie:
　　Whilst we surprisde with griefe cannot disclose them,
　　With sighing with the world for to suppose them.　　120

He that hath seene the sweete *Arcadian* boy
Wiping the purple from his forced wound,
His pretie teares betokening his annoy,
His sighes, his cries, his falling on the ground,
　　The Ecchoes ringing from the rockes his fall,　　　125
　　The trees with teares reporting of his thrall:

And *Venus* starting at her love-mates crie,
Forcing hir birds to hast her chariot on;
And full of griefe at last with piteous eie
Seene where all pale with death he lay alone,　　　130
　　Whose beautie quaild, as wont the Lillies droop
　　When wastfull winter windes doo make them stoop:

Her daintie hand addrest to dawe her deere,
Her roseall lip alied to his pale cheeke,
Her sighes, and then her lookes and heavie cheere,   135
Her bitter threates, and then her passions meeke;
    How on his senseles corpes she lay a crying,
    As if the boy were then but new a dying.

He that hath vewd *Angelica* the faire
Bestraught with fancie nere the *Caspian* springs: 140
Renting the tresses of her golden haire,
How on her harpe with pitious notes she sings
    Of *Rolands* ruth, of *Medors* false depart,
    Sighing each rest from center of her heart.

How now she writes upon a beechen bow   145
Her *Medors* name, and bedlam like againe
Calls all the heaven to witnes of his vow,
And straight againe begins a mournefull straine,
    And how in thought of her true faith forsooken
    He fled her bowres, and how his league was broken.   150

Aye me who markes her harpe hang up againe
Upon the willowes watered with her teares,
And how she rues to read her *Rolands* paine,
When but the shadowe of his name appeares;
    Would make more plainings from his eyes to flee   155
    Than teares distill from amber weeping tree.

He that hath knowne the passionate mishappes
That nere *Olimpus* faire *Lucina* felt
When as her *Latium* love her fancie trappes,
How with suspect her inward soule dooth melt: 160
    Or markt the Morne her *Cephalus* complaining,
    May then recount the course of all our paining.

But tender Nimphes to you belongs no teene;
Then favor me in flying from this bower
Whereas but care and thought of crosses been,   165
Leave me that loose my selfe through fancies power,
    Through fancies power which had I leave to loose it,
    No fancie then should see me for to choose it.

When you are fled the Heaven shall lowre for sorrowe,
The day orecast shalbe betimed with sable,   170
The aire from Sea such streaming showres shall borrow
As earth to beare the brunt shall not be able,
   And shippes shall safely saile whereas beforne
   The ploughman watcht the reaping of his corne.

Goe you in peace to *Neptunes* watrie sound,   175
No more may *Glaucus* play him with so prettie;
But shun resort where solace nill be found,
And plaine my *Scillaes* pride and want of pittie:
   Alas sweet Nimphs my Godhead's all in vaine,
   For why this brest includes immortall paine.   180

Scilla hath eyes, but too sweete eyes hath *Scilla*;
Scilla hath hands, faire hands but coy in touching;
Scilla in wit surpasseth grave *Sibilla*,
Scilla hath words, but words well storde with grutching;
   Scilla a Saint in looke, no Saint in scorning: 185
   Looke Saint-like *Scilla*, least I die with mourning.

Alas why talke I? Sea-god cease to mourne her,
For in her nay my joyes are ever ceasing:
Cease life or love, then shall I never blame her;
But neither love nor life may finde decreasing.   190
   A mortall wound is my immortall being,
   Which passeth thought, or eyes advised seeing.

Herewith his faltring tongue by sighs oppressed
Forsooke his office, and his bloud resorted
To feede the heart that wholly was distressed,   195
Whilst pale (like *Pallas* flowre) my knee supported
   His feeble head and arme, so full of anguish,
   That they which sawe his sorrowes gan to languish.

Themis the coyest of this beauteous traine
On hillie toppes the wonderous *Moly* found,   200
Which dipt in balmie deaw she gan to straine,
And brought her present to recure his wound:
   Clore she gathered *Amaranthus* flower,
   And *Nais Ajax* blossom in that stowre.

Some chafe his temples with their lovelie hands,   205
Some sprinkle water on his pale wan cheekes,
Some weepe, some wake, some curse affections bandes;
To see so young, so faire, become so weake:
    But not their pitious hearbs, or springs have working,
    To ease that heart where wanton love is lurking.   210

Naithles though loath to shewe his holy kindnes
On everie one he spent a looke for favour,
And prayed their pardon vouching *Cupids* blindnes,
(Oh fancies fond that naught but sorrowes savour);
    To see a lovely God leave Sea Nimphes so: 215
    Who cannot doome upon his deadly woe?

Themis that knewe, that waters long restrained
Breake foorth with greater billowes than the brookes
That swetely float through meades with flowres distained,
With cheerefull laies did raise his heavie lookes;   220
    And bad him speake and tell what him agreev'd:
    For griefes disclos'd (said she) are soone releev'd.

And as she wisht so all the rest did woe him;
By whose incessant suites at last invited,
He thus discovered that which did undoo him,   225
And orderlie his hideous harmes recited,
    When first with fingers wagge he gan to still them,
    And thus with drierie tearmes of love did fill them.

Ah Nimphes (quoth he) had I by reason learnt
That secret art which birdes have gaind by sence,   230
By due foresight misfortune to prevent;
Or could my wit controule mine eyes offence:
    You then should smile and I should tell such stories,
    As woods, and waves should triumph in our glories.

But *Nereus* daughters, Sea-borne Saints attend,   235
Lake breeding Geese when from the Easterne clime
They list unto the westerne waters wend
To choose their place of rest by course of time,
    Approaching *Taurus* haughtie topped hill
    They charme their cackle by this wondrous skill.   240

The climing mountaine neighbouring ayre welnie,
Hath harbored in his rockes and desart haunts
Whole airies of Eagles prest to flie
That gazing on the Sonne their birth right vaunts,
    Which birds of *Jove* with deadlie fewde pursue   245
    The wandering Geese, when so they presse in vewe.

These fearefull flitting troopes by nature tought,
Passing these dangerous places of pursuit:
When all the desart vales they through have sought,
With pibbles stop their beakes to make them mute,   250
    And by this meanes their dangerous deathes prevent
    And gaine their wished waters of frequent.

But I fond God (I God complaine thy follie)
Let birds by sense exceede my reason farre:
Whilom than I who was more strong and jollie   255
Who more contemnd affections wanton warre?
    Who lesse than I lov'd lustfull *Cupids* arrowes?
    Who now with curse and plagues poore *Glaucus* harrowes.

How have I leapt to heare the *Tritons* play
A harsh retreat unto the swelling flouds?   260
How have I kept the Dolphins at a bay,
When as I ment to charme their wanton moods?
    How have the angrie windes growne calme for love,
    When as these fingers did my harpe strings move?

Was any Nimph, you Nimphes was ever any   265
That tangled not her fingers in my tresse?
Some well I wot and of that some full many
Wisht or my faire, or their desire were lesse
    Even *Ariadne* gazing from the skie
    Became enamorde of poore *Glaucus* eye.   270

Amidst this pride of youth and beauties treasure
It was my chaunce, you floods can tell my chancing,
Fleeting along *Sicillian* bounds for pleasure,
To spie a Nimph of such a radiant glancing,
    As when I lookt, a beame of subtill firing   275
    From eye to heart incenst a deepe desiring.

Ah had the vaile of reason clad mine eye,
This foe of freedome had not burnt my heart:
But birds are blest, and most accurst am I
Who must reporte her glories to my smart,   280
   The Nimph I sawe and lov'de her, all to cruell
   Scilla, faire *Scilla*, my fond fancies juell.

Her haire not trust, but scatterd on her brow,
Surpassing *Hiblas* honnie for the view,
Or softned golden wires; I know not how   285
Love with a radiant beautie did pursue
   My too judiciall eyes, in darting fire
   That kindled straight in me my fond desire.

Within these snares first was my heart intrapped,
Till through those golden shrowdes mine eies did see   290
An yvorie shadowed front, wherein was wrapped
Those pretie bowres where Graces couched be:
   Next which her cheekes appeerd like crimson silk,
   Or ruddie rose bespred on whitest milk.

Twixt which the nose in lovely tenor bends,   295
(Too traitrous pretie for a Lovers view:)
Next which her lips like violets commends
By true proportion that which dooth insue;
   Which when they smile, present unto the eies
   The *Oceans* pride and yvorie paradice.   300

Her pollisht necke of milke white snowes doth shine,
As when the Moone in Winter night beholdes them:
Her breast of alablaster cleere and fine,
Whereon two rising apples faire unfolds them
   Like *Cinthias* face when in her full she shineth,   305
   And blushing to her Love-mates bower declineth.

From whence in length her armes doo sweetly spred
Like two rare branchie saples in the Spring,
Yeelding five lovely sprigs from everie head,
Proportioned alike in everie thing;   310
   Which featly sprout in length like springborne frends,
   Whose pretie tops with five sweet roses ends.

But why alas should I that Marble hide
That doth adorne the one and other flanke,
From whence a mount of quickned snow doth glide;   315
Or els the vale that bounds this milkwhite banke,
  Where *Venus* and her sisters hide the fount,
  Whose lovely *Nectar* dooth all sweetes surmount.

Confounded with descriptions, I must leave them;
Lovers must thinke, and Poets must report them: 320
For silly wits may never well conceave them,
Unlesse a speciall grace from heaven consort them.
  Aies me, these faires attending *Scilla* won me:
  But now (sweet Nimphes) attend what hath undon me.

The lovely breast where all this beautie rested,   325
Shrowded within a world of deepe disdaine:
For where I thought my fancie should be feasted
With kinde affect, alas (unto my paine)
  When first I woode the wanton straight was flying,
  And gave repulse before we talkt of trying.   330

How oft have I (too often have I done so)
In silent night when everie eye was sleeping,
Drawne neere her cave, in hope her love were won so,
Forcing the neighboring waters through my weeping
  To wake the windes, who did afflict her dwelling   335
  Whilst I with teares my passion was a telling.

When midst the *Caspian* seas the wanton plaid,
I drew whole wreaths of corrall from the rockes:
And in her lap my heavenly presents laid:
But she unkind rewarded me with mockes,   340
  Such are the fruites that spring from Ladies coying,
  Who smile at teares, and are intrapt with toying.

Tongue might grow wearie to report my wooings,
And heart might burst to thinke of her deniall:
May none be blamde but heaven for all these dooings,   345
That yeeld no helpes inmidst of all my triall.
  Heart, tongue, thought, pen nil serve me to repent me,
  Disdaine her selfe should strive for to lament me.

Wretched Love let me die, end my love by my death;
Dead alas still I live, flie my life, fade my love. 350
Out alas love abides, still I joy vitall breath:
Death in love, love is death, woe is me that doo prove.
   Paine and woe, care and griefe every day about me hovers:
   Then but death what can quel al the plages of haples lovers?

Aies me my moanings are like water drops 355
That neede an age to pearce her marble heart,
I sow'd true zeale, yet fruiteles were my crops:
I plighted faith, yet falsehoode wrought my smart:
   I praisd her lookes, her lookes dispised *Glaucus,*
   Was ever amorous Sea-god scorned thus? 360

A hundereth swelling tides my mother spent
Upon these lockes, and all hir Nimphes were prest,
To pleit them faire when to her bowre I went:
He that hath seene the wandring *Phœbus* crest,
   Toucht with the Christall of *Eurotas* spring, 365
   The pride of these my bushie locks might sing.

But short discourse beseemes my bad successe,
Eache office of a lover I performed:
So fervently my passions did her presse,
So sweete my laies, my speech so well reformed, 370
   That (cruell) when she sawe naught would begile me
   With angrie lookes the Nimph did thus exile me.

Packe hence thou fondling to the westerne Seas,
Within some calmy river shrowd thy head:
For never shall my faire thy love appease, 375
Since fancie from this bosome late is fled:
   And if thou love me shewe it in departing:
   For why thy presence dooth procure my smarting.

This said with angrie lookes, away she hasted
As fast as flie the flouds before the winds: 380
When I poore soule with wretched sorrowes wasted,
Exclaimde on love, which wit and reason blinds:
   And banisht from hir bowre with wofull poasting
   I bent my selfe to seeke a forreine coasting.

At last in wandring through the greater Seas 385
It was my chance to passe the noted streights:
And wearied sore in seeking after ease,
Amidst the creekes, and watrie coole receits,
   I spied from farre by helpe of sonnie beames
   A fruitefull Ile begirt with *Ocean* streames. 390

Westward I fleeted, and with heedfull eie
Beheld the chalkie cliffes that tempt the aire,
Till at the last it was my chance to spie
A pleasant entrance to the flouds repaire;
   Through which I prest, and wondring there beheld 395
   On either side a sweete and fruitfull field.

Isis (the Ladie of that lovely streame)
Made holiday in view of my resort;
And all the Nimphes of that her watrie realme
Gan trip for joy, to make me mickle sport: 400
   But I poore soule with no such joyes contented,
   Forsooke their bowers, and secretly lamented.

All solitarie rome I heere about,
Now on the shoare, now in the streame I weepe,
Fire burnes within, and gastly feare without, 405
No rest, no ease, no hope of any sleepe:
   Poore banisht God, heere have I still remained,
   Since time my *Scilla* hath my sutes disdained.

And heere consort I now with haplesse men,
Yeelding them comfort, (though my wound be curelesse) 410
Songs of remorse I warble now and then,
Wherein I curse fond Love and Fortune durelesse,
   Wanhope my weale, my trust but bad adventure,
   Circumference is care, my heart the center.

Whilest thus he spake, fierce *Ate* charmde his tongue, 415
His senses faild, his armes were folded straight,
And now he sighes, and then his heart is stung;
Againe he speakes gainst fancies fond deceit,
   And teares his tresses with his fingers faire,
   And rents his roabs, halfe mad with deepe dispaire. 420

The piteous Nimphes that viewd his heavie plight,
And heard the sequell of his bad successe,
Did loose the springs of their remorsefull sight,
And wept so sore to see his scant redresse:
    That of their teares there grew a pretie brooke,   425
    Whose Christall cleares the clowdes of pencive looke.

Alas woes me, how oft have I bewept
So faire, so yong, so lovely, and so kinde,
And whilst the God upon my bosome slept,
Behelde the scarres of his afflicted minde,   430
    Imprinted in his yvorie brow by care,
    That fruitlesse fancie left unto his share.

My wandring lines, bewitch not so my sences:
But gentle Muse direct their course aright,
Delayes in tragicke tales procure offences: 435
Yeeld me such feeling words, that whilst I wright
    My working lines may fill mine eyes with languish,
    And they to note my mones may melt with anguish.

The wofull *Glaucus* thus with woes attainted,
The pencive Nimphes agreevd to see his plight,   440
The flouds and fields with his laments acquainted,
My selfe amazd to see this heavie sight;
    On sodaine *Thetis* with her traine approched,
    And gravely thus her amorous sonne reproched.

My sonne (said she) immortall have I made thee,   445
Amidst my watrie realmes who may compare
Or match thy might? Why then should care invade thee,
That art so yong, so lovely, fresh and faire.
    Alas fond God, it merits great reproving
    In States of worth, to doate on foolish loving.   450

Come wend with me, and midst thy Fathers bowre
Let us disport and frolicke for a while
In spite of Love: although he powte and lowre,
Good exercise will idle lusts beguile;
    Let wanton *Scilla* coy her where she will,   455
    Live thou my sonne by reasons levell still.

Thus said the Goddesse: and although her words
Gave signes of counsaile, pompe and majestie:
Yet nathelesse her piteous eye affoords
Some pretie witnesse to the standers by,   460
 That in her thoughts (for all her outward show)
 She mournd to see her Sonne amated so.

But (welladay) her words have little force,
The haples lover worne with working woe,
Upon the ground lay pale as any corse,   465
And were not teares which from his eyes did flowe,
 And sighes that witnesse he enjoyd his breath,
 They might have thought him Citizen of death.

Which spectacle of care made *Thetis* bow,
And call on *Glaucus*, and command her Sonne   470
To yeelde her right: and hir advice allow,
But (woe) the man whome fancie had undone
 Nill marke her rules: nor words, nor weeping teares
 Can fasten counsaile in the lovers eares.

The Queene of Sea, with all hir Nimphes assured   475
That no perswasion might releeve his care:
Kneeling adowne, their faltring tongues enured
To tempt faire *Venus* by their vowed praier:
 The course whereof as I could beare in minde
 With sorrowing sobbes they uttered in this kinde.   480

Borne of the Sea, thou *Paphian* Queene of love,
Mistris of sweete conspiring harmonie:
Lady of *Cipris*, for whose sweete behove
The Shepeheards praise the youth of *Thessallie*:
 Daughter of *Jove* and Sister to the Sonne,   485
 Assist poore *Glaucus* late by love undone.

So maist thou baine thee in th'*Arcadian* brookes,
And play with *Vulcans* rivall when thou list,
And calme his jealous anger by thy lookes,
And knit thy temples with a roseat twist   490
 If thou thy selfe and thine almightie Sonne,
 Assist poore *Glaucus* late by love undone.

May earth still praise thee for her kinde increase:
And beasts adore thee for their fruitfull wombes,
And fowles with noates thy praises never cease,
And Bees admire thee for their honnie combes:
    So thou thy selfe and thine almightie Sonne,
    Assist poore *Glaucus* late by love undone.

No sooner from her reverent lips were past
Those latter lines, but mounting in the East,
Faire *Venus* in her ivorie coatch did hast,
And toward those pencive dames, her course addrest;
    Her doves so plied their waving wings with flight,
    That straight the sacred Goddesse came in sight.

Upon her head she bare that gorgeous Crowne,
Wherein the poore *Amyntas* is a starre;
Her lovely lockes, her bosome hang adowne
(Those netts that first insnar'd the God of warre:)
    Delicious lovely shine her prettie eies,
    And one her cheekes carnatioon cloudes arise,

The stately roab she ware upon her back
Was lillie white, wherein with cullored silke;
Her Nimphes had blaz'd the yong *Adonis* wrack,
And *Lædas* rape by Swan as white as milke,
    And on her lap her lovely Sonne was plaste,
    Whose beautie all his mothers pompe defaste.

A wreath of roses hem'd his Temples in,
His tresse was curlde and cleere as beaten gold;
Haught were his lookes, and lovely was his skin,
Each part as pure as Heavens eternall mold,
    And on his eies a milkewhite wreath was spred,
    Which longst his backe, with prettie pleits did shed.

Two daintie wings of partie coulored plumes
Adorne his shoulders dallying with the winde;
His left hand weelds a Torch, that ever fumes:
And in his right, his bowe that fancies bind,
    And on his back his Quiver hangs well stored
    With sundrie shaftes, that sundrie hearts have gored.

The Deities ariv'd in place desired;
Faire *Venus* her to *Thetis* first bespake,   530
Princesse of Sea (quoth she) as you required
From *Ceston* with my Sonne, my course I take:
   Frollick faire Goddesse, Nimphs forsake your plaining,
   My Sonne hath power and favour yet remaining.

With that the reverend powres each other kissed,   535
And Cupid smil'd upon the Nimphes for pleasure:
So naught but *Glaucus* solace there was missed,
Which to effect the Nimphes withouten measure
   Intreate the God, who at the last drewe nie
   The place, where *Glaucus* full of care did lie,   540

And from his bowe a furious dart hee sent
Into that wound which he had made before:
That like *Achilles* sworde became the teint
To cure the wound that it had carv'd before:
   And sodeinly the Sea-god started up: 545
   Revivde, relievd, and free from Fancies cup.

No more of love, no more of hate he spoke,
No more he forst the sighes from out his breast:
His sodaine joye his pleasing smiles provoke,
And all aloft he shakes his bushie creast,   550
   Greeting the Gods and Goddesses beside,
   And everie Nimph upon that happie tide.

Cupid and he together hand in hand
Approach the place of this renowned traine:
Ladies (said he) release from amorous band,   555
Receive my prisoner to your grace againe.
   Glaucus gave thankes, when *Thetis* glad with blisse
   Embrast his neck, and his kind cheekes did kisse.

To see the Nimphes in flockes about him play,
How *Nais* kempt his head, and washt his browes: 560
How *Thetis* checkt him with his welladay,
How *Clore* told him of his amorous vowes,
   How *Venus* praisd him for his faithfull love,
   Within my heart a sodein joy did move.

Whilst in this glee this holy troope delight,   565
Along the streame a farre faire *Scilla* floated,
And coilie vaunst hir creast in open sight:
Whose beauties all the tides with wonder noated,
 Fore whom *Palemon* and the *Tritons* danced
 Whilst she hir limmes upon the tide advanced.   570

Whose swift approach made all the Godheads wonder:
Glaucus gan smile to see his lovelie foe,
Rage almost rent poore *Thetis* heart asonder:
Was never happie troope confused so
 As were these deities and daintie dames,   575
 When they beheld the cause of *Glaucus* blames.

Venus commends the carriage of her eye,
Nais upbraides the dimple in her chinne,
Cupid desires to touch the wantons thie,
Clore she sweares that everie eie dooth sinne   580
 That likes a Nimph that so contemneth love,
 As no attempts her lawles heart may move.

Thetis impatient of her wrong sustained,
With envious teares her roseat cheekes afflicted;
And thus of *Scillas* former pride complained;   585
Cupid (said she) see her that hath inflicted
 The deadlie wound that harmde my lovelie sonne,
 From whome the ofspring of my care begonne.

Oh if there dwell within thy brest my boy
Or grace, or pittie, or remorse (said she)   590
Now bend thy bowe, abate yon wantons joy,
And let these Nimphes thy rightfull justice see.
 The God soone won, gan shoote, and cleft her heart
 With such a shaft as causd her endles smart.

The tender Nimph attainted unawares,   595
Fares like the *Libian* Lionesse that flies
The Hunters Launce that wounds her in his snares;
Now gins shee love, and straight on *Glaucus* cries;
 Whilst on the shore the goddesses rejoyce,
 And all the Nimphes afflict the ayre with noyse.   600

To shoare she flitts, and swift as *Affrick* wind
Her footing glides upon the yeelding grasse,
And wounded by affect recure to finde
She sodainely with sighes approcht the place
   Where *Glaucus* sat, and wearie with her harmes   605
   Gan claspe the Sea-god in her amorous armes.

Glaucus my love (quoth she) looke on thy lover,
Smile gentle *Glaucus* on the Nimph that likes thee;
But starke as stone sat he, and list not prove her:
(Ah silly Nimph the selfesame God that strikes thee   610
   With fancies darte, and hath thy freedome slaine)
   Wounds *Glaucus* with the arrowe of disdaine.

Oh kisse no more kind Nimph he likes no kindnes,
Love sleepes in him, to flame within thy brest,
Cleer'd are his eies, where thine are clad with blindnes;   615
Free'd be his thoughts, where thine must taste unrest:
   Yet nill she leave, for never love will leave her,
   But fruiteles hopes and fatall happes deceave her.

Lord how her lippes doo dwell upon his cheekes;
And how she lookes for babies in his eies: 620
And how she sighes, and sweares shee loves and leekes,
And how she vowes, and he her vowes envies:
   Trust me the envious Nimphs in looking on,
   Were forst with teares for to assist her mone.

How oft with blushes would she plead for grace,   625
How oft with whisperings would she tempt his eares:
How oft with Christall did she wet his face:
How oft she wipte them with her Amber heares:
   So oft me thought, I oft in heart desired
   To see the end whereto disdaine aspired.   630

Palemon with the *Tritons* roare for griefe,
To see the Mistris of their joyes amated:
But *Glaucus* scornes the Nimph, that waites reliefe:
And more she loves the more the Sea-god hated,
   Such change, such chance, such sutes, such storms beleeve
      me   635
   Poore silly wretch did hartely agreeve me.

As when the fatall bird of *Augurie*
Seeing a stormie dismall cloude arise
Within the South, foretells with piteous crie
The weeping tempest, that on sudden hies: 640
  So she poore soule, in view of his disdaine
  Began to descant on her future paine.

And fixing eye upon the fatall ground,
Whole hoasts of flouds drew deaw from out her eyes;
And when through inward griefe the lasse did sound,   645
The softned grasse like billowes did arise
  To woe her brests, and wed her limmes so daintie,
  Whom wretched love had made so weake and faintie.

(Ayes me), me thinks I see her *Thetis* fingers
Renting her locks as she were woe begon her;   650
And now her lippes upon his lipping lingers:
Oh lingring paine where love nill list to mone her:
  Rue me that writes, for why her ruth deserves it:
  Hope needs must faile, where sorrow scarce preserves it.

To make long tale were tedious to the wofull,   655
Wofull that read what wofull shee approoved:
In briefe her heart with deepe dispaire was so full,
As since she might not win her sweete beloved.
  With hideous cries like winde borne backe she fled
  Unto the Sea, and toward *Sicillia* sped.   660

Sweete *Zephirus* upon that fatall howre
In haples tide midst watrie world was walking;
Whose milder sighes, alas, had little power
To whisper peace amongst the Godheads talking:
  Who all in one conclude for to pursue,   665
  The haples Nimph, to see what would ensue.

Venus her selfe and her faire Sonne gan hie
Within their ivorie Coach drawne forth by doves
After this haples Nimph, their power to trie:
The Nimphes in hope to see their vowed loves,   670
  Gan cut the watrie boasom of the tide,
  As in *Cayster Phœbus* birds doe glide.

Thetis in pompe upon a *Tritons* back
Did poast her straight attended by her traine;
But *Glaucus* free from love by lovers wrack,   675
Seeing me pencive where I did remaine,
    Upon a *Dolphin* horst me (as he was)
    Thus on the *Ocean* hand in hand we passe.

Our talke midway was nought but still of wonder,
Of change, of chaunce, of sorrow, and her ending;   680
I wept for want: he said, time bringes men under,
And secret want can finde but small befrending.
    And as he said, in that before I tried it,
    I blamde my wit forewarnd, yet never spied it.

What neede I talke the order of my way,   685
Discourse was steeresman while my barke did saile,
My ship conceit, and fancie was my bay:
If these faile me, then faint my Muse and faile,
    Hast brought us where the haples Nimph sojourned,
    Beating the weeping waves that for her mourned.   690

He that hath seene the Northren blastes dispoile
The pompe of Prime, and with a whistling breath
Blast and dispearse the beauties of the soile;
May thinke upon her paines more worse than death.
    Alas poore Lasse the *Ecchoes* in the rockes   695
    Of *Sicilie*, her piteous plaining mockes.

Eccho her selfe when *Scilla* cried out *O love!*
With piteous voice from out her hollow den
Returnd these words, these words of sorrow, (*no love*)
No love (quoth she) then fie on traiterous men,   700
    Then fie on hope: then fie on hope (quoth *Eccho*)
    To everie word the Nimph did answere so.

For every sigh, the Rockes returnes a sigh;
For everie teare, their fountaines yeelds a drop;
Till we at last the place approached nigh,   705
And heard the Nimph that fed on sorrowes sop
    Make woods, and waves, and rockes, and hills admire
    The wonderous force of her untam'd desire.

Glaucus (quoth she) is faire: whilst *Eccho* sings
Glaucus is faire: but yet he hateth *Scilla*   710
The wretch reportes: and then her armes she wrings
Whilst *Eccho* tells her this, he hateth *Scilla*,
  No hope (quoth she): no hope (quoth *Eccho*) then.
  Then fie on men, when she said, fie on men.

Furie and *Rage*, *Wan-hope*, *Dispaire*, and *Woe*   715
From *Ditis* den by *Ate* sent, drewe nie:
Furie was red, with rage his eyes did gloe,
Whole flakes of fire from foorth his mouth did flie,
  His hands and armes ibath'd in blood of those
  Whome fortune, sinne, or fate made Countries foes.   720

Rage, wan and pale upon a Tiger sat,
Knawing upon the bones of mangled men;
Naught can he view, but he repinde thereat:
His lockes were Snakes bred foorth in Stigian den,
  Next whom, *Dispaire* that deepe disdained elf   725
  Delightlesse livde, still stabbing of her self.

Woe all in blacke, within her hands did beare
The fatall torches of a Funerall,
Her Cheekes were wet, dispearsed was hir heare,
Her voice was shrill (yet loathsome therewith all):   730
  Wan-hope (poore soule) on broken Ancker sitts,
  Wringing his armes as robbed of his witts.

These five at once the sorrowing Nimph assaile,
And captive lead her bound into the rocks,
Where howling still she strives for to prevaile,   735
With no availe yet strives she: for hir locks
  Are chang'd with wonder into hideous sands,
  And hard as flint become her snow-white hands.

The waters howle with fatall tunes about her,
The aire dooth scoule when as she turnes within them,   740
The winds and waves with puffes and billowes skout her;
Waves storme, aire scoules, both wind and waves begin them
  To make the place this mournful Nimph doth weepe in,
  A haples haunt whereas no Nimph may keepe in.

The Sea-man wandring by that famous Isle, 745
Shuns all with feare dispairing *Scillaes* bowre;
Nimphes, Sea-gods, Syrens when they list to smile
Forsake the haunt of *Scilla* in that stowre:
  Ah Nimphes thought I, if everie coy one felt
  The like misshappes, their flintie hearts would melt. 750

Thetis rejoyst to see her foe deprest,
Glaucus was glad, since *Scilla* was enthrald;
The Nimphs gan smile, to boast their *Glaucus* rest:
Venus and *Cupid* in their throanes enstald,
  At *Thetis* beck to *Neptunes* bowre repaire, 755
  Whereas they feast amidst his pallace faire.

Of pure immortall *Nectar* is their drinke,
And sweete *Ambrosia* dainties doo repast them,
The *Tritons* sing, *Palemon* smiles to thinke
Upon the chance, and all the Nimphs doo hast them 760
  To trick up mossie garlands where they woon,
  For lovely *Venus* and her conquering Sonne.

From foorth the fountaines of his mothers store,
Glaucus let flie a daintie Christall baine
That washt the Nimphs with labour tir'd before: 765
Cupid hee trips among this lovely traine,
  Alonely I apart did write this storie
  With many a sigh and heart full sad and sorie.

Glaucus when all the Goddesses tooke rest,
Mounted upon a Dolphin full of glee: 770
Conveide me friendly from this honored feast,
And by the way, such Sonnets song to me,
  That all the Dolphins neighbouring of his glide
  Daunst with delight, his reverend course beside.

At last he left me, where at first he found me, 775
Willing me let the world and ladies knowe
Of *Scillas* pride, and then by oath he bound me
To write no more, of that whence shame dooth grow:
  Or tie my pen to *Pennie-knaves* delight,
  But live with fame, and so for fame to wright. 780

L'envoy.

Ladies he left me, trust me I missay not,
But so he left me, as he wild me tell you:
That Nimphs must yeeld, when faithfull lovers straie not,
Least through contempt, almightie love compell you
   With *Scilla* in the rockes to make your biding   785
   A cursed plague, for womens proud back-sliding.

FINIS

Hero and Leander

CHRISTOPHER MARLOWE (1598, entered 1593)

THE ARGUMENT OF THE FIRST SESTYAD

Heros *description and her Loves,*
The Phane of Venus, *where he moves*
His worthie Love-suite, and attaines;
Whose blisse the wrath of Fates restraines,
For Cupids *grace to* Mercurie,
Which tale the Author doth implie.

On *Hellespont* guiltie of True-loves blood,
In view and opposit two citties stood,
Seaborderers, disjoin'd by *Neptunes* might:
The one *Abydos,* the other *Sestos* hight.
At *Sestos, Hero* dwelt; *Hero* the faire,   5
Whom young *Apollo* courted for her haire,
And offred as a dower his burning throne,
Where she should sit for men to gaze upon.
The outside of her garments were of lawne,
The lining, purple silke, with guilt starres drawne,   10
Her wide sleeves greene, and bordered with a grove,
Where *Venus* in her naked glory strove,
To please the carelesse and disdainfull eies,
Of proud *Adonis* that before her lies.
Her kirtle blew, whereon was many a staine,   15
Made with the blood of wretched Lovers slaine.
Upon her head she ware a myrtle wreath,
From whence her vaile reacht to the ground beneath.
Her vaile was artificiall flowers and leaves,
Whose workmanship both man and beast deceaves.   20
Many would praise the sweet smell as she past,
When t'was the odour which her breath foorth cast.
And there for honie, Bees have sought in vaine,

56

And beat from thence, have lighted there againe.
About her necke hung chaines of peble stone,   25
Which lightned by her necke, like Diamonds shone.
She ware no gloves, for neither sunne nor wind
Would burne or parch her hands, but to her mind,
Or warme or coole them, for they tooke delite
To play upon those hands, they were so white.   30
Buskins of shels all silvered, used she,
And brancht with blushing corall to the knee;
Where sparrowes pearcht, of hollow pearle and gold,
Such as the world would woonder to behold:
Those with sweet water oft her handmaid fils,   35
Which as shee went would cherupe through the bils.
Some say, for her the fairest *Cupid* pyn'd,
And looking in her face, was strooken blind.
But this is true, so like was one the other,
As he imagyn'd *Hero* was his mother.   40
And oftentimes into her bosome flew,
About her naked necke his bare armes threw,
And laid his childish head upon her brest,
And with still panting rockt, there tooke his rest.
So lovely faire was *Hero*, *Venus* Nun,   45
As nature wept, thinking she was undone;
Because she tooke more from her than she left,
And of such wondrous beautie her bereft:
Therefore in signe her treasure suffred wracke,
Since *Heroes* time, hath halfe the world beene blacke. 50
Amorous *Leander*, beautifull and yoong,
(Whose tragedie divine *Musæus* soong)
Dwelt at *Abidus*, since him, dwelt there none,
For whom succeeding times make greater mone.
His dangling tresses that were never shorne,   55
Had they beene cut, and unto *Colchos* borne,
Would have allu'rd the vent'rous youth of *Greece*,
To hazard more, than for the golden Fleece.
Faire *Cinthia* wisht, his armes might be her spheare,
Greefe makes her pale, because she mooves not there. 60
His bodie was as straight as *Circes* wand,
Jove might have sipt out *Nectar* from his hand.
Even as delicious meat is to the tast,

So was his necke in touching, and surpast
The white of *Pelops* shoulder. I could tell ye,   65
How smooth his brest was, and how white his bellie,
And whose immortall fingars did imprint,
That heavenly path, with many a curious dint,
That runs along his backe, but my rude pen,
Can hardly blazon foorth the loves of men,   70
Much lesse of powerfull gods, let it suffise,
That my slacke muse, sings of *Leanders* eies.
Those orient cheekes and lippes, exceeding his
That leapt into the water for a kis
Of his owne shadow, and despising many,   75
Died ere he could enjoy the love of any.
Had wilde *Hippolitus Leander* seene,
Enamoured of his beautie had he beene,
His presence made the rudest paisant melt,
That in the vast uplandish countrie dwelt,   80
The barbarous Thratian soldier moov'd with nought,
Was moov'd with him, and for his favour sought.
Some swore he was a maid in mans attire,
For in his lookes were all that men desire,
A pleasant smiling cheeke, a speaking eye,   85
A brow for love to banquet roiallye,
And such as knew he was a man would say,
Leander, thou art made for amorous play:
Why art thou not in love, and lov'd of all?
Though thou be faire, yet be not thine owne thrall.   90
    The men of wealthie *Sestos*, everie yeare,
(For his sake whom their goddesse held so deare,
Rose-cheekt *Adonis*) kept a solemne feast,
Thither resorted many a wandring guest,
To meet their loves; such as had none at all,   95
Came lovers home, from this great festivall.
For everie street like to a Firmament
Glistered with breathing stars, who where they went,
Frighted the melancholie earth, which deem'd,
Eternall heaven to burne, for so it seem'd,   100
As if another *Phaeton* had got
The guidance of the sunnes rich chariot.
But far above the loveliest *Hero* shin'd,

And stole away th'inchaunted gazers mind,
For like Sea-nimphs inveigling harmony, 105
So was her beautie to the standers by.
Nor that night-wandring pale and watrie starre,
(When yawning dragons draw her thirling carre,
From *Latmus* mount up to the glomie skie,
Where crown'd with blazing light and majestie, 110
She proudly sits) more over-rules the flood,
Than she the hearts of those that neere her stood.
Even as, when gawdie Nymphs pursue the chace,
Wretched *Ixions* shaggie footed race,
Incenst with savage heat, gallop amaine, 115
From steepe Pine-bearing mountains to the plaine:
So ran the people foorth to gaze upon her,
And all that view'd her, were enamour'd on her.
And as in furie of a dreadfull fight,
Their fellowes being slaine or put to flight, 120
Poore soldiers stand with fear of death dead strooken,
So at her presence all surpris'd and tooken,
Await the sentence of her scornefull eies:
He whom she favours lives, the other dies.
There might you see one sigh, another rage, 125
And some (their violent passions to asswage)
Compile sharpe satyrs, but alas too late,
For faithfull love will never turne to hate.
And many seeing great princes were denied,
Pyn'd as they went, and thinking on her died. 130
On this feast day, O cursed day and hower,
Went *Hero* thorow *Sestos*, from her tower
To *Venus* temple, where unhappilye,
As after chaunc'd, they did each other spye,
So faire a church as this, had *Venus* none, 135
The wals were of discoloured *Jasper* stone,
Wherein was *Proteus* carved, and o'rehead
A livelie vine of greene sea agget spread;
Where by one hand light headed *Bacchus* hoong,
And with the other, wine from grapes out wroong. 140
Of Christall shining faire, the pavement was,
The towne of *Sestos*, cal'd it *Venus* glasse,
There might you see the gods in sundrie shapes,

Committing headdie ryots, incest, rapes:
For know, that underneath this radiant floure,   145
Was *Danaes* statue in a brazen tower,
Jove, slylie stealing from his sisters bed,
To dallie with *Idalian Ganimed*:
And for his love *Europa*, bellowing loud,
And tumbling with the Rainbow in a cloud,   150
Blood-quaffing *Mars*, heaving the yron net,
Which limping *Vulcan* and his *Cyclops* set:
Love kindling fire, to burne such townes as *Troy*,
Sylvanus weeping for the lovely boy,
That now is turn'd into a *Cypres* tree,   155
Under whose shade the Wood-gods love to bee.
And in the midst a silver altar stood,
There *Hero* sacrificing turtles blood,
Vaild to the ground, vailing her eie-lids close,
And modestly they opened as she rose: 160
Thence flew Loves arrow with the golden head,
And thus *Leander* was enamoured.
Stone still he stood, and evermore he gazed,
Till with the fire that from his count'nance blazed,
Relenting *Heroes* gentle heart was strooke,   165
Such force and vertue hath an amorous looke.
   It lies not in our power to love, or hate,
For will in us is over-rul'd by fate.
When two are stript long ere the course begin,
We wish that one should loose, the other win.   170
And one especiallie doe we affect,
Of two gold Ingots like in each respect,
The reason no man knowes, let it suffise,
What we behold is censur'd by our eies.
Where both deliberat, the love is slight,   175
Who ever lov'd, that lov'd not at first sight?
   He kneel'd, but unto her devoutly praid;
Chast *Hero* to her selfe thus softly said:
Were I the saint hee worships, I would heare him,
And as shee spake those words, came somewhat nere him.
He started up, she blusht as one asham'd;   181
Wherewith *Leander* much more was inflam'd.
He toucht her hand, in touching it she trembled,

Love deepely grounded, hardly is dissembled,
These lovers parled by the touch of hands,   185
True love is mute, and oft amazed stands,
Thus while dum signs their yeelding harts entangled,
The aire with sparkes of living fire was spangled,
And night deepe drencht in mystie *Acheron*,
Heav'd up her head, and halfe the world upon,   190
Breath'd darkenesse forth (darke night is *Cupids* day).
And now begins *Leander* to display
Loves holy fire, with words, with sighs and teares,
Which like sweet musicke entred *Heroes* eares,
And yet at everie word shee turn'd aside,   195
And alwaies cut him off as he replide,
At last, like to a bold sharpe Sophister,
With chearefull hope thus he accosted her.
     Faire creature, let me speake without offence,
I would my rude words had the influence,   200
To lead thy thoughts, as thy faire lookes doe mine,
Then shouldst thou bee his prisoner who is thine.
Be not unkind and faire, mishapen stuffe
Are of behaviour boisterous and ruffe.
O shun me not, but heare me ere you goe,   205
God knowes I cannot force love, as you doe.
My words shall be as spotlesse as my youth,
Full of simplicitie and naked truth.
This sacrifice (whose sweet perfume descending,
From *Venus* altar to your footsteps bending)   210
Doth testifie that you exceed her farre,
To whom you offer, and whose Nunne you are,
Why should you worship her? her you surpasse,
As much as sparkling Diamonds flaring glasse.
A Diamond set in lead his worth retaines,   215
A heavenly Nimph, belov'd of humane swaines,
Receives no blemish, but oft-times more grace,
Which makes me hope, although I am but base,
Base in respect of thee, divine and pure,
Dutifull service may thy love procure,   220
And I in dutie will excell all other,
As thou in beautie doest exceed Loves mother.
Nor heaven, nor thou, were made to gaze upon,

As heaven preserves all things, so save thou one.
A stately builded ship, well rig'd and tall,   225
The Ocean maketh more majesticall:
Why vowest thou then to live in *Sestos* here,
Who on Loves seas more glorious wouldst appeare?
Like untun'd golden strings all women are,
Which long time lie untoucht, will harshly jarre.   230
Vessels of Brasse oft handled, brightly shine,
What difference betwixt the richest mine
And basest mold, but use? for both not us'de,
Are of like worth. Then treasure is abus'de,
When misers keepe it; being put to lone,   235
In time it will returne us two for one.
Rich robes, themselves and others do adorne,
Neither themselves nor others, if not worne.
Who builds a pallace and rams up the gate,
Shall see it ruinous and desolate.   240
Ah simple *Hero*, learne thy selfe to cherish,
Lone women like to emptie houses perish.
Lesse sinnes the poore rich man that starves himselfe,
In heaping up a masse of drossie pelfe,
Than such as you: his golden earth remains,   245
Which after his disceasse some other gains.
But this faire jem, sweet in the losse alone,
When you fleet hence, can be bequeath'd to none.
Or if it could, downe from th'enameld skie,
All heaven would come to claime this legacie,   250
And with intestine broiles the world destroy,
And quite confound natures sweet harmony.
Well therefore by the gods decreed it is,
We humane creatures should enjoy that blisse.
One is no number, mayds are nothing then,   255
Without the sweet societie of men.
Wilt thou live single still? one shalt thou bee,
Though never-singling *Hymen* couple thee.
Wild savages, that drinke of running springs,
Thinke water farre excels all earthly things: 260
But they that dayly tast neat wine, despise it.
Virginitie, albeit some highly prise it,
Compar'd with marriage, had you tried them both,

Differs as much, as wine and water doth.
Base boullion for the stampes sake we allow,   265
Even so for mens impression do we you:
By which alone, our reverend fathers say,
Women receave perfection everie way.
This idoll which you terme *Virginitie*,
Is neither essence subject to the eie,   270
No, nor to any one exterior sence,
Nor hath it any place of residence,
Nor is't of earth or mold celestiall,
Or capable of any forme at all.
Of that which hath no being, doe not boast,   275
Things that are not at all, are never lost.
Men foolishly doe call it vertuous,
What vertue is it, that is borne with us?
Much lesse can honour bee ascrib'd thereto,
Honour is purchac'd by the deedes wee do.   280
Beleeve me *Hero*, honour is not wone,
Untill some honourable deed be done.
Seeke you for chastitie, immortall fame,
And know that some have wrong'd *Dianas* name?
Whose name is it, if she be false or not,   285
So she be faire, but some vile toongs will blot?
But you are faire (aye me) so wondrous faire,
So yoong, so gentle, and so debonaire,
As *Greece* will thinke, if thus you live alone,
Some one or other keepes you as his owne.   290
Then *Hero* hate me not, nor from me flie,
To follow swiftly blasting infamie.
Perhaps, thy sacred Priesthood makes thee loath,
Tell me, to whom mad'st thou that heedlesse oath?
    To *Venus*, answered shee, and as shee spake,   295
Foorth from those two tralucent cesternes brake,
A streame of liquid pearle, which downe her face
Made milk-white paths, wheron the gods might trace
To *Joves* high court. Hee thus replide: The rites
In which Loves beauteous Empresse most delites,   300
Are banquets, Dorick musicke, midnight-revell,
Plaies, maskes, and all that stern age counteth evill.
Thee as a holy Idiot doth she scorne,

For thou in vowing chastitie, hast sworne
To rob her name and honour, and thereby   305
Commit'st a sinne far worse than perjurie,
Even sacrilege against her Dietie,
Through regular and formall puritie.
To expiat which sinne, kisse and shake hands,
Such sacrifice as this, *Venus* demands.   310
   Thereat she smild, and did denie him so,
As put thereby, yet might he hope for mo.
Which makes him quickly re-enforce his speech,
And her in humble manner thus beseech.
   Though neither gods nor men may thee deserve,   315
Yet for her sake whom you have vow'd to serve,
Abandon fruitlesse cold Virginitie,
The gentle queene of Loves sole enemie.
Then shall you most resemble *Venus* Nun,
When *Venus* sweet rites are perform'd and done.   320
Flint-brested *Pallas* joies in single life,
But *Pallas* and your mistresse are at strife.
Love *Hero* then, and be not tirannous,
But heale the heart, that thou hast wounded thus,
Nor staine thy youthfull years with avarice,   325
Faire fooles delight to be accounted nice.
The richest corne dies, if it be not reapt,
Beautie alone is lost, too warily kept.
These arguments he us'de, and many more,
Wherewith she yeelded, that was woon before,   330
Heroes lookes yeelded, but her words made warre,
Women are woon when they begin to jarre.
Thus having swallow'd *Cupids* golden hooke,
The more she striv'd the deeper was she strooke.
Yet evilly faining anger, strove she still,   335
And would be thought to graunt against her will.
So having paus'd a while, at last shee said:
Who taught thee Rethoricke to deceive a maid?
Aye me, such words as these should I abhor,
And yet I like them for the Orator.   340
   With that *Leander* stoopt, to have imbrac'd her,
But from his spreading armes away she cast her,
And thus bespake him. Gentle youth forbeare

To touch the sacred garments which I weare.
Upon a rocke, and underneath a hill,   345
Far from the towne (where all is whist and still,
Save that the sea playing on yellow sand,
Sends foorth a ratling murmure to the land,
Whose sound allures the golden *Morpheus*,
In silence of the night to visite us).   350
My turret stands, and there God knowes I play
With *Venus* swannes and sparrowes all the day.
A dwarfish beldame beares me companie,
That hops about the chamber where I lie,
And spends the night (that might be better spent)   355
In vaine discourse, and apish merriment.
Come thither; As she spake this, her toong tript,
For unawares (*Come thither*) from her slipt,
And sodainly her former colour chang'd,
And here and there her eies through anger rang'd.   360
And like a planet, mooving severall waies,
At one selfe instant, she poore soule assaies,
Loving, not to love at all, and everie part,
Strove to resist the motions of her hart.
And hands so pure, so innocent, nay such,   365
As might have made heaven stoope to have a touch,
Did she uphold to *Venus*, and againe,
Vow'd spotlesse chastitie, but all in vaine,
Cupid beats downe her praiers with his wings,
Her vowes above the emptie aire he flings: 370
All deepe enrag'd, his sinowie bow he bent,
And shot a shaft that burning from him went,
Wherewith she strooken, look'd so dolefully,
As made Love sigh, to see his tirannie.
And as she wept, her teares to pearle he turn'd,   375
And wound them on his arme, and for her mourn'd.
Then towards the pallace of the destinies,
Laden with languishment and griefe he flies.
And to those sterne nymphs humblie made request,
Both might enjoy ech other, and be blest.   380
But with a ghastly dreadfull countenaunce,
Threatning a thousand deaths at everie glaunce,
They answered Love, nor would vouchsafe so much

As one poore word, their hate to him was such.
Harken a while, and I will tell you why: 385
Heavens winged herrald, *Jove-borne Mercury*,
The selfe-same day that he asleepe had layd
Inchaunted *Argus*, spied a countrie mayd,
Whose carelesse haire, in stead of pearle t'adorne it,
Glist'red with deaw, as one that seem'd to skorne it: 390
Her breath as fragrant as the morning rose,
Her mind pure, and her toong untaught to glose.
Yet prowd she was, (for loftie pride that dwels
In tow'red courts, is oft in sheapheards cels.)
And too too well the faire vermilion knew,   395
And silver tincture of her cheekes, that drew
The love of everie swaine: On her, this god
Enamoured was, and with his snakie rod,
Did charme her nimble feet, and made her stay,
The while upon a hillocke downe he lay,   400
And sweetly on his pipe began to play,
And with smooth speech her fancie to assay,
Till in his twining armes he lockt her fast,
And then he woo'd with kisses, and at last,
As sheap-heards do, her on the ground hee layd, 405
And tumbling in the grasse, he often strayd
Beyond the bounds of shame, in being bold
To eie those parts, which no eie should behold.
And like an insolent commaunding lover,
Boasting his parentage, would needs discover   410
The way to new *Elisium*: but she,
Whose only dower was her chastitie,
Having striv'ne in vaine, was now about to crie,
And crave the helpe of sheap-heards that were nie.
Herewith he stayd his furie, and began   415
To give her leave to rise, away she ran,
After went *Mercurie*, who us'd such cunning,
As she to heare his tale, left off her running.
Maids are not woon by brutish force and might,
But speeches full of pleasure and delight.   420
And knowing *Hermes* courted her, was glad
That she such lovelinesse and beautie had,
As could provoke his liking, yet was mute,

And neither would denie, nor graunt his sute.
Still vowd he love, she wanting no excuse   425
To feed him with delaies, as women use:
Or thirsting after immortalitie,
(All women are ambitious naturallie,)
Impos'd upon her lover such a taske,
As he ought not performe, nor yet she aske.   430
A draught of flowing *Nectar* she requested,
Wherewith the king of Gods and men is feasted.
He readie to accomplish what she wil'd,
Stole some from *Hebe* (*Hebe*, *Joves* cup fil'd,)
And gave it to his simple rustike love,   435
Which being knowne (as what is hid from *Jove?*)
He inly storm'd, and waxt more furious,
Than for the fire filcht by *Prometheus*;
And thrusts him down from heaven, he wandring here,
In mournfull tearmes, with sad and heavie cheare   440
Complaind to *Cupid*, *Cupid* for his sake,
 To be reveng'd on *Jove*, did undertake,
And those on whom heaven, earth, and hell relies,
I mean the Adamantine Destinies,
He wounds with love, and forst them equallie,   445
To dote upon deceitfull *Mercurie*.
They offred him the deadly fatall knife,
That sheares the slender threads of humane life,
At his faire feathered feet, the engins layd,
Which th'earth from ougly *Chaos* den up-wayd: 450
These he regarded not, but did intreat,
That *Jove*, usurper of his fathers seat,
Might presently be banisht into hell,
And aged *Saturne* in *Olympus* dwell.
They granted what he crav'd, and once againe,   455
Saturne and *Ops*, began their golden raigne.
Murder, rape, warre, lust and trecherie,
Were with *Jove* clos'd in *Stigian* Emperie.
But long this blessed time continued not,
As soone as he his wished purpose got;   460
He recklesse of his promise, did despise
The love of th'everlasting Destinies.
They seeing it, both Love and him abhor'd,

And *Jupiter* unto his place restor'd.
And but that Learning, in despight of Fate, 465
Will mount aloft, and enter heaven gate,
And to the seat of *Jove* it selfe advaunce,
Hermes had slept in hell with ignoraunce.
Yet as a punishment they added this,
That he and *Povertie* should alwaies kis. 470
And to this day is everie scholler poore,
Grosse gold, from them runs headlong to the boore.
Likewise the angrie sisters thus deluded,
To venge themselves on *Hermes*, have concluded
That *Midas* brood shall sit in Honors chaire, 475
To which the *Muses* sonnes are only heire:
And fruitfull wits that in aspiring are,
Shall discontent run into regions farre;
And few great lords in vertuous deeds shall joy,
But be surpris'd with every garish toy. 480
And still inrich the loftie servile clowne,
Who with incroching guile, keepes learning downe.
Then muse not, *Cupids* sute no better sped,
Seeing in their loves the Fates were injured.

The end of the first Sestyad.

THE ARGUMENT OF THE SECOND SESTYAD

Hero of love takes deeper sence,
And doth her love more recompence.
Their first nights meeting, where sweet kisses
Are th'only crownes of both their blisses.
He swims t'Abydus, and returnes;
Cold Neptune with his beautie burnes,
Whose suite he shuns, and doth aspire
Heros faire towre, and his desire.

By this, sad *Hero*, with love unacquainted,
Viewing *Leanders* face, fell downe and fainted.
He kist her, and breath'd life into her lips,
Wherewith as one displeas'd, away she trips.

Yet as she went, full often look'd behind,   5
And many poore excuses did she find,
To linger by the way, and once she stayd,
And would have turn'd againe, but was afrayd,
In offring parlie, to be counted light.
So on she goes, and in her idle flight,   10
Her painted fanne of curled plumes let fall,
Thinking to traine *Leander* therewithall.
He being a novice, knew not what she meant,
But stayd, and after her a letter sent.
Which joyfull *Hero* answerd in such sort,   15
As he had hope to scale the beauteous fort,
Wherein the liberall graces lock'd their wealth,
And therefore to her tower he got by stealth.
Wide open stood the doore, he need not clime;
And she her selfe before the pointed time,   20
Had spread the boord, with roses strowed the roome,
And oft look't out, and mus'd he did not come.
At last he came, O who can tell the greeting
These greedie lovers had at their first meeting.
He askt, she gave, and nothing was denied,   25
Both to each other quickly were affied.
Looke how their hands, so were their hearts united,
And what he did, she willingly requited.
(Sweet are the kisses, the imbracements sweet,
When like desires and affections meet,   30
 For from the earth to heaven, is *Cupid* rais'd,
Where fancie is in equall ballance pais'd.)
Yet she this rashnesse sodainly repented,
And turn'd aside, and to her selfe lamented,
As if her name and honour had beene wrong'd,   35
By being possest of him for whom she long'd:
I, and shee wisht, albeit not from her hart,
That he would leave her turret and depart.
The mirthfull God of amorous pleasure smil'd,
To see how he this captive Nymph beguil'd.   40
For hitherto hee did but fan the fire,
And kept it downe that it might mount the hier.
Now waxt she jealous, least his love abated,
Fearing her owne thoughts made her to be hated.

Therefore unto him hastily she goes,   45
And like light *Salmacis*, her body throes
Upon his bosome, where with yeelding eyes,
She offers up her selfe a sacrifice,
To slake his anger, if he were displeas'd.
O what god would not therewith be appeas'd?   50
Like *Æsops* cocke, this jewell he enjoyed,
And as a brother with his sister toyed,
Supposing nothing else was to be done,
Now he her favour and good will had wone.
But know you not that creatures wanting sence,   55
By nature have a mutuall appetence,
And wanting organs to advaunce a step,
Mov'd by Loves force, unto ech other lep?
Much more in subjects having intellect,
Some hidden influence breeds like effect.   60
Albeit *Leander* rude in love, and raw,
Long dallying with *Hero*, nothing saw
That might delight him more, yet he suspected
Some amorous rites or other were neglected.
Therefore unto his bodie, hirs he clung,   65
She, fearing on the rushes to be flung,
Striv'd with redoubled strength, the more she strived,
The more a gentle pleasing heat revived,
Which taught him all that elder lovers know,
And now the same gan so to scorch and glow,   70
As in plaine termes (yet cunningly) he crav'd it,
Love alwaies makes those eloquent that have it.
Shee, with a kind of graunting, put him by it,
And ever as he thought himselfe most nigh it,
Like to the tree of *Tantalus* she fled,   75
And seeming lavish, sav'de her maydenhead.
Ne're king more sought to keepe his diademe,
Than *Hero* this inestimable gemme.
Above our life we love a stedfast friend,
Yet when a token of great worth we send,   80
We often kisse it, often looke thereon,
And stay the messenger that would be gon:
No marvell then, though *Hero* would not yeeld
So soone to part from that she deerely held.

Jewels being lost are found againe, this never,   85
T'is lost but once, and once lost, lost for ever.
   Now had the morne espy'de her lovers steeds,
Whereat she starts, puts on her purple weeds,
And red for anger that he stayd so long,
All headlong throwes her selfe the clouds among,   90
And now *Leander* fearing to be mist,
Imbrast her sodainly, tooke leave, and kist,
Long was he taking leave, and loath to go,
And kist againe, as lovers use to do.
Sad *Hero* wroong him by the hand, and wept,   95
Saying, let your vowes and promises be kept.
Then standing at the doore, she turnd about,
As loath to see *Leander* going out.
And now the sunne that through th'orizen peepes,
As pittying these lovers, downeward creepes,   100
So that in silence of the cloudie night,
Though it was morning, did he take his flight.
But what the secret trustie night conceal'd,
Leanders amorous habit soone reveal'd,
With *Cupids* myrtle was his bonet crownd,   105
About his armes the purple riband wound,
Wherewith she wreath'd her largely spreading heare,
Nor could the youth abstaine, but he must weare
The sacred ring wherewith she was endow'd,
When first religious chastitie she vow'd: 110
Which made his love through *Sestos* to bee knowne,
And thence unto *Abydus* sooner blowne,
Than he could saile, for incorporeal Fame,
Whose waight consists in nothing but her name,
Is swifter than the wind, whose tardie plumes,   115
Are reeking water, and dull earthlie fumes.
Home when he came, he seem'd not to be there,
But like exiled aire thrust from his sphere,
Set in a forren place, and straight from thence,
Alcides like, by mightie violence,   120
He would have chac'd away the swelling maine,
That him from her unjustly did detaine.
Like as the sunne in a Dyameter,
Fires and inflames objects remooved farre,

And heateth kindly, shining lat'rally;   125
So beautie, sweetly quickens when t'is ny,
But being separated and remooved,
Burnes where it cherisht, murders where it loved.
Therefore even as an Index to a booke,
So to his mind was yoong *Leanders* looke,   130
O none but gods have power their love to hide,
Affection by the count'nance is describe.
The light of hidden fire it selfe discovers,
And love that is conceal'd, betraies poore lovers.
His secret flame apparantly was seene,   135
Leanders Father knew where hee had beene,
And for the same mildly rebuk't his sonne,
Thinking to quench the sparckles new begonne.
But love resisted once, growes passionate,
And nothing more than counsaile, lovers hate.   140
For as a hote prowd horse highly disdaines,
To have his head control'd, but breakes the raines,
Spits foorth the ringled bit, and with his hoves,
Checkes the submissive ground: so hee that loves,
The more he is restrain'd, the woorse he fares,   145
What is it now, but mad *Leander* dares?
O *Hero, Hero,* thus he cry'de full oft,
And then he got him to a rocke aloft.
Where having spy'de her tower, long star'd he on't,
And pray'd the narrow toyling *Hellespont*   150
To part in twaine, that hee might come and go,
But still the rising billowes answered no.
With that hee stript him to the yv'rie skin,
And crying, Love I come, leapt lively in.
Whereat the saphir visag'd god grew prowd,   155
And made his capring *Triton* sound alowd,
Imagining, that *Ganimed* displeas'd,
Had left the heavens, therefore on him hee seaz'd.
Leander striv'd, the waves about him wound,
And puld him to the bottome, where the ground   160
Was strewd with pearle, and in low corrall groves
Sweet singing Meremaids, sported with their loves
On heapes of heavie gold, and tooke great pleasure
To spurne in carelesse sort, the shipwracke treasure.

For here the stately azure pallace stood,   165
Where kingly *Neptune* and his traine abode,
The lustie god imbrast him, cald him love,
And swore he never should returne to *Jove*.
But when he knew it was not *Ganimed*,
For underwater he was almost dead,   170
He heav'd him up, and looking on his face,
Beat downe the bold waves with his triple mace,
Which mounted up, intending to have kist him,
And fell in drops like teares, because they mist him.
Leander being up began to swim,   175
And looking backe, saw *Neptune* follow him.
Whereat agast, the poore soule gan to crie,
O let mee visite *Hero* ere I die.
The god put *Helles* bracelet on his arme,
And swore the sea should never doe him harme.   180
He clapt his plumpe cheekes, with his tresses playd,
And smiling wantonly, his love bewrayd.
He watcht his armes, and as they opend wide,
At every stroke, betwixt them would he slide,
And steale a kisse, and then run out and daunce,   185
And as he turnd, cast many a lustfull glaunce,
And threw him gawdie toies to please his eie,
And dive into the water, and there prie
Upon his brest, his thighs, and everie lim,
And up againe, and close beside him swim,   190
And talke of love: *Leander* made replie,
You are deceav'd, I am no woman I.
Thereat smilde *Neptune*, and then told a tale,
How that a sheapheard sitting in a vale,
Playd with a boy so faire and kind,   195
As for his love, both earth and heaven pyn'd;
That of the cooling river durst not drinke,
Least water-nymphs should pull him from the brinke.
And when hee sported in the fragrant lawnes,
Gote-footed Satyrs, and up-staring Fawnes,   200
Would steale him thence. Ere halfe this tale was done,
Aye me, *Leander* cryde, th'enamoured sunne,
That now should shine on *Thetis* glassie bower,
Descends upon my radiant *Heroes* tower.

O that these tardie armes of mine were wings,   205
And as he spake, upon the waves he springs.
Neptune was angrie that hee gave no eare,
And in his heart revenging malice bare:
He flung at him his mace, but as it went,
He cald it in, for love made him repent.   210
The mace returning backe, his owne hand hit,
As meaning to be veng'd for darting it.
When this fresh bleeding wound *Leander* viewd,
His colour went and came, as if he rewd
The greefe which *Neptune* felt. In gentle brests,   215
Relenting thoughts, remorse and pittie rests.
And who have hard hearts, and obdurat minds,
But vicious, harebraind, and illit'rat hinds?
The god seeing him with pittie to be moved,
Thereon concluded that he was beloved.   220
(Love is too full of faith, too credulous,
With follie and false hope deluding us.)
Wherefore *Leanders* fancie to surprize,
To the rich *Ocean* for gifts he flies.
'Tis wisedome to give much, a gift prevailes,   225
When deepe perswading Oratorie failes.
By this *Leander* being nere the land,
Cast downe his wearie feet, and felt the sand.
Breathlesse albeit he were, he rested not,
Till to the solitarie tower he got,   230
And knockt and cald, at which celestiall noise,
The longing heart of *Hero* much more joies
Then nymphs and sheapheards, when the timbrell rings,
Or crooked Dolphin when the sailer sings;
She stayd not for her robes, but straight arose,   235
And drunke with gladnesse, to the dore she goes,
Where seeing a naked man, she scriecht for feare,
Such sights as this, to tender maids are rare.
And ran into the darke her selfe to hide,
Rich jewels in the darke are soonest spide.   240
Unto her was he led, or rather drawne,
By those white limmes, which sparckled through the lawne.
The neerer that he came, the more she fled,
And seeking refuge, slipt into her bed.

Whereon *Leander* sitting, thus began,   245
Through numming cold, all feeble, faint and wan:
  If not for love, yet love for pittie sake,
Me in thy bed and maiden bosome take,
At least vouchsafe these armes some little roome,
Who hoping to imbrace thee, cherely swome.   250
This head was beat with manie a churlish billow,
And therefore let it rest upon thy pillow.
Herewith afrighted *Hero* shrunke away,
And in her luke-warme place *Leander* lay.
Whose lively heat like fire from heaven fet,   255
Would animate grosse clay, and higher set
The drooping thoughts of base declining soules,
Then drerie *Mars*, carowsing *Nectar* boules.
His hands he cast upon her like a snare,
She overcome with shame and sallow feare,   260
Like chast *Diana*, when *Acteon* spyde her,
Being sodainly betraide, dyv'd downe to hide her.
And as her silver body downeward went,
With both her hands she made the bed a tent,
And in her owne mind thought her selfe secure,   265
O'recast with dim and darksome coverture.
And now she lets him whisper in her eare,
Flatter, intreat, promise, protest and sweare,
Yet ever as he greedily assayd,
To touch those dainties, she the *Harpey* playd,   270
And every lim did as a soldier stout,
Defend the fort, and keep the foe-man out.
For though the rising yv'rie mount he scal'd,
Which is with azure circling lines empal'd,
Much like a globe, (a globe may I tearme this,   275
By which love sailes to regions full of blis,)
Yet there with *Sysiphus* he toyld in vaine,
Till gentle parlie did the truce obtaine.
Wherein *Leander* on her quivering brest,
Breathlesse spoke some thing, and sigh'd out the rest;   280
Which so prevail'd, as he with small ado,
Inclos'd her in his armes and kist her to.
And everie kisse to her was as a charme,
And to *Leander* as a fresh alarme.

So that the truce was broke, and she alas,   285
(Poore sillie maiden) at his mercie was.
Love is not ful of pittie (as men say)
But deaffe and cruell, where he meanes to pray.
Even as a bird, which in our hands we wring,
Foorth plungeth, and oft flutters with her wing,   290
She trembling strove, this strife of hers (like that
Which made the world) another world begat,
Of unknowne joy. Treason was in her thought,
And cunningly to yeeld her selfe she sought.
Seeming not woon, yet woon she was at length,   295
In such warres women use but halfe their strength.
Leander now like Theban *Hercules*,
Entred the orchard of th'*Esperides*.
Whose fruit none rightly can describe, but hee
That puls or shakes it from the golden tree: 300
And now she wisht this night were never done,
And sigh'd to thinke upon th'approching sunne,
For much it greev'd her that the bright day-light,
Should know the pleasure of this blessed night.
And then like *Mars* and *Ericine* displayd,   305
Both in each others armes chaind as they layd.
Againe she knew not how to frame her looke,
Or speake to him who in a moment tooke,
That which so long so charily she kept,
And faine by stealth away she would have crept,   310
And to some corner secretly have gone,
Leaving *Leander* in the bed alone.
But as her naked feet were whipping out,
He on the suddaine cling'd her so about,
That Meremaid-like unto the floore she slid,   315
One halfe appear'd the other halfe was hid.
Thus neere the bed she blushing stood upright,
And from her countenance behold ye might,
A kind of twilight breake, which through the heare,
As from an orient cloud, glymse here and there.   320
And round about the chamber this false morne,
Brought foorth the day before the day was borne.
So *Heroes* ruddie cheeke *Hero* betrayd,
And her all naked to his sight displayd.

Whence his admiring eyes more pleasure tooke,   325
Than *Dis*, on heapes of gold fixing his looke.
By this *Apollos* golden harpe began,
To sound foorth musicke to the *Ocean*,
Which watchfull *Hesperus* no sooner heard,
But he the day bright-bearing Car prepar'd.   330
And ran before, as Harbenger of light,
And with his flaring beames mockt ougly night,
Till she o'recome with anguish, shame, and rage,
Dang'd downe to hell her loathsome carriage.

The end of the second Sestyad.

Hero and Leander

GEORGE CHAPMAN (1598)

THE ARGUMENT OF THE THIRD SESTYAD

Leander to the envious light
Resignes his night-sports with the night,
And swims the Hellespont againe;
Thesme the Deitie soveraigne
Of Customes and religious rites
Appeares, improving his delites
Since Nuptiall honors he neglected;
Which straight he vowes shall be effected.
Faire Hero left Devirginate
Waies, and with furie wailes her state:
But with her love and womans wit
She argues, and approveth it.

New light gives new directions, Fortunes new
To fashion our indevours that ensue,
More harsh (at lest more hard) more grave and hie
Our subject runs, and our sterne *Muse* must flie,
Loves edge is taken off, and that light flame,   5
Those thoughts, joyes, longings, that before became,
High unexperienst blood, and maids sharpe plights,
Must now grow staid, and censure the delights,
That being enjoyd aske judgement; now we praise,
As having parted: Evenings crowne the daies.   10
  And now ye wanton loves, and yong desires,
Pied vanitie, the mint of strange Attires;
Ye lisping Flatteries, and obsequious Glances,
Relentfull Musicks, and attractive Dances,
And you detested Charmes constraining love,   15
Shun loves stolne sports by that these Lovers prove.

By this the Soveraigne of Heavens golden fires,
And yong *Leander*, Lord of his desires,
Together from their lovers armes arose:
Leander into *Hellespontus* throwes   20
His *Hero*-handled bodie, whose delight
Made him disdaine each other Epethite.
And as amidst the enamourd waves he swims,
The God of gold of purpose guilt his lims,
That this word guilt, including double sence,   25
The double guilt of his *Incontinence*,
Might be exprest, that had no stay t'employ
The treasure which the Love-god let him joy
In his deare *Hero*, with such sacred thrift,
As had beseemd so sanctified a gift: 30
But like a greedie vulgar Prodigall
Would on the stock dispend, and rudely fall
Before his time, to that unblessed blessing,
Which for lusts plague doth perish with possessing.
   Joy graven in sence, like snow in water wasts;   35
   Without preserve of vertue, nothing lasts.
What man is he that with a welthie eie,
Enjoyes a beautie richer than the skie,
Through whose white skin, softer then soundest sleep,
With damaske eyes, the rubie blood doth peep,   40
And runs in branches through her azure vaines,
Whose mixture and first fire, his love attaines;
Whose both hands limit, both Loves deities,
And sweeten humane thoughts like Paradise;
Whose disposition silken is and kinde,   45
Directed with an earth-exempted minde;
Who thinks not heaven with such a love is given?
And who like earth would spend that dower of heaven,
With ranke desire to joy it all at first?
What simply kils our hunger, quencheth thirst,   50
Clothes but our nakednes, and makes us live?
Praise doth not any of her favours give:
But what doth plentifully minister
Beautious apparell and delicious cheere,
So orderd that it still excites desire,   55
And still gives pleasure freenes to aspire

The palme of *Bountie*, ever moyst preserving:
To loves sweet life this is the courtly carving.
Thus *Time*, and all-states-ordering *Ceremonie*
Had banisht all offence: *Times* golden *Thie*   60
Upholds the flowrie bodie of the earth,
In sacred harmonie, and every birth
Of men, and actions makes legitimate,
Being usde aright; *The use of time is Fate.*

Yet did the gentle flood transfer once more,   65
This prize of Love home to his fathers shore;
Where he unlades himselfe of that false welth
That makes few rich; treasures composde by stelth.
And to his sister kinde *Hermione*,
(Who on the shore kneeld, praying to the sea   70
For his returne) he all Loves goods did show
In *Hero* seasde for him, in him for *Hero*.

His most kinde sister all his secrets knew,
And to her singing like a shower he flew,
Sprinkling the earth, that to their tombs tooke in   75
Streames dead for love, to leave his ivorie skin,
Which yet a snowie fome did leave above,
As soule to the dead water that did love;
And from thence did the first white Roses spring,
(For love is sweet and faire in every thing)   80
And all the sweetned shore as he did goe,
Was crownd with odrous roses white as snow.
Love-blest *Leander* was with love so filled,
That love to all that toucht him he instilled.
And as the colours of all things we see,   85
To our sights powers communicated bee:
So to all objects that in compasse came
Of any sence he had; his sences flame
Flowd from his parts, with force so virtuall,
It fir'd with sence things meere insensuall.   90

Now (with warme baths and odours comforted)
When he lay downe he kindly kist his bed,
As consecrating it to *Heros* right,
And vowd thereafter that what ever sight
Put him in minde of *Hero*, or her blisse,   95
Should be her Altar to prefer a kisse.

Then laid he forth his late inriched armes,
In whose white circle Love writ all his charmes,
And made his characters sweet *Heros* lims,
When on his breasts warme sea she sideling swims.   100
And as those armes (held up in circle) met,
He said; see sister *Heros* Carquenet,
Which she had rather weare about her neck,
Then all the jewels that doth *Juno* deck.

But as he shooke with passionate desire,   105
To put in flame his other secret fire,
A musick so divine did pierce his eare,
As never yet his ravisht sence did heare:
When suddenly a light of twentie hews
Brake through the roofe, and like the Rainbow views 110
Amazd *Leander*; in whose beames came downe
The Goddesse *Ceremonie*, with a Crowne
Of all the stars, and heaven with her descended,
Her flaming haire to her bright feete extended,
By which hung all the bench of Deities;   115
And in a chaine, compact of eares and eies,
She led Religion; all her bodie was
Cleere and transparent as the purest glasse:
For she was all presented to the sence;
Devotion, Order, State, and Reverence,   120
Her shadowes were; Societie, Memorie;
All which her sight made live; her absence die.
A rich disparent Pentackle she weares,
Drawne full of circles and strange characters:
Her face was changeable to everie eie;   125
One way lookt ill, another graciouslie;
Which while men viewd, they cheerfull were and holy:
But looking off, vicious, and melancholy:
The snakie paths to each observed law,
Did *Policie* in her broad bosome draw: 130
One hand a Mathematique Christall swayes,
Which gathering in one line a thousand rayes
From her bright eyes, *Confusion* burnes to death,
And all estates of men distinguisheth.
By it *Morallitie* and *Comelinesse*,   135
Themselves in all their sightly figures dresse.

Her other hand a lawrell rod applies,
To beate back *Barbarisme*, and *Avarice*,
That followd eating earth, and excrement
And humane lims; and would make proud ascent   140
To seates of Gods, were *Ceremonie* slaine;
The *Howrs* and *Graces* bore her glorious traine,
And all the sweetes of our societie
Were Spherde, and treasurde in her bountious eie.
Thus she appeard, and sharply did reprove   145
Leanders bluntnes in his violent love;
Tolde him how poore was substance without rites,
Like bils unsignd, desires without delites;
Like meates unseasond; like ranke corne that growes
On Cottages, that none or reapes or sowes: 150
Not being with civill forms confirm'd and bounded,
For humane dignities and comforts founded:
But loose and secret all their glories hide,
Feare fils the chamber, darknes decks the Bride.
    She vanisht, leaving pierst *Leanders* hart   155
With sence of his unceremonious part,
In which with plaine neglect of Nuptiall rites,
He close and flatly fell to his delites:
And instantly he vowd to celebrate
All rites pertaining to his maried state.   160
So up he gets and to his father goes,
To whose glad eares he doth his vowes disclose:
The Nuptials are resolv'd with utmost powre,
And he at night would swim to *Heros* towre.
From whence he ment to *Sestus* forked Bay   165
To bring her covertly, where ships must stay,
Sent by his father throughly rigd and mand,
To waft her safely to *Abydus* Strand.
There leave we him, and with fresh wing pursue
Astonisht *Hero*, whose most wished view   170
I thus long have forborne, because I left her
So out of countnance, and her spirits bereft her.
To looke on one abasht is impudence,
When of sleight faults he hath too deepe a sence.
Her blushing het her chamber: she lookt out,   175
And all the ayre she purpled round about,

And after it a foule black day befell,
Which ever since a red morne doth foretell:
And still renewes our woes for *Heros* wo,
And foule it prov'd, because it figur'd so   180
The next nights horror, which prepare to heare;
I faile if it prophane your daintiest eare.
   Then thou most strangely-intellectuall fire,
That proper to my soule hast power t'inspire
Her burning faculties, and with the wings   185
Of thy unspheared flame visitst the springs
Of spirits immortall; Now (as swift as Time
Doth follow Motion) finde th'eternall Clime
Of his free soule, whose living subject stood
Up to the chin in the Pyerean flood,   190
And drunke to me halfe this Musean storie,
Inscribing it to deathles Memorie:
Confer with it, and make my pledge as deepe,
That neithers draught be consecrate to sleepe.
Tell it how much his late desires I tender,   195
(If yet it know not) and to light surrender
My soules darke ofspring, willing it should die
To loves, to passions, and societie.
   Sweet *Hero* left upon her bed alone,
Her maidenhead, her vowes, *Leander* gone,   200
And nothing with her but a violent crew
Of new come thoughts that yet she never knew,
Even to her selfe a stranger; was much like
Th'*Iberian* citie that wars hand did strike
By English force in princely *Essex* guide,   205
When peace assur'd her towres had fortifide;
And golden-fingred *India* had bestowd
Such wealth on her, that strength and Empire flowd
Into her Turrets; and her virgin waste
The wealthie girdle of the Sea embraste: 210
Till our *Leander* that made *Mars* his *Cupid*,
For soft love-sutes, with iron thunders chid:
Swum to her Towers, dissolv'd her virgin zone;
Lead in his power, and made Confusion
Run through her streets amazd, that she supposde   215
She had not been in her owne walls inclosde:

But rapt by wonder to some forraine state,
Seeing all her issue so disconsolate:
And all her peacefull mansions possest
With wars just spoyle, and many a forraine guest   220
From every corner driving an enjoyer,
Supplying it with power of a destroyer.
So far'd fayre *Hero* in th'expugned fort
Of her chast bosome, and of every sort
Strange thoughts possest her, ransacking her brest   225
For that that was not there, her wonted rest.
She was a mother straight and bore with paine,
Thoughts that spake straight and wisht their mother slaine;
She hates their lives, and they their own and hers:
Such strife still growes where sin the race prefers.   230
Love is a golden bubble full of dreames,
That waking breakes, and fils us with extreames.
She mus'd how she could looke upon her Sire,
And not shew that without, that was intire.
For as a glasse is an inanimate eie,   235
And outward formes imbraceth inwardlie:
So is the eye an animate glasse that showes
In-formes without us. And as *Phœbus* throwes
His beames abroad, though he in clowdes be closde,
Still glancing by them till he finde opposde,   240
A loose and rorid vapour that is fit
T'event his searching beames, and useth it
To forme a tender twentie-coloured eie,
Cast in a circle round about the skie.
So when our firie soule, our bodies starre,   245
(That ever is in motion circulare)
Conceives a forme; in seeking to display it
Through all our clowdie parts, it doth convey it
Forth at the eye, as the most pregnant place,
And that reflects it round about the face.   250
And this event uncourtly *Hero* thought,
Her inward guilt would in her lookes have wrought:
For yet the worlds stale cunning she resisted
To beare foule thoughts, yet forge what lookes she listed,
And held it for a very sillie sleight,   255
To make a perfect mettall counterfeit:

Glad to disclaime her selfe; proud of an Art,
That makes the face a Pandar to the hart.
Those be the painted Moones, whose lights prophane
Beauties true Heaven, at full still in their wane.   260
Those be the Lapwing faces that still crie,
Here tis, when that they vow is nothing nie.
Base fooles, when every moorish fowle can teach
That which men thinke the height of humane reach.
But custome that the Apoplexie is   265
Of beddred nature, and lives led amis,
And takes away all feeling of offence:
Yet brazde not *Heros* brow with impudence;
And this she thought most hard to bring to pas,
To seeme in countnance other then she was.   270
As if she had two soules; one for the face,
One for the hart; and that they shifted place
As either list to utter, or conceale
What they conceiv'd: or as one soule did deale
With both affayres at once, keeps and ejects   275
Both at an instant contrarie effects:
Retention and ejection in her powrs
Being acts alike: for this one vice of ours,
That forms the thought, and swaies the countenance,
Rules both our motion and our utterance.   280
   These and more grave conceits toyld *Heros* spirits:
For though the light of her discoursive wits,
Perhaps might finde some little hole to pas
Through all these worldly cinctures; yet (alas)
There was a heavenly flame incompast her;   285
Her Goddesse, in whose Phane she did prefer
Her virgin vowes; from whose impulsive sight
She knew the black shield of the darkest night
Could not defend her, nor wits subtilst art:
This was the point pierst *Hero* to the hart.   290
Who heavie to the death, with a deep sigh
And hand that languisht, tooke a robe was nigh,
Exceeding large, and of black Cypres made,
In which she sate, hid from the day in shade,
Even over head and face downe to her feete;   295
Her left hand made it at her bosome meete;

Her right hand leand on her hart-bowing knee,
Wrapt in unshapefull foulds: twas death to see
Her knee stayd that, and that her falling face
Each limme helpt other to put on disgrace.   300
No forme was seene, where forme held all her sight:
But like an Embrion that saw never light:
Or like a scorched statue made a cole
With three-wingd lightning: or a wretched soule
Muffled with endles darknes, she did sit: 305
The night had never such a heavie spirit.
Yet might an imitating eye well see,
How fast her cleere teares melted on her knee
Through her black vaile, and turnd as black as it,
Mourning to be her teares: then wrought her wit   310
With her broke vow, her Goddesse wrath, her fame,
All tooles that enginous despayre could frame:
Which made her strow the floore with her torne haire,
And spread her mantle peece-meale in the aire.
Like *Joves* sons club, strong passion strook her downe,
And with a piteous shrieke inforst her swoune: 316
Her shrieke, made with another shrieke ascend
The frighted Matron that on her did tend:
And as with her owne crie her sence was slaine,
So with the other it was calde againe.   320
She rose and to her bed made forced way,
And layd her downe even where *Leander* lay:
And all this while the red sea of her blood
Ebd with *Leander*: but now turnd the flood,
And all her fleete of sprites came swelling in   325
With childe of saile, and did hot fight begin
With those severe conceits, she too much markt,
And here *Leanders* beauties were imbarkt.
He came in swimming painted all with joyes,
Such as might sweeten hell: his thought destroyes   330
All her destroying thoughts: she thought she felt
His heart in hers: with her contentions melt,
And chid her soule that it could so much erre,
To check the true joyes he deserv'd in her.
Her fresh heat blood cast figures in her eyes,   335
And she supposde she saw in *Neptunes* skyes

How her star wandred, washt in smarting brine
For her loves sake, that with immortall wine
Should be embath'd, and swim in more hearts ease,
Than there was water in the Sestian seas.   340
Then said her *Cupid* prompted spirit: shall I
Sing mones to such delightsome harmony?
Shall slick-tongde fame patcht up with voyces rude,
The drunken bastard of the multitude,
(Begot when father Judgement is away,   345
And gossip-like, sayes because others say,
Takes newes as if it were too hot to eate,
And spits it slavering forth for dog-fees meate)
Make me for forging a phantastique vow,
Presume to beare what makes grave matrons bow?   350
Good vowes are never broken with good deedes,
For then good deedes were bad: vowes are but seedes,
And good deeds fruits; even those good deedes that grow
From other stocks, than from th'observed vow.
That is a good deede that prevents a bad: 355
Had I not yeelded, slaine my selfe I had.
Hero Leander is, Leander Hero:
Such vertue love hath to make one of two.
If then *Leander* did my maydenhead git,
Leander being my selfe I still retaine it.   360
We breake chast vowes when we live loosely ever:
But bound as we are, we live loosely never.
Two constant lovers being joynd in one,
Yeelding to one another, yeeld to none.
We know not how to vow, till love unblinde us,   365
And vowes made ignorantly never binde us.
Too true it is that when t'is gone men hate
The joyes as vaine they tooke in loves estate:
But that's, since they have lost, the heavenly light
Should shew them way to judge of all things right. 370
When life is gone death must implant his terror,
As death is foe to life, so love to error.
Before we love how range we through this sphere,
Searching the sundrie fancies hunted here:
Now with desire of wealth transported quite   375
Beyond our free humanities delight:

Now with ambition climing falling towrs,
Whose hope to scale, our feare to fall devours:
Now rapt with pastimes, pomp, all joyes impure;
In things without us no delight is sure.   380
But love with all joyes crownd, within doth sit;
O Goddesse pitie love and pardon it.
This spake she weeping: but her Goddesse eare
Burnd with too sterne a heat, and would not heare.
Aie me, hath heavens straight fingers no more graces,
For such as *Hero*, then for homeliest faces?   386
Yet she hopte well, and in her sweet conceit
Waying her arguments, she thought them weight:
And that the logick of *Leanders* beautie,
And them together would bring proofes of dutie.   390
And if her soule, that was a skilfull glance
Of Heavens great essence, found such imperance
In her loves beauties; she had confidence
Jove lov'd him too, and pardond her offence.
    Beautie in heaven and earth this grace doth win,   395
    It supples rigor, and it lessens sin.
Thus, her sharpe wit, her love, her secrecie,
Trouping together, made her wonder why
She should not leave her bed, and to the Temple?
Her health sayd she must live; her sex dissemble.   400
She viewd *Leanders* place, and wisht he were
Turnd to his place, so his place were *Leander*.
Aye me (sayd she) that loves sweet life and sence
Should doe it harme! my love had not gone hence,
Had he been like his place. O blessed place,   405
Image of Constancie. Thus my loves grace
Parts no where but it leaves some thing behinde
Worth observation: he renowmes his kinde.
His motion is like heavens Orbiculer:
For where he once is, he is ever there.   410
This place was mine: *Leander* now t'is thine;
Thou being my selfe, then it is double mine:
Mine, and *Leanders* mine, *Leanders* mine.
O see what wealth it yeelds me, nay yeelds him:
For I am in it, he for me doth swim.   415
Rich, fruitfull love, that doubling selfe estates

Elixer-like contracts, though separates.
Deare place I kisse thee, and doe welcome thee,
As from *Leander* ever sent to mee.

The end of the third Sestyad.

THE ARGUMENT OF THE FOURTH SESTYAD

Hero, in sacred habit deckt,
Doth private sacrifice effect.
Her Skarfs description wrought by fate,
Ostents, that threaten her estate.
The strange, yet Phisicall events,
Leanders counterfeit presents.
In thunder, Ciprides *descends,*
Presaging both the lovers ends.
Ecte the Goddesse of remorce,
With vocall and articulate force
Inspires Leucote, Venus *swan,*
T"excuse the beautious Sestian.
Venus, to wreake her rites abuses,
Creates the monster Eronusis;
Enflaming Heros *Sacrifice,*
With lightning darted from her eyes:
And thereof springs the painted beast,
That ever since taints every breast.

Now from *Leanders* place she rose, and found
Her haire and rent robe scattred on the ground:
Which taking up, she every peece did lay
Upon an Altar; where in youth of day
She usde t'exhibite private Sacrifice: 5
Those would she offer to the Deities
Of her faire Goddesse, and her powerfull son,
As relicks of her late-felt passion:
And in that holy sort she vowd to end them,
In hope her violent fancies that did rend them,   10
Would as quite fade in her loves holy fire,
As they should in the flames she ment t'inspire.

Then put she on all her religious weedes,
That deckt her in her secret sacred deedes:
A crowne of Isickles, that sunne nor fire   15
Could ever melt, and figur'd chast desire.
A golden star shinde in her naked breast,
In honour of the Queene-light of the East.
In her right hand she held a silver wand,
On whose bright top *Peristera* did stand,   20
Who was a Nymph, but now transformd a Dove,
And in her life was deare in *Venus* love:
And for her sake she ever since that time,
Chusde Doves to draw her Coach through heavens blew clime.
Her plentious haire in curled billowes swims   25
On her bright shoulder: her harmonious lims
Sustainde no more but a most subtile vaile
That hung on them, as it durst not assaile
Their different concord: for the weakest ayre
Could raise it swelling from her bewties fayre: 30
Nor did it cover, but adumbrate onelie
Her most heart-piercing parts, that a blest eie
Might see (as it did shadow) fearfullie,
All that all-love-deserving Paradise:
It was as blew as the most freezing skies   35
Neere the Seas hew, for thence her Goddesse came:
On it a skarfe she wore of wondrous frame;
In midst whereof she wrought a virgins face,
From whose each cheeke a firie blush did chace
Two crimson flames, that did two waies extend,   40
Spreading the ample skarfe to either end,
Which figur'd the division of her minde,
Whiles yet she rested bashfully inclinde,
And stood not resolute to wed *Leander*.
This serv'd her white neck for a purple sphere,   45
And cast it selfe at full breadth downe her back.
There (since the first breath that begun the wrack
Of her free quiet from *Leanders* lips)
She wrought a Sea in one flame full of ships:
But that one ship where all her wealth did passe   50
(Like simple marchants goods) *Leander* was:
For in that Sea she naked figured him;

Her diving needle taught him how to swim,
And to each thred did such resemblance give,
For joy to be so like him, it did live. 55
  Things senceles live by art, and rationall die,
  By rude contempt of art and industrie.
Scarce could she work but in her strength of thought,
She feard she prickt *Leander* as she wrought:
And oft would shrieke so, that her Guardian frighted, 60
Would staring haste, as with some mischiefe cited.
  They double life that dead things griefs sustayne:
  They kill that feele not their friends living payne.
Sometimes she feard he sought her infamie,
And then as she was working of his eie, 65
She thought to pricke it out to quench her ill:
But as she prickt, it grew more perfect still.
  Trifling attempts no serious acts advance;
  The fire of love is blowne by dalliance.
In working his fayre neck she did so grace it, 70
She still was working her owne armes t'imbrace it:
That, and his shoulders, and his hands were seene
Above the streame, and with a pure Sea greene
She did so queintly shadow every lim,
All might be seene beneath the waves to swim. 75
  In this conceited skarfe she wrought beside
A Moone in change, and shooting stars did glide
In number after her with bloodie beames,
Which figur'd her affects in their extreames,
Pursuing Nature in her Cynthian bodie, 80
And did her thoughts running on change implie:
For maids take more delights when they prepare
And thinke of wives states, than when wives they are.
Beneath all these she wrought a Fisherman,
Drawing his nets from forth that Ocean; 85
Who drew so hard ye might discover well,
The toughned sinewes in his neck did swell:
His inward straines drave out his blood-shot eyes,
And springs of sweat did in his forehead rise:
Yet was of nought but of a Serpent sped, 90
That in his bosome flew and stung him dead.
And this by fate into her minde was sent,

Not wrought by meere instinct of her intent.
At the skarfs other end her hand did frame,
Neere the forkt point of the devided flame,   95
A countrie virgin keeping of a Vine,
Who did of hollow bulrushes combine
Snares for the stubble-loving Grashopper,
And by her lay her skrip that nourisht her.
Within a myrtle shade she sate and sung,   100
And tufts of waving reedes about her sprung:
Where lurkt two Foxes, that while she applide
Her trifling snares, their theeveries did devide:
One to the vine, another to her skrip,
That she did negligently overslip: 105
By which her fruitfull vine and holesome fare,
She suffred spoyld to make a childish snare.
These omenous fancies did her soule expresse,
And every finger made a Prophetesse,
To shew what death was hid in loves disguise,   110
And make her judgement conquer destinies.
O what sweet formes fayre Ladies soules doe shrowd,
Were they made seene and forced through their blood,
If through their beauties like rich work through lawn,
They would set forth their minds with vertues drawn,   115
In letting graces from their fingers flie,
To still their eyas thoughts with industrie:
That their plied wits in numbred silks might sing
Passions huge conquest, and their needels leading
Affection prisoner through their own-built citties,   120
Pinniond with stories and Arachnean ditties.
    Proceed we now with *Heros* sacrifice;
She odours burnd, and from their smoke did rise
Unsavorie fumes, that ayre with plagues inspired,
And then the consecrated sticks she fired.   125
On whose pale flame an angrie spirit flew,
And beate it downe still as it upward grew.
The virgin Tapers that on th'altar stood,
When she inflam'd them burnd as red as blood:
All sad ostents of that too neere successe,   130
That made such moving beauties motionlesse.
Then *Hero* wept; but her affrighted eyes

She quickly wrested from the sacrifice:
Shut them, and inwards for *Leander* lookt,
Searcht her soft bosome, and from thence she pluckt 135
His lovely picture: which when she had viewd,
Her beauties were with all loves joyes renewd.
The odors sweetned, and the fires burnd cleere,
Leanders forme left no ill object there.
Such was his beautie that the force of light,   140
Whose knowledge teacheth wonders infinite.
The strength of number and proportion,
Nature had plaste in it to make it knowne,
Art was her daughter, and what humane wits
For studie lost, intombd in drossie spirits.   145
After this accident (which for her glorie
Hero could not but make a historie)
Th'inhabitants of *Sestus*, and *Abydus*,
Did every yeare with feasts propitious,
To fayre *Leanders* picture sacrifice,   150
And they were persons of especiall prize
That were allowd it, as an ornament
T'inrich their houses; for the continent
Of the strange vertues all approv'd it held:
For even the very looke of it repeld   155
All blastings, witchcrafts, and the strifes of nature
In those diseases that no hearbs could cure.
The woolfie sting of Avarice it would pull,
And make the rankest miser bountifull.
It kild the feare of thunder and of death;   160
The discords that conceits ingendereth
Twixt man and wife, it for the time would cease:
The flames of love it quencht, and would increase:
Held in a princes hand it would put out
The dreadfulst Comet: it would ease all doubt   165
Of threatned mischiefes: it would bring asleepe
Such as were mad: it would enforce to weepe
Most barbarous eyes: and many more effects
This picture wrought, and sprung *Leandrian* sects,
Of which was *Hero* first: For he whose forme   170
(Held in her hand) cleerd such a fatall storme,
From hell she thought his person would defend her,

Which night and *Hellespont* would quickly send her.
With this confirmd, she vowd to banish quite
All thought of any check to her delite: 175
And in contempt of sillie bashfulnes,
She would the faith of her desires professe:
Where her Religion should be Policie,
To follow love with zeale her pietie:
Her chamber her Cathedrall Church should be,   180
And her *Leander* her chiefe Deitie.
For in her love these did the gods forego;
And though her knowledge did not teach her so,
Yet did it teach her this, that what her hart
Did greatest hold in her selfe greatest part,   185
That she did make her god; and t'was lesse nought
To leave gods in profession and in thought,
Than in her love and life: for therein lies
Most of her duties, and their dignities,
And raile the brain-bald world at what it will;   190
Thats the grand Atheisme that raignes in it still.
Yet singularitie she would use no more,
For she was singular too much before:
But she would please the world with fayre pretext;
Love would not leave her conscience perplext.   195
Great men that will have lesse doe for them still,
Must beare them out though th'acts be nere so ill.
Meannes must Pandar be to Excellence,
Pleasure attones Falshood and Conscience:
Dissembling was the worst (thought *Hero* then)   200
And that was best now she must live with men.
O vertuous love that taught her to doe best,
When she did worst, and when she thought it lest.
Thus would she still proceed in works divine,
And in her sacred state of priesthood shine,   205
Handling the holy rites with hands as bold,
As if therein she did *Joves* thunder hold;
And need not feare those menaces of error,
Which she at others threw with greatest terror.
O lovely *Hero*, nothing is thy sin,   210
Wayd with those foule faults other Priests are in;
That having neither faiths, nor works, nor bewties,

T'engender any scuse for slubberd duties;
With as much countnance fill their holie chayres,
And sweat denouncements gainst prophane affayres, 215
As if their lives were cut out by their places,
And they the only fathers of the Graces.
    Now as with setled minde she did repaire,
Her thoughts to sacrifice, her ravisht haire
And her torne robe which on the altar lay,   220
And only for Religions fire did stay;
She heard a thunder by the Cyclops beaten,
In such a volley as the world did threaten,
Given *Venus* as she parted th'ayrie Sphere,
Discending now to chide with *Hero* here: 225
When suddenly the Goddesse waggoners,
The Swans and Turtles that in coupled pheres,
Through all worlds bosoms draw her influence,
Lighted in *Heros* window, and from thence
To her fayre shoulders flew the gentle Doves.   230
Gracefull *Ædone* that sweet pleasure loves,
And ruffoot *Chreste* with the tufted crowne,
Both which did kisse her, though their Goddes frownd.
The Swans did in the solid flood her glasse,
Proyne their fayre plumes; of which the fairest was, 235
Jove-lov'd *Leucote*, that pure brightnes is;
The other bountie-loving *Dapsilis*.
All were in heaven, now they with *Hero* were:
But *Venus* lookes brought wrath, and urged feare.
Her robe was skarlet, black her heads attire,   240
And through her naked breast shinde streames of fire,
As when the rarefied ayre is driven
In flashing streames, and opes the darkned heaven.
In her white hand a wreath of yew she bore,
And breaking th'icie wreath sweet *Hero* wore,   245
She forst about her browes her wreath of yew,
And sayd, now minion to thy fate be trew,
Though not to me, indure what this portends;
Begin where lightnes will, in shame it ends.
Love makes thee cunning; thou art currant now,   250
By being counterfeit: thy broken vow,
Deceit with her pide garters must rejoyne,

And with her stampe thou countnances must coyne:
Coynes, and pure deceits for purities,
And still a mayd wilt seeme in cosoned eies,   255
And have an antike face to laugh within,
While thy smooth lookes make men digest thy sin.
But since thy lips (lest thought forsworne) forswore,
Be never virgins vow worth trusting more.

When Beauties dearest did her Goddesse heare,   260
Breathe such rebukes gainst that she could not cleare;
Dumbe sorrow spake alowd in teares, and blood
That from her griefe-burst vaines in piteous flood,
From the sweet conduits of her savor fell:
The gentle Turtles did with moanes make swell   265
Their shining gorges: the white black-eyde Swans
Did sing as wofull Epicedians,
As they would straightwaies dye: when pities Queene
The Goddesse *Ecte*, that had ever beene
Hid in a watrie clowde neere *Heros* cries,   270
Since the first instant of her broken eies,
Gave bright *Leucote* voyce, and made her speake,
To ease her anguish, whose swolne breast did breake
With anger at her Goddesse, that did touch
Hero so neere for that she usde so much.   275
And thrusting her white neck at *Venus*, sayd;
Why may not amorous *Hero* seeme a mayd,
Though she be none, as well as you suppresse
In modest cheekes your inward wantonnesse?
How often have wee drawne you from above,   280
T'exchange with mortals, rites for rites in love?
Why in your preist then call you that offence
That shines in you, and is your influence?
With this the furies stopt *Leucotes* lips,
Enjoynd by *Venus*; who with Rosie whips   285
Beate the kind Bird. Fierce lightning from her eyes
Did set on fire faire *Heros* sacrifice,
Which was her torne robe, and inforced hayre;
And the bright flame became a mayd most faire
For her aspect: her tresses were of wire,   290
Knit like a net, where harts all set on fire,
Strugled in pants and could not get releast:

Her armes were all with golden pincers drest,
And twentie fashiond knots, pullies, and brakes,
And all her bodie girdled with painted Snakes. 295
Her doune parts in a Scorpions taile combinde,
Freckled with twentie colours; pyed wings shinde
Out of her shoulders; Cloth had never die,
Nor sweeter colours never viewed eie,
In scorching *Turkie*, *Cares*, *Tartarie*, 300
Than shinde about this spirit notorious;
Nor was *Arachnes* web so glorious.
Of lightning and of shreds she was begot;
More hold in base dissemblers is there not.
Her name was *Eronusis*. *Venus* flew 305
From *Heros* sight, and at her Chariot drew
This wondrous creature to so steepe a height,
That all the world she might command with sleight
Of her gay wings: and then she bad her hast,
Since *Hero* had dissembled, and disgrast 310
Her rites so much, and every breast infect
With her deceits, she made her Architect
Of all dissimulation, and since then
Never was any trust in maides nor men.
      O it spighted, 315
Fayre *Venus* hart to see her most delighted.
And one she chusde for temper of her minde,
To be the only ruler of her kinde,
So soone to let her virgin race be ended;
Not simply for the fault a whit offended: 320
But that in strife for chastnes with the Moone,
Spitefull *Diana* bad her shew but one,
That was her servant vowd, and liv'd a mayd,
And now she thought to answer that upbrayd,
Hero had lost her answer; who knowes not 325
Venus would seeme as farre from any spot
Of light demeanour, as the very skin
Twixt *Cynthias* browes; Sin is asham'd of Sin.
Up *Venus* flew, and scarce durst up for feare
Of *Phœbes* laughter, when she past her Sphere: 330
And so most ugly clowded was the light,
That day was hid in day; night came ere night,

And *Venus* could not through the thick ayre pierce,
Till the daies king, god of undanted verse,
Because she was so plentifull a theame,   335
To such as wore his Lawrell *Anademe:*
Like to a firie bullet made descent,
And from her passage those fat vapours rent,
That being not throughly rarefide to raine,
Melted like pitch as blew as any vaine,   340
And scalding tempests made the earth to shrinke
Under their fervor, and the world did thinke
In every drop a torturing Spirit flew,
It pierst so deeply, and it burnd so blew.

    Betwixt all this and *Hero*, *Hero* held   345
Leanders picture as a Persian shield:
And she was free from feare of worst successe;
The more ill threats us, we suspect the lesse:
As we grow haples, violence subtle growes,
Dumb, deafe, and blind, and comes when no man knowes. 350

The end of the fourth Sestyad.

THE ARGUMENT OF THE FIFT SESTYAD

Day doubles her accustomd date,
As loth the night, incenst by fate,
Should wrack our lovers; Heros plight,
Longs for Leander, *and the night:*
Which, ere her thirstie wish recovers,
She sends for two betrothed lovers,
And marries them, that (with their crew
Their sports and ceremonies due)
She covertly might celebrate,
With secret joy her owne estate.
She makes a feast, at which appeares
The wilde Nymph Teras, *that still beares*
An Ivory Lute, tels Omenous tales,
And sings at solemne festivales.

Now was bright *Hero* weary of the day,
Thought an Olympiad in *Leanders* stay.

Sol, and the soft-foote *Howrs* hung on his armes,
And would not let him swim, foreseeing his harmes:
That day *Aurora* double grace obtainde   5
Of her love *Phœbus;* she his Horses rainde,
Set on his golden knee, and as she list
She puld him back; and as she puld, she kist
To have him turne to bed; he lov'd her more,
To see the love *Leander Hero* bore.   10
Examples profit much ten times in one,
In persons full of note, good deedes are done.
 Day was so long, men walking fell asleepe,
The heavie humors that their eyes did steepe,
Made them feare mischiefs. The hard streets were beds   15
For covetous churles, and for ambitious heads,
That spight of Nature would their busines plie.
All thought they had the falling *Epilepsie*,
Men groveld so upon the smotherd ground,
And pittie did the hart of heaven confound.   20
The Gods, the Graces, and the Muses came
Downe to the Destinies, to stay the frame
Of the true lovers deaths, and all worlds teares:
But death before had stopt their cruell eares.
All the Celestials parted mourning then,   25
Pierst with our humane miseries more then men.
Ah, nothing doth the world with mischiefe fill,
But want of feeling one anothers ill.
 With their descent the day grew something fayre,
And cast a brighter robe upon the ayre.   30
Hero to shorten time with merriment,
For yong *Alcmane*, and bright *Mya* sent,
Two lovers that had long crav'd mariage dues
At *Heros* hands: but she did still refuse,
For lovely *Mya* was her consort vowd   35
In her maids state, and therefore not allowd
To amorous Nuptials: yet faire *Hero* now
Intended to dispence with her cold vow,
Since hers was broken, and to marrie her:
The rites would pleasing matter minister   40
To her conceits, and shorten tedious day.
They came; sweet Musick usherd th'odorous way,

And wanton Ayre in twentie sweet forms danst
After her fingers; Beautie and Love advanst
Their ensignes in the downles rosie faces   45
Of youths and maids, led after by the Graces.
For all these, *Hero* made a friendly feast,
Welcomd them kindly, did much love protest,
Winning their harts with all the meanes she might,
That when her fault should chance t'abide the light,   50
Their loves might cover or extenuate it,
And high in her worst fate make pittie sit.
  She married them, and in the banquet came
Borne by the virgins: *Hero* striv'd to frame
Her thoughts to mirth. Aye me, but hard it is   55
To imitate a false and forced blis.
Ill may a sad minde forge a merrie face,
Nor hath constrained laughter any grace.
Then layd she wine on cares to make them sinke;
Who feares the threats of fortune, let him drinke.   60
  To these quick Nuptials entred suddenly,
Admired *Teras* with the Ebon Thye,
A Nymph that haunted the greene *Sestyan* groves,
And would consort soft virgins in their loves,
At gaysome Triumphs, and on solemne dayes,   65
Singing prophetike Elegies and Layes:
And fingring of a silver Lute she tide,
With black and purple skarfs by her left side.
Apollo gave it, and her skill withall,
And she was term'd his Dwarfe she was so small.   70
Yet great in vertue, for his beames enclosde
His vertues in her: never was proposde
Riddle to her, or Augurie, strange or new,
But she resolv'd it: never sleight tale flew
From her charmd lips, without important sence,   75
Shewne in some grave succeeding consequence.
  This little Silvane with her songs and tales,
Gave such estate to feasts and Nuptiales,
That though oft times she forewent Tragedies,
Yet for her strangenes still she pleasde their eyes,   80
And for her smalnes they admir'd her so,
They thought her perfect borne and could not grow.

All eyes were on her: *Hero* did command
An Altar deckt with sacred state should stand,
At the Feasts upper end close by the Bride,   85
On which the pretie Nymph might sit espide.
Then all were silent; every one so heares,
As all their sences climbd into their eares:
And first this amorous tale that fitted well,
Fayre *Hero* and the Nuptials she did tell: 90

The tale of Teras.

Hymen that now is god of Nuptiall rites,
And crownes with honor love and his delights,
Of *Athens* was a youth so sweet of face,
That many thought him of the femall race:
Such quickning brightnes did his cleere eyes dart,   95
Warme went their beames to his beholders hart:
In such pure leagues his beauties were combinde,
That there your Nuptiall contracts first were signde.
For as proportion, white, and crimsine, meet
In Beauties mixture, all right cleere, and sweet;   100
The eye responsible, the golden haire,
And none is held without the other, faire:
All spring together, all together fade;
Such intermixt affections should invade
Two perfect lovers: which being yet unseene,   105
Their vertues and their comforts copied beene,
In Beauties concord, subject to the eie;
And that, in *Hymen*, pleasde so matchleslie,
That lovers were esteemde in their full grace,
Like forme and colour mixt in *Hymens* face;   110
And such sweete concord was thought worthie then
Of torches, musick, feasts, and greatest men:
So *Hymen* lookt, that even the chastest minde
He mov'd to joyne in joyes of sacred kinde:
For onely now his chins first doune consorted   115
His heads rich fleece, in golden curles contorted;
And as he was so lov'd, he lov'd so too,
So should best bewties, bound by Nuptialls doo.
   Bright *Eucharis*, who was by all men saide
The noblest, fayrest, and the richest maide,   120

Of all th'*Athenian* damzels, *Hymen* lov'd;
With such transmission, that his heart remov'd
From his white brest to hers, but her estate
In passing his, was so interminate
For wealth and honor, that his love durst feede   125
On nought but sight and hearing, nor could breede
Hope of requitall, the grand prise of love;
Nor could he heare or see but he must prove
How his rare bewties musick would agree
With maids in consort: therefore robbed he   130
His chin of those same few first fruits it bore,
And clad in such attire, as Virgins wore,
He kept them companie, and might right well,
For he did all but *Eucharis* excell
In all the fayre of Beautie: yet he wanted   135
Vertue to make his owne desires implanted
In his deare *Eucharis*; for women never
Love beautie in their sex, but envie ever.
His judgement yet (that durst not suite addresse,
Nor past due meanes, presume of due successe)   140
Reason gat fortune in the end to speede
To his best prayers: but strange it seemd indeede,
That fortune should a chast affection blesse,
Preferment seldome graceth bashfulnesse.
Nor grast it *Hymen* yet; but many a dart   145
And many an amorous thought enthrald his hart,
Ere he obtaind her; and he sick became,
Forst to abstaine her sight, and then the flame
Rag'd in his bosome. O what griefe did fill him:
Sight made him sick, and want of sight did kill him. 150
The virgins wondred where *Diætia* stay'd,
For so did *Hymen* terme himselfe a mayd.
At length with sickly lookes he greeted them:
Tis strange to see gainst what an extreame streame
A lover strives; poore *Hymen* lookt so ill,   155
That as in merit he increased still,
By suffring much, so he in grace decreast.
Women are most wonne when men merit least:
If merit looke not well, love bids stand by,
Loves speciall lesson is to please the eye.   160

And *Hymen* soone recovering all he lost,
Deceiving still these maids, but himselfe most.
His love and he with many virgin dames,
Noble by birth, noble by beauties flames,
Leaving the towne with songs and hallowed lights,   165
To doe great *Ceres Eleusina* rites
Of zealous Sacrifice; were made a pray
To barbarous Rovers that in ambush lay,
And with rude hands enforst their shining spoyle,
Farre from the darkned Citie, tir'd with toyle.   170
And when the yellow issue of the skie
Came trouping forth, jelous of crueltie,
To their bright fellowes of this under heaven,
Into a double night they saw them driven,
A horride Cave, the theeves black mansion,   175
Where wearie of the journey they had gon,
Their last nights watch, and drunke with their sweete gains,
Dull *Morpheus* entred, laden with silken chains,
Stronger then iron, and bound the swelling vaines
And tyred sences of these lawles Swaines.   180
But when the virgin lights thus dimly burnd;
O what a hell was heaven in! how they mournd
And wrung their hands, and wound their gentle forms
Into the shapes of sorrow! Golden storms
Fell from their eyes: As when the Sunne appeares,   185
And yet it raines, so shewd their eyes their teares.
And as when funerall dames watch a dead corse,
Weeping about it, telling with remorse
What paines he felt, how long in paine he lay,
How little food he eate, what he would say;   190
And then mixe mournfull tales of others deaths,
Smothering themselves in clowds of their owne breaths.
At length, one cheering other, call for wine,
The golden boale drinks teares out of their eine,
As they drinke wine from it; and round it goes,   195
Each helping other to relieve their woes:
So cast these virgins beauties mutuall raies,
One lights another, face the face displaies;
Lips by reflexion kist, and hands hands shooke,
Even by the whitenes each of other tooke.   200

But *Hymen* now usde friendly *Morpheus* aide,
Slew every theefe, and rescue every maide.
And now did his enamourd passion take
Hart from his hartie deede, whose worth did make
His hope of bounteous *Eucharis* more strong;   205
And now came *Love* with *Proteus*, who had long
Inggl'd the little god with prayers and gifts,
Ran through all shapes, and varied all his shifts,
To win *Loves* stay with him, and make him love him:
And when he saw no strength of sleight could move him   210
To make him love, or stay, he nimbly turnd
Into *Loves* selfe, he so extreamely burnd.
And thus came *Love* with *Proteus* and his powre,
T'encounter *Eucharis:* first like the flowre
That *Junos* milke did spring the silver Lillie,   215
He fell on *Hymens* hand, who straight did spie
The bounteous Godhead, and with wondrous joy
Offred it *Eucharis*. She wondrous coy
Drew back her hand: the subtle flowre did woo it,
And drawing it neere, mixt so you could not know it.   220
As two cleere Tapers mixe in one their light,
So did the Lillie and the hand their white:
She viewd it, and her view the forme bestowes
Amongst her spirits: for as colour flowes
From superficies of each thing we see,   225
Even so with colours formes emitted bee:
And where Loves forme is, love is, love is forme;
He entred at the eye, his sacred storme
Rose from the hand, loves sweetest instrument:
It stird her bloods sea so, that high it went,   230
And beate in bashfull waves gainst the white shore
Of her divided cheekes; it rag'd the more,
Because the tide went gainst the haughtie winde
Of her estate and birth: And as we finde
In fainting ebs, the flowrie Zephire hurles   235
The greene-hayrd *Hellespont*, broke in silver curles
Gainst *Heros* towre: but in his blasts retreate,
The waves obeying him, they after beate,
Leaving the chalkie shore a great way pale,
Then moyst it freshly with another gale: 240

So ebd and flowde the blood in *Eucharis* face,
Coynesse and Love striv'd which had greatest grace,
Virginitie did fight on Coynesse side;
Feare of her parents frownes, and femall pride,
Lothing the lower place, more then it loves   245
The high contents, desert and vertue moves.
With love fought *Hymens* beautie and his valure,
Which scarce could so much favour yet allure
To come to strike, but fameles idle stood,
Action is firie valours soveraigne good.   250
But Love once entred, wisht no greater ayde
Then he could find within; thought, thought betrayd,
The bribde, but incorrupted Garrison,
Sung *Io Hymen*; there those songs begun,
And Love was growne so rich with such a gaine,   255
And wanton with the ease of his free raigne,
That he would turne into her roughest frownes
To turne them out; and thus he *Hymen* crownes
King of his thoughts, mans greatest Emperie:
This was his first brave step to deitie.   260
    Home to the mourning cittie they repayre,
With newes as holesome as the morning ayre,
To the sad parents of each saved maid:
But *Hymen* and his *Eucharis* had laid
This plat, to make the flame of their delight   265
Round as the Moone at full, and full as bright.
    Because the parents of chast *Eucharis*
Exceeding *Hymens* so, might crosse their blis;
And as the world rewards deserts, that law
Cannot assist with force: so when they saw   270
Their daughter safe, take vantage of their owne,
Praise *Hymens* valour much, nothing bestowne.
Hymen must leave the virgins in a Grove
Farre off from Athens, and go first to prove
If to restore them all with fame and life,   275
He should enjoy his dearest as his wife.
This told to all the maids; the most agree:
The riper sort knowing what t'is to bee
The first mouth of a newes so farre deriv'd,
And that to heare and beare newes brave folks liv'd,   280

As being a carriage speciall hard to beare,
Occurrents, these occurrents being so deare,
They did with grace protest, they were content
T'accost their friends with all their complement,
For *Hymens* good: but to incurre their harme,   285
There he must pardon them. This wit went warme
To *Adolesches* braine, a Nymph borne hie,
Made all of voyce and fire, that upwards flie:
Her hart and all her forces neither traine,
Climbd to her tongue, and thither fell her braine,   290
Since it could goe no higher: and it must go,
All powers she had, even her tongue did so.
In spirit and quicknes she much joy did take,
And lov'd her tongue, only for quicknes sake,
And she would hast and tell. The rest all stay,   295
Hymen goes on; the Nymph another way:
And what became of her Ile tell at last:
Yet take her visage now: moyst lipt, long fa'st,
Thin like an iron wedge, so sharpe and tart,
As twere of purpose made to cleave *Loves* hart.   300
Well were this lovely Beautie rid of her,
And *Hymen* did at *Athens* now prefer
His welcome suite, which he with joy aspirde:
A hundred princely youths with him retirde
To fetch the Nymphs: Chariots and Musick went,   305
And home they came: heaven with applauses rent.
The Nuptials straight proceed, whiles all the towne,
Fresh in their joyes might doe them most renowne.
First gold-lockt *Hymen* did to Church repaire,
Like a quick offring burnd in flames of haire.   310
And after, with a virgin firmament,
The Godhead-proving Bride, attended went
Before them all, she lookt in her command,
As if forme-giving *Cyprias* silver hand
Gripte all their beauties, and crusht out one flame,   315
She blusht to see how beautie overcame
The thoughts of all men. Next before her went
Five lovely children deckt with ornament
Of her sweet colours, bearing Torches by,
For light was held a happie Augurie   320

Of generation, whose efficient right
Is nothing else but to produce to light.
The od disparent number they did chuse,
To shew the union married loves should use,
Since in two equall parts it will not sever,   325
But the midst holds one to rejoyne it ever,
As common to both parts: men therfore deeme,
That equall number Gods doe not esteeme,
Being authors of sweet peace and unitie,
But pleasing to th'infernall Emperie,   330
Under whose ensignes Wars and Discords fight,
Since an even number you may disunite
In two parts equall, nought in middle left,
To reunite each part from other reft:
And five they hold in most especiall prise,   335
Since t'is the first od number that doth rise
From the two formost numbers unitie
That od and even are; which are two, and three,
For one no number is: but thence doth flow
The powerfull race of number. Next did go   340
A noble Matron that did spinning beare
A huswifes rock and spindle, and did weare
A Weathers skin, with all the snowy fleece,
To intimate that even the daintiest peece,
And noblest borne dame should industrious bee,   345
That which does good, disgraceth no degree.
    And now to *Junos* Temple they are come,
Where her grave Priest stood in the mariage rome.
On his right arme did hang a skarlet vaile,
And from his shoulders to the ground did traile,   350
On either side, Ribands of white and blew;
With the red vaile he hid the bashfull hew
Of the chast Bride, to shew the modest shame,
In coupling with a man should grace a dame.
Then tooke he the disparent Silks and tide   355
The Lovers by the wasts, and side to side,
In token that thereafter they must binde
In one selfe sacred knot each others minde.
Before them on an Altar he presented
Both fire and water: which was first invented,   360

Since to ingenerate every humane creature,
And every other birth produ'st by Nature,
Moysture and heate must mixe: so man and wife
For humane race must joyne in Nuptiall life.
Then one of *Junos* Birds, the painted Jay,   365
He sacrifisde, and tooke the gall away.
All which he did behinde the Altar throw,
In signe no bitternes of hate should grow
Twixt maried loves, nor any least disdaine.
Nothing they spake, for twas esteemd too plaine   370
For the most silken mildnes of a maid,
To let a publique audience heare it said
She boldly tooke the man: and so respected
Was bashfulnes in *Athens:* it erected
To chast *Agneia*, which is Shamefastnesse,   375
A sacred Temple, holding her a Goddesse.
And now to Feasts, Masks, and triumphant showes,
The shining troupes returnd, even till earths throwes
Brought forth with joy the thickest part of night,
When the sweet Nuptiall song that usde to cite   380
All to their rest, was by *Phemonoe* sung:
First *Delphian* Prophetesse, whose graces sprung
Out of the *Muses* well, she sung before
The Bride into her chamber: at which dore
A Matron and a Torch-bearer did stand;   385
A painted box of Confits in her hand
The Matron held, and so did other some
That compast round the honourd Nuptiall rome.
The custome was that every maid did weare,
During her maidenhead, a silken Sphere   390
About her waste, above her inmost weede,
Knit with *Minervas* knot, and that was freede
By the faire Bridegrome on the mariage night,
With many ceremonies of delight:
And yet eternisde *Hymens* tender Bride,   395
To suffer it dissolv'd so sweetly cride.
The maids that heard, so lov'd, and did adore her,
They wisht with all their hearts to suffer for her.
So had the Matrons, that with Confits stood
About the chamber, such affectionate blood,   400

And so true feeling of her harmeles paines,
That every one a showre of Confits raines.
For which the Brideyouths scrambling on the ground,
In noyse of that sweet haile their cryes were drownd.
And thus blest *Hymen* joyde his gracious Bride,   405
And for his joy was after deifide.

   The Saffron mirror by which *Phœbus* love,
Greene *Tellus* decks her, now he held above
The clowdy mountaines: and the noble maide,
Sharp-visag'd *Adolesche*, that was straide   410
Out of her way, in hasting with her newes,
Not till this houre th'*Athenian* turrets viewes,
And now brought home by guides: she heard by all
That her long kept occurrents would be stale,
And how faire *Hymens* honors did excell   415
For those rare newes, which she came short to tell.
To heare her deare tongue robd of such a joy,
Made the well-spoken Nymph take such a toy,
That downe she sunke: when lightning from above,
Shrunk her leane body, and for meere free love,   420
Turnd her into the pied-plum'd *Psittacus*,
That now the Parrat is surnam'd by us,
Who still with counterfeit confusion prates,
Nought but newes common to the commonst mates.
This tolde, strange *Teras* toucht her Lute and sung   425
This dittie, that the Torchie evening sprung.

Epithalamion Teratos.

Come come deare night, Loves Mart of kisses,
Sweet close of his ambitious line,
The fruitfull summer of his blisses,
Loves glorie doth in darknes shine.   430
O come soft rest of Cares, come night,
Come naked vertues only tire,
The reaped harvest of the light,
Bound up in sheaves of sacred fire.
   Love cals to warre,   435
   Sighs his Alarmes,
   Lips his swords are,
   The field his Armes.

Come Night and lay thy velvet hand
On glorious Dayes outfacing face;   440
And all thy crouned flames command,
For Torches to our Nuptiall grace.
    Love cals to warre,
    Sighs his Alarmes,
    Lips his swords are,   445
    The field his Armes.
No neede have we of factious Day,
To cast in envie of thy peace,
Her bals of Discord in thy way:
Here beauties day doth never cease,   450
Day is abstracted here,
And varied in a triple sphere.
Hero, Alcmane, Mya, so outshine thee,
Ere thou come here let *Thetis* thrice refine thee.
    Love cals to warre,   455
    Sighs his Alarmes,
    Lips his swords are,
    The field his Armes.
The Evening starre I see,
Rise youths the Evening starre,   460
Helps Love to summon warre,
Both now imbracing bee.
Rise youths, loves right claims more then banquets, rise.
Now the bright Marygolds that deck the skies,
Phœbus celestiall flowrs, that (contrarie   465
To his flowers here) ope when he shuts his eie,
And shuts when he doth open, crowne your sports:
Now love in night, and night in love exhorts
Courtship and Dances: All your parts employ,
And suite nights rich expansure with your joy,   470
Love paints his longings in sweet virgins eyes:
Rise youths, loves right claims more then banquets, rise.
Rise virgins, let fayre Nuptiall loves enfolde
Your fruitles breasts: the maidenheads ye holde
Are not your owne alone, but parted are;   475
Part in disposing them your Parents share,
And that a third part is: so must ye save
Your loves a third, and you your thirds must have.

Love paints his longings in sweet virgins eyes:
Rise youths, loves right claims more then banquets, rise.   480

   Herewith the amorous spirit that was so kinde
To *Teras* haire, and combd it downe with winde,
Still as it Comet-like brake from her braine,
Would needes have *Teras* gone, and did refraine
To blow it downe: which staring up, dismaid   485
The timorous feast, and she no longer staid:
But bowing to the Bridegrome and the Bride,
Did like a shooting exhalation glide
Out of their sights: the turning of her back
Made them all shrieke, it lookt so ghastly black.   490
O haples *Hero*, that most haples clowde,
Thy soone-succeeding Tragedie foreshowde.
Thus all the Nuptiall crew to joyes depart,
But much-wrongd *Hero*, stood Hels blackest dart:
Whose wound because I grieve so to display,   495
I use digressions thus t'encrease the day.

The end of the fift Sestyad.

THE ARGUMENT OF THE SIXT SESTYAD

Leucote flyes to all the windes,
And from the fates their outrage bindes,
That Hero *and her love may meete.*
Leander (*with* Loves *compleate Fleete*
Mand in himselfe) *puts forth to Seas,*
When straight the ruthles Destinies,
With Ate *stirre the windes to warre*
Upon the Hellespont: *Their jarre*
Drownes poore Leander. Heros *eyes*
Wet witnesses of his surprise
Her Torch blowne out: Griefe casts her downe
Upon her love, and both doth drowne.
In whose just ruth the God of Seas,
Transformes them to th'Acanthides.

No longer could the day nor Destinies
Delay the night, who now did frowning rise
Into her Throne; and at her humorous brests,
Visions and Dreames lay sucking: all mens rests
Fell like the mists of death upon their eyes,   5
Dayes too long darts so kild their faculties.
The windes yet, like the flowrs to cease began:
For bright *Leucote*, *Venus* whitest Swan,
That held sweet *Hero* deare, spread her fayre wings,
Like to a field of snow, and message brings   10
From *Venus* to the Fates, t'entreate them lay
Their charge upon the windes their rage to stay,
That the sterne battaile of the Seas might cease,
And guard *Leander* to his love in peace.
The Fates consent, (aye me dissembling Fates)   15
They shewd their favours to conceale their hates,
And draw *Leander* on, least Seas too hie
Should stay his too obsequious destinie:
Who like a fleering slavish Parasite,
In warping profit or a traiterous sleight,   20
Hoopes round his rotten bodie with devotes,
And pricks his descant face full of false notes,
Praysing with open throte (and othes as fowle
As his false heart) the beautie of an Owle,
Kissing his skipping hand with charmed skips,   25
That cannot leave, but leapes upon his lips
Like a cock-sparrow, or a shameles queane
Sharpe at a red-lipt youth, and nought doth meane
Of all his antick shewes, but doth repayre
More tender fawnes, and takes a scattred hayre   30
From his tame subjects shoulder; whips, and cals
For every thing he lacks; creepes gainst the wals
With backward humblesse, to give needles way:
Thus his false fate did with *Leander* play.
    First to black *Eurus* flies the white *Leucote*,   35
Borne mongst the *Negros* in the *Levant* Sea,
On whose curld head the glowing Sun doth rise,⎤
And shewes the soveraigne will of Destinies,   ⎬
To have him cease his blasts, and downe he lies.⎦
Next, to the fennie *Notus*, course she holds,   40

And found him leaning with his armes in folds
Upon a rock, his white hayre full of showres,
And him she chargeth by the fatall powres,
To hold in his wet cheekes his clowdie voyce,
To *Zephire* then that doth in flowres rejoyce.　　45
To snake-foote *Boreas* next she did remove,
And found him tossing of his ravisht love,
To heate his frostie bosome hid in snow,
Who with *Leucotes* sight did cease to blow.
Thus all were still to *Heros* harts desire,　　50
Who with all speede did consecrate a fire
Of flaming Gummes, and comfortable Spice,
To light her Torch, which in such curious price
She held, being object to *Leanders* sight,
That nought but fires perfum'd must give it light.　　55
She lov'd it so, she griev'd to see it burne,
Since it would waste and soone to ashes turne:
Yet if it burnd not, twere not worth her eyes,
What made it nothing, gave it all the prize.
Sweet Torch, true Glasse of our societie;　　60
What man does good, but he consumes thereby?
But thou wert lov'd for good, held high, given show:
Poore vertue loth'd for good, obscur'd, held low.
Doe good be pinde, be deedles good, disgrast:
Unles we feede on men, we let them fast.　　65
Yet *Hero* with these thoughts her Torch did spend.
When Bees makes waxe, Nature doth not intend
It shall be made a Torch: but we that know
The proper vertue of it make it so,
And when t'is made we light it: nor did Nature　　70
Propose one life to maids, but each such creature
Makes by her soule the best of her free state,
Which without love is rude, disconsolate,
And wants loves fire to make it milde and bright,
Till when, maids are but Torches wanting light.　　75
Thus gainst our griefe, not cause of griefe we fight,
The right of nought is gleande, but the delight.
Up went she, but to tell how she descended,
Would God she were not dead, or my verse ended.
She was the rule of wishes, summe and end　　80

For all the parts that did on love depend:
Yet cast the Torch his brightnes further forth;
But what shines neerest best, holds truest worth.
Leander did not through such tempests swim
To kisse the Torch, although it lighted him: 85
But all his powres in her desires awaked,
Her love and vertues cloth'd him richly naked.
Men kisse but fire that only shewes pursue,
Her Torch and *Hero*, figure, shew, and vertue.

   Now at opposde *Abydus* nought was heard,   90
But bleating flocks, and many a bellowing herd,
Slaine for the Nuptials, cracks of falling woods,
Blowes of broad axes, powrings out of floods.
The guiltie *Hellespont* was mixt and stainde
With bloodie Torrents, that the shambles raind;   95
Not arguments of feast, but shewes that bled,
Foretelling that red night that followed.
More blood was spilt, more honors were addrest,
Then could have graced any happie feast.
Rich banquets, triumphs, every pomp employes   100
His sumptuous hand: no misers nuptiall joyes.
Ayre felt continuall thunder with the noyse,
Made in the generall mariage violence:
And no man knew the cause of this expence,
But the two haples Lords, *Leanders* Sire,   105
And poore *Leander*, poorest where the fire
Of credulous love made him most rich surmisde,
As short was he of that himselfe he prisde,
As is an emptie Gallant full of forme,
That thinks each looke an act, each drop a storme,   110
That fals from his brave breathings; most brought up
In our *Metropolis*, and hath his cup
Brought after him to feasts; and much Palme beares,
For his rare judgement in th'attire he weares,
Hath seene the hot Low Countries, not their heat,   115
Observes their rampires and their buildings yet.
And for your sweet discourse with mouthes is heard,
Giving instructions with his very beard.
Hath gone with an Ambassadour, and been
A great mans mate in travailing, even to *Rhene*,   120

And then puts all his worth in such a face,
As he saw brave men make, and strives for grace
To get his newes forth; as when you descrie
A ship with all her sayle contends to flie
Out of the narrow Thames with windes unapt,   125
Now crosseth here, then there, then this way rapt,
And then hath one point reacht; then alters all,
And to another crooked reach doth fall
Of halfe a burdbolts shoote; keeping more coyle,
Then if she danst upon the Oceans toyle: 130
So serious is his trifling companie,
In all his swelling ship of vacantrie.
And so short of himselfe in his high thought,
Was our *Leander* in his fortunes brought.
And in his fort of love that he thought won,   135
But otherwise, he skornes comparison.
    O sweet *Leander*, thy large worth I hide
In a short grave; ill favour'd stormes must chide
Thy sacred favour; I, in floods of inck
Must drowne thy graces, which white papers drink,   140
Even as thy beauties did the foule black Seas:
I must describe the hell of thy disease,
That heaven did merit: yet I needes must see
Our painted fooles and cockhorse Pessantrie
Still still usurp, with long lives, loves and lust, 145
The seates of vertue, cutting short as dust
Her deare bought issue; ill, to worse converts,
And tramples in the blood of all deserts.
    Night close and silent now goes fast before
The Captaines and their souldiers to the shore,   150
On whom attended the appointed Fleete
At *Sestus* Bay, that should *Leander* meete.
Who fainde he in another ship would passe:
Which must not be, for no one meane there was
To get his love home, but the course he tooke.   155
Forth did his beautie for his beautie looke,
And saw her through her Torch, as you beholde
Sometimes within the Sunne a face of golde,
Form'd in strong thoughts, by that traditions force,
That saies a God sits there and guides his course.   160

His sister was with him, to whom he shewd
His guide by Sea: and sayd, oft have you viewd
In one heaven many starres, but never yet
In one starre many heavens till now were met.
See lovely sister, see, now *Hero* shines   165
No heaven but her appeares: each star repines,
And all are clad in clowdes, as if they mournd,
To be by influence of Earth out-burnd.
Yet doth she shine, and teacheth vertues traine,
Still to be constant in Hels blackest raigne: 170
Though even the gods themselves do so entreat them
As they did hate, and Earth as she would eate them.
    Off went his silken robe, and in he leapt;
Whom the kinde waves so licorously cleapt,
Thickning for haste one in another so,   175
To kisse his skin, that he might almost go
To *Heros* Towre, had that kind minuit lasted.
But now the cruell fates with *Ate* hasted
To all the windes, and made them battaile fight
Upon the *Hellespont*, for eithers right   180
Pretended to the windie monarchie.
And forth they brake, the Seas mixt with the skie,
And tost distrest *Leander*, being in hell,
As high as heaven; Blisse not in height doth dwell.
The Destinies sate dancing on the waves,   185
To see the glorious windes with mutuall braves
Consume each other: O true glasse to see,
How ruinous ambitious Statists bee
To their owne glories! Poore *Leander* cried
For help to Sea-borne *Venus*; she denied   190
To *Boreas*, that for his *Atthæas* sake,
He would some pittie on his *Hero* take,
And for his owne loves sake, on his desires:
But Glorie never blowes cold Pitties fires.
Then calde he *Neptune*, who through all the noise,   195
Knew with affright his wrackt *Leanders* voice:
And up he rose, for haste his forehead hit
Gainst heavens hard Christall; his proud waves he smit
With his forkt scepter, that could not obay,
Much greater powers then *Neptunes* gave them sway,   200

They lov'd *Leander* so, in groanes they brake
When they came neere him; and such space did take
Twixt one another, loth to issue on,
That in their shallow furrowes earth was shone,
And the poore lover tooke a little breath: 205
But the curst Fates sate spinning of his death
On every wave, and with the servile windes
Tumbled them on him: And now *Hero* findes
By that she felt her deare *Leanders* state,
She wept and prayed for him to every fate, 210
And every winde that whipt her with her haire
About the face, she kist and spake it faire,
Kneeld to it, gave it drinke out of her eyes
To quench his thirst: but still their cruelties
Even her poore Torch envied, and rudely beate 215
The bating flame from that deare foode it eate:
Deare, for it nourisht her *Leanders* life,
Which with her robe she rescude from their strife:
But silke too soft was, such hard hearts to breake,
And she deare soule, even as her silke, faint, weake, 220
Could not preserve it: out, O out it went.
Leander still cald *Neptune*, that now rent
His brackish curles, and tore his wrinckled face ⎫
Where teares in billowes did each other chace, ⎬
And (burst with ruth) he hurld his marble Mace ⎭ 225
At the sterne Fates, it wounded *Lachesis*
That drew *Leanders* thread, and could not misse
The thread it selfe, as it her hand did hit,
But smote it full and quite did sunder it.
The more kinde Neptune rag'd, the more he raste 230
His loves lives fort, and kild as he embraste.
Anger doth still his owne mishap encrease;
If any comfort live, it is in peace.
O theevish Fates, to let Blood, Flesh, and Sence, ⎫
Build two fayre Temples for their Excellence, ⎬ 235
To rob it with a poysoned influence. ⎭
Though soules gifts starve, the bodies are held deare
In ugliest things; Sence-sport preserves a Beare.
But here nought serves our turnes; O heaven and earth,
How most most wretched is our humane birth? 240

And now did all the tyrannous crew depart,
Knowing there was a storme in *Heros* hart,
Greater then they could make, and skornd their smart.
She bowd her selfe so low out of her Towre,
That wonder twas she fell not ere her howre,   245
With searching the lamenting waves for him;
Like a poore Snayle, her gentle supple lim
Hung on her Turrets top so most downe right,
As she would dive beneath the darknes quite,
To finde her Jewell; Jewell, her *Leander*,   250
A name of all earths Jewels pleasde not her,
Like his deare name; *Leander*, still my choice,
Come nought but my *Leander*; O my voice
Turne to *Leander*: hence-forth be all sounds,
Accents, and phrases that shew all griefes wounds,   255
Analisde in *Leander*. O black change!
Trumpets doe you with thunder of your clange,
Drive out this changes horror, my voyce faints:
Where all joy was, now shrieke out all complaints.
Thus cryed she, for her mixed soule could tell   260
Her love was dead: And when the morning fell
Prostrate upon the weeping earth for woe,
Blushes that bled out of her cheekes did show,
Leander brought by *Neptune*, brusde and torne,
With Cities ruines he to Rocks had worne,   265
To filthie usering Rocks that would have blood,
Though they could get of him no other good.
She saw him, and the sight was much much more,
Then might have serv'd to kill her; should her store
Of giant sorrowes speake? Burst, dye, bleede,   270
And leave poore plaints to us that shall succeede.
She fell on her loves bosome, hugg'd it fast,
And with *Leanders* name she breath'd her last.
    Neptune for pittie in his armes did take them,
Flung them into the ayre, and did awake them.   275
Like two sweet birds surnam'd th'*Acanthides*,
Which we call Thistle-warps, that neere no Seas
Dare ever come, but still in couples flie,
And feede on Thistle tops, to testifie
The hardnes of their first life in their last: 280

The first in thornes of love, and sorrowes past,
And so most beautifull their colours show,
As none (so little) like them: her sad brow
A sable velvet feather covers quite,
Even like the forehead cloths that in the night,   285
Or when they sorrow, Ladies use to weare:
Their wings, blew, red and yellow mixt appeare,
Colours, that as we construe colours paint
Their states to life; the yellow shewes their saint,
The devill *Venus* left them; blew their truth,   290
The red and black, ensignes of death and ruth.
And this true honor from their love-deaths sprung,
They were the first that ever Poet sung.

FINIS

The Second Part of Hero and Leander Conteyning their further Fortunes

HENRY PETOWE (1598)

When young *Apollo* heavens sacred beautie,
Gan on his silver harpe with reverent dutie,
To blazen foorth the faire of *Tellus* wonder,
Whose faire, all other faires brought subject under:
Heaven gan to frowne at earthes fragilitie,   5
Made proude with such adored Majestie.
Hero the faire, so doe I name this faire,
With whome immortall faires might not compare,
Such was her beautie fram'd in heavens scorne,
Her spotles faire caus'd other faires to mourne: 10
Heaven frown'd, *Earth* sham'd, that none so faire as she,
Base borne of earth in heaven might equall be.
Fell moodie *Venus* pale with fretting ire,
Aye mee (quoth she) for want of her desire,
Earthes basest mould, fram'd of the baser dust,   15
Strumpet to filth, bawde to loathed lust:
Worse then *Mædeas* charmes, are thy inticements,
Worse then the Mermaides songs, are thy allurements.
Worse then the snakie hag *Tysiphone*,
To mortall soules is thy inveagling beautie: 20
Thus she exclaimes gainst harmeles *Hero's* faire,
And would the Gods consent, her dangling haire,
Wherewith the busie ayre doth often play,
(As wanton birdes upon a Sunne-shine day:)
Should be transform'd to snakes all ugly blacke,   25
To be a meanes of her eternall wracke.
But wanton *Jove* sweete beauties favorite,
Demaunds of beautie beauties worthy merite:
Yf beauties guerdon merit paine (quoth he,)

Your faire deserves no lesse as faire as she,   30
Then moodie *Juno* frowning gan replie,
Ile want my will, but strumpet she shall die.
Juno (quoth he) we ought not tyrannize,
On such (saide she) as you doe wantonnize.
But since our continent the scope of Heaven,   35
Containes her not, unlesse from earth beryven,
Ile make a transformation of her hue,
And force the hautie Mother earth to rue:
That her base wombe dare yeilde such bastard faires,
That *Jove* must seeke on earth immortall heires.   40
Ile cause a second desperat *Phaeton*,
To rule the fierie Charriot of the Sunne:
That topsie turvie Heaven and Earth may turne,
That *Heaven, Earth, Sea,* and *Hell* may endlesse burne.
Stay head-strong goddesse *Jove* to *Juno* sayde,   45
Can you doe this without your husbands ayde?
With that she gan intreate it might be so,
But *Jove* would not sweete beautie overthrow:
But this he graunted *Juno*, that *Apollo*
Should never more extoll the faire of *Hero*.   50
His censure past the irefull *Queene* doth hie,
To set a period to his harmony.
From foorth his yeilding armes she soone bereaves
Apollo's Lute, whom comfortlesse she leaves,
Making a Thousand parts of two gould stringes,   55
Into oblivions Cell the same she flinges.
Quicke sighted spirits, this suppos'd *Apollo*,
Conceit no other, but th'admired *Marlo*:
Marlo admir'd, whose honney flowing vaine,
No English writer can as yet attaine.   60
Whose name in Fames immortall treasurie,
Truth shall record to endles memorie,
Marlo late mortall, now fram'd all divine,
What soule more happy, then that soule of thine?
Live still in heaven thy soule, thy fame on earth,   65
(Thou dead) of *Marlo's Hero* findes a dearth.
Weepe aged *Tellus*, all earth on earth complaine,
Thy chiefe borne faire, hath lost her faire againe:
Her faire in this is lost, that *Marlo's* want,

Inforceth *Hero's* faire be wonderous scant.   70
Oh had that King of poets breathed longer,
Then had faire beauties fort been much more stronger:
His goulden pen had clos'd her so about,
No bastard *Æglets* quill the world throughout,
Had been of force to marre what he had made,   75
For why they were not expert in that trade:
What mortall soule with *Marlo* might contend,
That could gainst reason force him stoope or bend?
Whose silver charming toung, mov'd such delight,
That men would shun their sleepe in still darke night. 80
To meditate upon his goulden lynes,
His rare conceyts and sweete according rimes.
But *Marlo*, still admired *Marlo's* gon,
To live with beautie in *Elyzium*,
Immortall beautie, who desires to heare,   85
His sacred Poesies sweete in every eare:
Marlo must frame to *Orpheus* melodie,
Himnes all divine to make heaven harmonie.
There ever live the Prince of Poetrie,
Live with the living in eternitie.   90
Apollo's Lute bereav'd of silver string,
Fond *Mercury* doth harshly gin to sing.
A counterfeit unto his honney note,
But I doe feare he'le chatter it by rote:
Yet if his ill according voice be such,   95
That (hearing part) you thinke you heare too much,
Beare with his rashnes and he will amende,
His follie blame, but his good will commend.
Yet rather discommend what I intreate,
For if you like it, some wil storme and fret.   100
And then insulting *Ægles* soaring hie,
Will pray upon the sillie harmeles flie:
(*Nil refert*) for Ile pawne my better part,
Ere sweete fac't beautie loose her due desart.
   Avaunt base Steele where shrill tong'd silver rings, 105
The chatt'ring Pie may range when black-birdes sings:
Birdes blacke as Jet with sweete according voices,
Like to *Elyziums* Saincts with heavenly noises.
Why should harsh *Mercury* recount againe,

What sweet *Apollo* (living) did maintaine?   110
Which was of *Hero* her all pleasing faire,
Her prettie browes, her lip, her amber haire,
Her roseat cheeke, her lillie fingers white,
Her sparkling eyes that lend the day his light:
What should I say, her all in all he praysed,   115
Wherewith the spacious world was much amazed.
Leanders love, and lovers sweetest pleasure,
He wrought a full discourse of beauties treasure:
And left me nothing pleasing to recite,
But of unconstant chance, and fortunes spight.   120
Then in this glasse view beauties frayltie,
Faire *Hero*, and *Leanders* miserie.

The virgin Princesse of the westerne Ile,
Faire *Cambarina* of the goulden soile,
And yet not faire, but of a swartie hew,   125
For by her gould, her beautie did renew:
Renew as thus, that having gould to spare,
Men helde it dutie to protest and sweare,
Her faire was such, as all the world admir'd it,
Her blushing beautie such, all men desir'd it.   130
The scornefull *Queene* made proude with fained praises,
Her black-fram'd soule, to a hier rate she raises:
That men bewitched with her gould, not beautie,
A Thousand Knights as homage proffer dutie,
Yf such a base deformed lumpe of clay,   135
In whome no sweete content had any stay,
No pleasure residence, no sweet delight,
Shelter from heate of day, or cold of night:
Yf such a she so many sutors had,
Hero whose angrie frownes made heaven sad: 140
Hero whose gaze gracing darke *Plutos* cell,
Pluto would deeme *Phœbus* came there to dwell.
Hero whose eyes heavens fierie tapors staine,
Hero whose beautie makes night day againe,
How much more love merits so sweet a *Queene*,   145
Whose like no out-worne world hath ever seene.
Of sweete *Leanders* love, to *Hero's* beautie,
Heaven, *Earth*, and *Hell*, and all the world is guiltie,

Of *Hero's* kindnes, to her trustie Phere,
By lost *Apollo's* tale it doth appere,   150
Recorded in the Register of Fame,
The workes of *Marlo* doe expresse the same.
But ere he gan of fickle chance to tell,
How bad chance gainst the Better did rebell:
When love in loves sweet garden newly planted,   155
Remorcefull *Hero* to *Leander* graunted,
Free libertie, to yeild the world increase,
Unconstant *Fortune* foe to harmeles peace:
Playde such unruly prancks in loves despight,
That love was forced from his true-loves sight.   160
    Duke *Archilaus* cruell, voyd of pitie,
Where *Hero* dwelt was regent of that Citie:
Woe worth that towne where bloody homicides,
And Tyrants are elected cities guides.
Woe woorth that countrey where unlawfull lust,   165
Sitts in a Regall throne, of force it must
Downe to the low layde bowells of the earth,
Like to a still borne Childes untimely byrth:
Duke *Archilaus* lov'd; but whome lov'd he?
He courted *Hero*, but it would not be.   170
Why should he plant where other Knights have sowen,
The land is his, therefore the fruit his owne,
Must it be thus, alas it is not so,
Lust may not force true-lovers overthrow.
Lust hath no limits, lust will have his will,   175
Like to a ravening wolfe that's bent to kill,
The Duke affecting her that was belov'd,
(*Hero* whose firme fixt love *Leander* prov'd,)
Gave on-set to the still resisting fort,
But fearefull hate set period to his sport.   180
Lust egg'd him on to further his desire,
But fell disdaine inforc't him to retire.
When *Archilaus* sawe that thundering threates
Could not prevaile, he mildly then intreates.
But all in vaine, the Doo had choose her make,   185
And whome she tooke, she never would forsake,
The Doo's sweet Deere, this hunter seekes to chace,
Harmeles *Leander* whose all smiling face

Grac't with unspotted faire to all mens sight,
Would force the houndes retire, and not to bite: 190
Which when the Duke perceav'd, an other curre,
Was forced from his den, that made much sturre,
And treason he was nam'd, which helde so fast,
That feares swift winges did lend some ayde at last.
For force perforce *Leander* must depart   195
From *Sestos*, yet behind he left his hart.
His hart in *Hero's* brest, *Leander* left,
Leanders absence, *Heroes* joyes bereft:
Leanders want, the cruell Duke thought sure
Some ease to discontent would soone procure.   200
Leander having heard his wofull doome,
Towards his weeping Lady he doth come,
Dewing her cheekes with his distilling teares,
Which *Hero* dryeth with her dangling haires:
They weeping greete each other with sweete kisses,   205
(Kindly imbracing) thus they gan their wishes.
Oh that these foulding armes might nere undoe;
As she desir'd: so wisht *Leander* too:
Then with her hand, she toucht his sacred brest,
Where in his bosome she desires to rest.   210
Like to a snake she clung unto him fast,
And wound about him, which snatcht-up in hast,
By the Prince of birdes, borne lightly up aloft,
Doth wrythe her selfe about his necke, and oft
About his winges displayed in the winde,   215
Or like as Ivie on trees cling bout the rinde:
Or as the Crab-fish having caught in seas
His enemies, doth claspe him with his cleas.
So joynd in one, these two together stood,
Even as *Hermaphroditus* in the flood: 220
Untill the Duke did bannish him away,
Then gan *Leander* to his *Hero* say.
⎰(Let me goe where the Sunne doth parch the greene,
⎱ In temperate heate, where he is felt and seene:
⎰Or where his beames doe not dissolve the ice,   225
⎱ In presence prest, of people mad or wise.
Set mee in high, or else in low degree,
In clearest skie, or where clowdes thickest bee,

In longest night, or in the shortest day,
In lustie youth, or when my haires be gray: 230
Goe I to heaven, to earth, or else to hell,
Thrall or at large, alive where so I dwell,
On hill or dale, or on the foaming flood,
⎧ Sicke or in health, in evill fame or good:
⎨ Thine will I be, and onely with this thought,   235
⎩ Content thy selfe: although my chance be naught.)
Thus parted these two lovers full of woes,
She staies behinde, on pilgrimage he goes.
Leave we a while, *Leander* wandring Knight,
To *Delphos* taking his all speedie flight,   240
That by the Oracle of *Apollo*,
His further Fortunes he may truely knowe.
    True-love quite bannisht, lust began to pleade,
To *Hero* like a scholler deepely reade:
The flaming sighes, that boyle within my brest,   245
Faire love (quoth he) are cause of my unrest.
Unrest I entertaine for thy sweet sake,
And in my tent choose sorrow for my make.
Why dost thou frowne (quoth he) and then she turn'd
Oh coole the fainting soule, that flaming burn'd: 250
Forc't by desire, to touch thy matchles beautie,
To whome thy servant vowes all reverent dutie.
With that her irefull browes clowded with frownes,
His soule already drencht, in woes sea drownes.
But floating on the waves thus he gan say,   255
Flint harted Lady canst thou be so coy?
Can pittie take no place, is kinde remorce
Quite bannisht, quite fled? then gan he to be horce,
Unable to exclaime, against her longer,
Whose woe lament made *Hero's* hart more stronger. 260
Hero that gave no eare to her commaunder,
But ever weepes for her exil'd *Leander*:
And weeping sore among'st her liquid teares,
These words she spake, wherewith her sorrow weares.
(The piller perisht is, whereto I lent,   265
To my unhap, for lust away hath sent,
Of all my Joy, the verie barke and rinde,
The strongest stay of my unquiet minde:

And I alas am forc't without consent,
Dayly to mourne, till death doe it relent.)   270
Oh my *Leander* he is banished,
From his sweete *Hero's* sight he is exiled.
Oh yee just heavens, if that heaven be just,
Raine the unbridled head, of hautie lust,
Make him to stoope, that forceth others bend,   275
Bereave his joyes, that reft me of my friend.
I want my selfe, for *Hero* wants her love,
And where *Leander* is, my selfe doth move.
What can I more, but have a woefull hart,
My minde in woe, my body full of smart,   280
And I my selfe, my selfe alwayes to hate,
Till dreadfull death doe ease my dolefull state.
The angry Duke lay listning to her words,
And till she ends no speech at all affords,
Untill at length; exclaiming gainst her kinde,   285
Thus he breath'd foorth the venome of his minde.
{ (Oh timerous taunters that delights in toyes,
{ Jangling jesters, deprivers of sweete joyes,
{ Tumbling cock-boats tottering too and fro,
Grown'd of the graft, whence all my griefe doth grow:
Sullen Serpents environ'd with despight,   291
That ill for good at all times doth requite.
As *Cypresse* tree that rent is by the roote,
As well sowen seede, for drought that cannot sprout.
As braunch or slip bitter from whence it growes,   295
As gaping ground that raineles cannot close:
As filth on lande to whome no water flowes,
{ As flowers doe fade when *Phœbus* rarest showes,
{ As *Salamandra* repulsed from the fier,
{ Wanting my wish, I die for my desire.)   300
Speaking those words death seiz'd him for his owne,
Wherewith she thought her woes were overthrowne:
Hero so thought, but yet she thought amisse,
Before she was belov'd: now findes no blisse.
Duke *Archilaus* being sodaine dead,   305
Young *Euristippus* ruled in his stead:
The next succeeding heire to what was his,
Then *Hero's* woes increast, and fled all blis.

Looke how the sillie harmeles bleating lambe,
Bereft from his kinde make the gentle dam,   310
Left as a pray to Butchers crueltie,
In whome she findes not any drop of mercie.
Or like a warriour whom his Souldiors flies,
At his shrill eccho of his foes dread cries.
He all unable to withstand so many,   315
Not having wherewith to combat, nor any
Assured friend that dares to comfort him,
Nor any way for feare dares succour him.
But as a pray he yeildes to him he would not,
Yf he had helpe, but (helplesse) strive he could not. 320
So far'd it with the meeke distressed *Hero*,
That sweet *Leander*, bannished her fro.
She had no *Hercules*, to defend her cause,
She had no *Brandamore* disdaining lawes,
To combat for her safetie; this sweet *Io*,   325
Had no kinde *Jove* to keepe her from her foe.
This *Psiches* had no *Cupid*, love was bannisht,
And love from love exild, love needs must famish.
Wood *Euristippus* for his brothers death,
Like as a toyled huntsman wanting breath,   330
Stormeth that bad chance in the games pursute,
Should cause him panting, rest as dead and mute.
Or like sad *Orphey* for *Euridice*,
Whom *Cerberus* bereft so hastilie,
Like to the thundering threates of *Hercules*,   335
The worldes admired Prince the great *Alcides*,
When *Nessus* got the height of his desire;
By ravishing his fairest *Deianire*.
Such was his ire, and more if more may be,
Which he gainst *Hero* breathed spightfully: 340
Thou damned hag: thus gan he to exclaime,
Thou base borne Strumpet one of *Circes* traine.
Durst thou presume, poore sillie simple flie,
With *Venum's* force, to force an Ægle die?
What though my brother *Leander* bannished,   345
Must he by thee therefore be poysoned?
Die cursed wretch, with that he cast her from him,
And would not suffer her to looke upon him.

The still amazed Lady musing stood,
Admiring why the Duke should be so wood.   350
Humbly she prostrates her at Angers feete,
And with downe dropping teares, like liquid sleete,
She watereth the Summer thirstie ground,
Weeping so long, she fell into a sound.
Againe revived by the standers by,   355
She doth intreate them to resolve her why,
Duke *Euristippus* wrongeth her so much,
As to dishonour her with such a touch.
Well know the Gods my guiltlesse soule (quoth she,)
Was *Archilaus* poysoned by me,   360
Yf so? Just heavens and immortall powers,
Raine vengeance downe in all consuming showers:
And cause that *Hero*, that was counted faire,
Like a mad hellish furie to dispaire.
The more she weepes, the more the heavens smile,   365
Scorning that beautie should take any soile,
Juno commaunded *Argos* to defend her,
But *Jupiter* would not so much befriend her.
Argos starke dead; sweet *Hero* might not live,
For of her life the Duke will her deprive.   370
Her doome was thus, ere three moneths date tooke end,
If she found none, that would her cause defend:
Untimely death should seize her as a pray,
And unresisting life, should death obay.
Meane time within a rocke-fram'd castle strong,   375
She was imprisoned traytors vile among:
Where (discontented) when she should have rested,
Her foode bad fare, with sighes and teares she feasted.
And when the breathlesse horses of the Sunne,
Had made their stay, and *Luna* had begun,   380
With cheerefull smyling browes to grace darke night,
Clad in blacke sable weedes, for want of light.
This all alone sad Lady gan to play,
Framing sweet musick to her welladay:
Th'effect whereof this Sonnet plainely showes,   385
The fountaine whence springs *Hero's* heavie woes.

Hero's *lamentation in Prison.*

Nights mourning blacke and mistie vailing hew,
Shadowes the blessed comfort of the Sunne:
At whose bright gaze I wonted to renew
My liveles life, when life was almost done.   390
Done is my life, and all my pleasure done,
For he is gone, in whome my life begun:
Unhappie I poore I, and none as I,
But pilgrim he, poore he, that should be by.

My love exil'd, and I in prison fast,   395
Out streaming teares breake into weeping raine,
He too soone banisht, I in dungeon cast,
He for me mourneth, I for him complaine.
He's banished, yet lives at libertie,
And I exil'd, yet live in miserie: 400
He weepes for me far off, I for him here,
I would I were with him, and he more nere.

But this imprisoning cave, this woefull cell,
This house of sorrow and increasing woe,
Griefes tearie chamber where sad care doth dwell,   405
Where liquid teares, like top fil'd Seas doe flow:
Beating their waves gainst still relentles stone,
Still still they smile on me, and I still mone;
I weepe to stone, and stone of stone I finde,
Colde stone, colde comfort yeilds (oh most unkinde.)   410

Oft have I read that stone relents at raine,
And I impleat their barren wombe with store,
Teares streaming downe, they wet and wet againe,
Yet pittilesse they harden more and more.
And when my longing soule lookes they should sonder,
I touch the flintie stone, and they seeme stronger,   416
They stronge, I weake: alas what hope have I?
Hero wants comfort, *Hero* needs must die.

When the melodious shrill toung'd Nightingale,
With heavie cheere had warbled this sad tale: 420

Nights drowsie God an ivorie Cannopie,
Curtaines before the windowes of faire beautie.
Drown'd thus in sleepe, she spent the wearie night,
There leave I *Hero* in a heavie plight.
Now to the woefull Pilgrime I returne,   425
Whose passions force the gentle birdes to mourne.
They see Leander weepe, with heavie note
They faintly singe, as when they singe by rote:
While he gan descant on his miserie,
The pretie fowles doe make him melodie.   430

        Leanders complaint of his *restles estate.*

Bright Heavens immortall moving *Spheares*,
    and *Phœbus* all divine,
Rue on lowe *Earths* unfained teares:
    that issue from *Earths* eyne.
Eyes, were these no eyes, whilst eies eye-sight lasted, 435
But these darke eyes cleere sight, sad sorrow wasted.

What creature living lives in griefe,
    that breathes on *Tellus* soile?
But *Heavens* pitie with reliefe,
    save me, a slave to spoyle.   440
Spoyle doe his worst, spoyle cannot spoile me more,
Spoyle never spoyl'd, so true a Love before.

The stricken Deere stands not in awe
    of blacke grym irefull Death,
For he findes hearbes that can withdrawe   445
    the shaft, to save his breath.
The chased Deere hath soile to coole his heate,
The toyled Steed is up in stable set.

The sillie Owles lurke in the leaves,
    shine Sunne or nights Queene whether: 450
The Sparrowe shrowdes her in the eaves,
    from stormes of huffing weather.
Fowles comfort finde, *Leander* findes no friend,
Then (comfortlesse) *Leanders* life must end.

By this it pleas'd the smiling browes of **Heaven,** 455
Whose deadly frownes, him erst of joy beryven:
To set a period to *Leanders* toyle,
Having enjoy'd that long desired soyle.
When he had viewd the stately territories,
And *Delphos* sacred hie erected towers, 460
Unto *Apollo's* Oracle he goes,
In hope to finde reliefe for many woes;
He craves long lookt-for rest, or else to die,
To whome the Oracle gan thus reply.

The Oracle

He loveth thine that loves not thee, 465
His love to thine shall fatall bee.
Upon suspect she shalbe slaine,
Unles thou doe returne againe.

These harsh according rimes to mickle paine,
Did but renewe *Leanders* woes againe: 470
Yet as he might, with Fortunes sweet consent,
He gins returne all dangers to prevent.
Within short time at *Sestos* he ariveth,
On *Loves* light winges, desire *Leander* driveth,
Desire that longs to view a blessed end, 475
Of *Love* and *Fortune* that so long contend.
This backe retired Pilgrime liv'd secure,
And in unknowen disguise, he did indure,
Full two moneths space untill the time drew nie,
To free faire *Hero*, or inforce her die: 480
The date outworne of the prefixed day,
When combatants their valour should display.
(All thinges prepar'd) as blazing fame reported,
T'were wonder to behould how men resorted.
Knights neighboring by, and Ladies all divine, 485
Darting daies splendour from their Sunne-like eyne:
Spectatum veniunt, veniunt spectentur ut ipsae,
But wanting faire, they come to gaze on beautie,
Beautie faire Heavens beautie, worlds wonder,
Hero whose beautie keepes all beautie under. 490
This faire fac't beautie, from a fowle fac't cell,

A loath-some dungeon like to nights darke hell,
At the fell Dukes commaund in open view,
Was sent for, on whose never spotted hew,
Earths mortall soules doe feed and gaze upon her,   495
So long they gaze, that they doe surfet on her.
For when this Earthes admir'd immortall Sunne,
To peepe from under sable hould begun.
Like as the pearcing eye of cloudie Heaven,
Whose sight the blacke thicke cloudes have quite beriven.
But by the huffing windes being overblowen,   501
And all their blacke expeld and overthrowen.
The day doth gin, be jocond secure playing,
The faire of Heaven, his beautie so displaying:
So when the fairest *Hero* did begin,   505
(Whilome yclad in darknes blacke tan'd skin.)
To passe the noysome portall of the prison,
Like to the gorgeous *Phœbus* newly risen,
She doth illuminate the morning day,
Clad in a sable Mantle of blacke Say.   510
Which *Hero's* eyes transformed to faire white,
Making the lowring-morne darke, pure light.
As many mortall eyes beheld her eies,
As there are fierie Tapors in the skies:
As many eyes gaz'd on faire *Hero's* beautie,   515
As there be eyes that offer Heaven dutie:
As many servitors attended on her,
As *Venus*, servants had to waite upon her.
Though by the sterne Duke she was dishonored,
Yet of the people she was honored: 520
Mong'st whome exil'd *Leander* all unseene,
And all unknowne attended on his *Queene*.
When to the neere-adjoyning pallaice gate,
The place appointed for the Princely combate,
They did approch; there might all eies behold,   525
The Duke in armour of pure beaten gold,
Mounted upon a Steed as white as snow,
The proud Duke *Euristippus Hero's* foe.
Hero being seated in rich Majestie,
A servile hand-mayd to Captivitie.   530
From whence she might behold that gentle Knight,

That for her sake durst hazard life in fight.
For this was all the comfort *Hero* had,
So many eyes shed teares to see her sad.
Her hand-maide hope, perswaded her some one,   535
Undaunted Knight would be her Champion.
Yet since her Lord *Leander* was not nie,
She was resolv'd eyther to live or die;
But her *Leander* carefull of his love,
Intending loves firme constancie to prove: 540
(Yf to his lot the honour did befall,)
Withdrew himselfe into the Pallaice hall,
Where he was armed to his soules content,
And privily conducted to a tent,
From whence he issu'd foorth at trumpets sound,   545
Who at the first encounter, on the ground,
Forced the mazed Duke sore panting lie,
Drown'd in the ryver of sad extacie.
At length reviving, he doth mount againe,
Whome young *Leander* in short time had slaine.   550
The Duke quite dead, this all unknowne young Knight,
Was foorthwith made the heire of *Sestos* right.
The Princesse *Hero* set at libertie,
Kept by the late dead Duke in miserie:
Whose constancie *Leander* gan to prove,   555
And now anew begins to court his love.
To walke on ground where danger is unseene,
Doth make men doubt, where they have never been.
As blind men feare what footing they shall finde:
So doth the wise mistrust the straungers minde.   560
I strange to you, and you unknowen to me,
Yet may not love twixt us two grafted bee?
What I have done, for *Hero's* love was done,
Say then you love, and end as I begun.
I hazard life, to free thy beauties faire,   565
From Tyrants force and hellish soule dispaire:
Then sacred *Faire* ballance my good desart,
Inrich my soule with thy affecting hart.
Hero repli'd: (to rue on all false teares,
And forged tales, wherein craft oft appeares,   570
To trust each fained face, and forcing charme,

Betrayes the simple soule that thinks no harme.)
(Not every teare doth argue inward paine,
Not every sigh warrants, men doe not faine,
Not every smoke doth prove a present fier,   575
Not all that glisters, goulden soules desire,
Not every word is drawen out of the deepe,
For oft men smile, when they doe seeme to weepe:
Oft malice makes the minde to powre forth brine,
And envie leakes the conduits of the eyne.   580
Craft oft doth cause men make a seeming showe,
Of heavie woes where griefe did never growe.
Then blame not those that wiselie can beware,
To shun dissimulations dreadfull snare.
Blame not the stopped eares gainst *Syrens* songe,   585
Blame not the minde not mov'd with falshood tonge.)
But rest content and satisfied with this,
Whilst true *Leander* lives, true *Hero's* his.
And thy *Leander* lives sweete soule sayde he,
Praysing thy all admired chastitie.   590
Though thus disguis'd, I am that banisht Knight,
That for affecting thee was put to flight.
Hero, I am *Leander* thy true phere,
As true to thee, as life to me is deere.
When *Hero* all amazed gan revive,   595
And she that then seem'd dead, was now alive:
With kinde imbracements kissing at each straine,
She welcoms him, and kisses him againe.
By thee, my joyes have shaken of dispaire,
All stormes be past, and weather waxeth faire,   600
By thy returne *Hero* receaves more Joye,
Then *Paris* did when *Hellen* was in *Troy*.
By thee my heavy doubts and thoughts are fled,
And now my wits with pleasant thoughts are fed.
Feed sacred Sainct on *Nectar* all divine,   605
While these my eyes (quoth he) gaze on thy eyne.
And ever after may these eyes beware,
That they on strangers beautie never stare:
(My wits I charme henceforth they take such heede,
They frame no toyes, my fancies new to feede.   610
Deafe be my eares to heare another voice,

To force me smile, or make my soule rejoyce,
Lame be my feete when they presume to move,
To force *Leander* seeke another love.)
And when thy faire (sweet faire) I gin disgrace,   615
Heaven to my soule afford no resting place.
What he to her, she vow'd the like to him,
(All sorrowes fled) their joyes anew begin.
Full many yeares those lovers liv'd in fame,
That all the world did much admire the same.   620
Their lives spent date, and unresisted death,
At hand to set a period to their breath,
They were transform'd by all divine decrees,
Into the forme, and shape of two Pine trees.
Whose *Natures* such, the *Female* pine will die,   625
Unles the *Male* be ever planted by:
A map for all succeeding times to come,
To view true-love, which in their loves begun.

FINIS

Qualis vita, finis ita

Ovids Banquet of Sence

GEORGE CHAPMAN (1595)

The Argument

Ovid, newly enamoured of *Julia*, (daughter to *Octavius Augustus Cæsar*, after by him called *Corynna*,) secretly convaid himselfe into a Garden of the Emperors Court: in an Arbor whereof, *Corynna* was bathing; playing upon her Lute, and singing: which *Ovid* over-hearing, was exceedingly pleasde with the sweetnes of her voyce, and to himselfe uttered the comfort he conceived in his sence of Hearing. — Auditus.

Then the odors shee usde in her bath, breathing a rich savor, hee expresseth the joy he felt in his sence of Smelling. — Olfactus.

Thus growing more deeplie enamoured, in great contentation with himselfe, he venters to see her in the pride of her nakednesse: which dooing by stealth, he discovered the comfort hee conceived in Seeing, and the glorie of her beautie. — Visus.

Not yet satisfied, hee useth all his Art to make knowne his being there, without her offence: or (being necessarily offended) to appease her: which done, he entreats a kisse to serve for satisfaction of his Tast, which he obtaines. — Gustus.

Then proceedes he to entreaty for the fift sence and there is interrupted. — Tactus.

NARRATIO

The Earth, from heavenly light conceived heat,
Which mixed all her moyst parts with her dry,
When with right beames the Sun her bosome beat,
And with fit foode her Plants did nutrifie;
    They (which to Earth, as to theyr Mother cling   5
In forked rootes) now sprinckled plenteously

With her warme breath; did hasten to the spring,
Gather their proper forces, and extrude
All powre but that, with which they stood indude.

Then did *Cyrrhus* fill his eyes with fire,   10
Whose ardor curld the foreheads of the trees,
And made his greene-love burne in his desire,
When youth, and ease, (Collectors of loves fees)
    Entic'd *Corynna* to a silver spring,
Enchasing a round Bowre; which with it sees,   15
    (As with a Diamant dooth an ameld Ring.)
Into which eye, most pittifully stood
Niobe, shedding teares, that were her blood.

Stone *Niobe*, whose statue to this Fountaine,
In great *Augustus Cæsars* grace was brought   20
From *Sypilus*, the steepe *Mygdonian* Mountaine:
That statue tis, still weepes for former thought,
    Into thys spring *Corynnas* bathing place;
So cunningly to optick reason wrought,
    That a farre of, it shewd a womans face,   25
Heavie, and weeping; but more neerely viewed,
Nor weeping, heavy, nor a woman shewed.

In Sommer onely wrought her exstasie;
And that her story might be still observed,
Octavius caus'd in curious imagrie,   30
Her fourteene children should at large be carved,
    Theyr fourteene brests, with fourteene arrowes gored
And set by her, that for her seede so starved
    To a stone Sepulcher herselfe deplored,
In Ivory were they cut; and on each brest,   35
In golden Elements theyr names imprest.

Her sonnes, were *Sypilus, Agenor, Phædimus,*
Ismenus, Argus, and *Damasicthen,*
The seaventh calde like his Grandsire, *Tantalus.*
Her Daughters, were the fayre *Astiochen,*   40
    Chloris, Næera, and *Pelopie,*
Phaeta, proud *Phthia,* and *Eugigen,*

All these apposde to violent *Niobe*
Had lookes so deadly sad, so lively doone,
As if Death liv'd in theyr confusion.   45

Behind theyr Mother two Pyramides
Of freckled Marble, through the Arbor viewed,
On whose sharp brows, *Sol*, and *Tytanides*
In purple and transparent glasse were hewed,
  Through which the Sun-beames on the statues staying,
Made theyr pale bosoms seeme with blood imbrewed, 51
  Those two sterne Plannets rigors still bewraying
To these dead forms, came living beauties essence
Able to make them startle with her presence.

In a loose robe of Tynsell foorth she came,   55
Nothing but it betwixt her nakednes
And envious light. The downward-burning flame,
Of her rich hayre did threaten new accesse,
  Of ventrous *Phaeton* to scorch the fields:
And thus to bathing came our Poets Goddesse,   60
  Her handmaides bearing all things pleasure yeelds
To such a service; Odors most delighted,
And purest linnen which her lookes had whited.

Then cast she off her robe, and stood upright,
As lightning breakes out of a laboring cloude;   65
Or as the Morning heaven casts off the Night,
Or as that heaven cast off it selfe, and showde
  Heavens upper light, to which the brightest day
Is but a black and melancholy shroude:
  Or as when *Venus* striv'd for soveraine sway   70
Of charmfull beautie, in yong Troyes desire,
So stood *Corynna* vanishing her tire.

A soft enflowred banck embrac'd the founte;
Of *Chloris* ensignes, an abstracted field;
Where grew Melanthy, great in Bees account,   75
Amareus, that precious Balme dooth yeeld,
  Enameld Pansies, us'd at Nuptials still,
Dianas arrow, *Cupids* crimson shielde,

Ope-morne, night-shade, and *Venus* navill,
Solemne Violets, hanging head as shamed,   80
And verdant Calaminth, for odor famed.

Sacred Nepenthe, purgative of care,
And soveraine Rumex that doth rancor kill,
Sya, and Hyacinth, that Furies weare,
White and red Jessamines, Merry, Melliphill: 85
    Fayre Crowne-imperiall, Emperor of Flowers,
Immortall Amaranth, white Aphrodill,
    And cup-like Twillpants, stroude in *Bacchus* Bowres,
These cling about this Natures naked Jem,
To taste her sweetes, as Bees doe swarme on them.   90

And now shee usde the Founte, where *Niobe*,
Toomb'd in her selfe, pourde her lost soule in teares,
Upon the bosome of this Romaine *Phœbe*;
Who; bathd and Odord; her bright lyms she rears,
    And drying her on that disparent rounde;   95
Her Lute she takes t'enamoure heavenly eares,
    And try if with her voyces vitall sounde,
She could warme life through those colde statues spread,
And cheere the Dame that wept when she was dead.

And thus she sung, all naked as she sat,   100
Laying the happy Lute upon her thigh,
Not thinking any neere to wonder at
The blisse of her sweete brests divinitie,

The Song of CORYNNA.

T'is better to contemne then love,
And to be fayre then wise;   105
For soules are rulde by eyes:
And *Joves* Bird, ceaz'd by *Cypris* Dove,
It is our grace and sport to see,
Our beauties sorcerie,
That makes (like destinie)   110
Men followe us the more wee flee;
That sets wise Glosses on the foole,
And turns her cheekes to bookes,

Where wisdome sees in lookes
Derision, laughing at his schoole, 115
  Who (loving) proves, prophanenes, holy;
Nature, our fate, our wisdome, folly.

While this was singing, *Ovid* yong in love
With her perfections, never proving yet
How mercifull a Mistres she would prove, 120
Boldly embrac'd the power he could not let
  And like a fiery exhalation
Followd the sun, he wisht might never set;
  Trusting heerein his constellation
Rul'd by loves beames, which *Julias* eyes erected, 125
Whose beauty was the star his life directed.

And having drencht his anckles in those seas,
He needes woulde swimme, and car'd not if he drounde:
Loves feete are in his eyes; for if he please
The depth of beauties gulfye floodd to sounde, 130
  He goes upon his eyes, and up to them,
At the first steap he is; no shader grounde
  Coulde *Ovid* finde; but in loves holy streame
Was past his eyes, and now did wett his eares,
For his high Soveraignes silver voice he heares. *Auditus.*

Whereat his wit, assumed fierye wings, 136
Soring above the temper of his soule,
And he the purifying rapture sings
Of his eares sence, takes full the Thespian boule
  And it carrouseth to his Mistres health, 140
Whose sprightfull verdure did dull flesh controle,
  And his conceipt he crowneth with the wealth
Of all the Muses in his pleased sences,
When with the eares delight he thus commences:

Now Muses come, repayre your broken wings, 145
(Pluckt, and prophan'd by rusticke Ignorance,)
With feathers of these notes my Mistres sings;
And let quick verse hir drooping head advance

From dungeons of contempt to smite the starrs;
In *Julias* tunes, led forth by furious trance   150
  A thousand Muses come to bid you warrs,
Dive to your Spring, and hide you from the stroke,
All Poets furies will her tunes invoke.

Never was any sence so sette on fire
With an immortall ardor, as myne eares;   155
Her fingers to the strings doth speeche inspire
And numberd laughter; that the deskant beares
  To hir sweete voice; whose species through my sence
My spirits to theyr highest function reares;
  To which imprest with ceaseles confluence   160
It useth them, as propper to her powre
Marries my soule, and makes it selfe her dowre;

Me thinks her tunes flye guilt, like *Attick* Bees
To my eares hives, with hony tryed to ayre;
My braine is but the combe, the wax, the lees,   165
My soule the Drone, that lives by their affayre.
  O so it sweets, refines, and ravisheth,
And with what sport they sting in theyr repayre?
  Rise then in swarms, and sting me thus to death
Or turne me into swounde; possesse me whole,   170
Soule to my life, and essence to my soule.

Say gentle Ayre, ô does it not thee good
Thus to be smit with her correcting voyce?
Why daunce ye not, ye daughters of the wood?
Wither for ever, if not now rejoyce.   175
  Rise stones, and build a Cittie with her notes,
And notes infuse with your most Cynthian noyse,
  To all the Trees, sweete flowers, and christall Flotes,
That crowne, and make this cheerefull Garden quick,
Vertue, that every tuch may make such Musick.   180

O that as man is cald a little world
The world might shrink into a little man,
To heare the notes about this Garden hurld,
That skill disperst in tunes so Orphean

Might not be lost in smiting stocks and trees   185
That have no eares; but growne as it began
  Spred theyr renownes, as far as *Phœbus* sees
Through earths dull vaines; that shee like heaven might move,
In ceaseles Musick, and be fill'd with love.

In precious incense of her holy breath,   190
My love doth offer Hecatombs of notes
To all the Gods; who now despise the death
Of Oxen, Heifers, Wethers, Swine, and Goates.
  A Sonnet in her breathing sacrifiz'd,
Delights them more then all beasts bellowing throates,   195
  As much with heaven, as with my hearing priz'd.
And as guilt Atoms in the sunne appeare,
So greete these sounds the grissells of myne eare.

Whose pores doe open wide to theyr regreete,
And my implanted ayre, that ayre embraceth   200
Which they impresse; I feele theyr nimble feete
Tread my eares Labyrinth; theyr sport amazeth
  They keepe such measure; play themselves and dance.
And now my soule in *Cupids* Furnace blazeth,
  Wrought into furie with theyr daliance: 205
And as the fire the parched stuble burns,
So fades my flesh, and into spyrit turns.

Sweete tunes, brave issue, that from *Julia* come;
Shooke from her braine, armd like the Queene of Ire;
For first conceived in her mentall wombe,   210
And nourisht with her soules discursive fire,
  They grew into the power of her thought;
She gave them dounye plumes from her attire,
  And them to strong imagination brought:
That, to her voice; wherein most movinglye   215
Shee (blessing them with kysses) letts them flye.

Who flye rejoysing; but (like noblest mindes)
In giving others life themselves do dye,
Not able to endure earthes rude unkindes
Bred in my soveraigns parts too tenderly;   220

O that as Intellects themselves transite
To eache intellegible quallitie,
   My life might passe into my loves conceit,
Thus to be form'd in words, her tunes, and breath,
And with her kysses, sing it selfe to death.   225

This life were wholy sweete, this onely blisse,
Thus would I live to dye; Thus sence were feasted,
My life that in my flesh a Chaos is
Should to a Golden worlde be thus dygested;
   Thus should I rule her faces Monarchy,   230
Whose lookes in severall Empires are invested
   Crown'd now with smiles, and then with modesty,
Thus in her tunes division I should raigne,
For her conceipt does all, in every vaine.

My life then turn'd to that, t'each note, and word   235
Should I consorte her looke; which sweeter sings,
Where songs of solid harmony accord,
Rulde with Loves rule; and prickt with all his stings;
   Thus should I be her notes, before they be;
While in her blood they sitte with fierye wings   240
   Not vapord in her voyces stillerie,
Nought are these notes her breast so sweetely frames,
But motions, fled out of her spirits flames.

For as when steele and flint together smit,
With violent action spitt forth sparkes of fire,   245
And make the tender tynder burne with it;
So my loves soule doth lighten her desire
   Uppon her spyrits in her notes pretence;
And they convaye them (for distinckt attire)
   To use the Wardrobe of the common sence: 250
From whence in vailes of her rich breath they flye,
And feast the eare with this felicitye.

Me thinks they rayse me from the heavy ground
And move me swimming in the yeelding ayre:
As Zephirs flowry blasts doe tosse a sounde;   255
Upon their wings will I to Heaven repayre,

And sing them so, Gods shall descend and heare
Ladies must bee ador'd that are but fayre,
   But apt besides with art to tempt the eare
In notes of Nature, is a Goddesse part,   260
Though oft, men Natures notes, please more then Art.

But heere are Art and Nature both confinde,
Art casting Nature in so deepe a trance
That both seeme deade, because they be divinde,
Buried is Heaven in earthly ignorance,   265
   Why breake not men then strumpet Follies bounds,
To learne at this pure virgine utterance?
   No; none but *Ovids* eares can sound these sounds,
Where sing the harts of Love and Poesie,
Which make my Muse so strong she works too hye.   270

Now in his glowing eares her tunes did sleepe,
And as a silver Bell, with violent blowe
Of Steele or Iron, when his soundes most deepe,
Doe from his sides and ayres soft bosome flowe,
   A great while after murmures at the stroke,   275
Letting the hearers eares his hardnes knowe,
   So chid the Ayre to be no longer broke:
And left the accents panting in his eare
Which in this Banquet his first service were.

Heerewith, as *Ovid* something neerer drew,   *Olfactus* 280
Her Odors, odord with her breath and brest,
Into the sensor of his savor flew,
As if the Phenix hasting to her rest
   Had gatherd all th'Arabian Spicerie
T'enbalme her body in her Tombe, her nest,   285
   And there lay burning gainst *Apollos* eye,
Whose fiery ayre straight piercing *Ovids* braine
Enflamde his Muse with a more odorouse vaine.

And thus he sung, come soveraigne Odors, come
Restore my spirits now in love consuming,   290
Wax hotter ayre, make them more savorsome,
My fainting life with fresh-breath'd soule perfuming,

The flames of my disease are violent,
And many perish on late helps presuming,
    With which hard fate must I yet stand content,   295
As Odors put in fire most richly smell,
So men must burne in love that will excell.

And as the ayre is rarefied with heate
But thick and grosse with Summer-killing colde,
So men in love aspire perfections seate,   300
When others, slaves to base desire are sold,
    And if that men neere *Ganges* liv'd by sent
Of Flowres, and Trees, more I a thousand fold
    May live by these pure fumes that doe present
My Mistres quickning, and consuming breath   305
Where her wish flyes with power of life and death.

Me thinks, as in these liberall fumes I burne
My Mistres lips be neere with kisse-entices,
And that which way soever I can turne,
She turns withall, and breaths on me her spices   310
    As if too pure for search of humaine eye
She flewe in ayre disburthening Indian prizes,
    And made each earthly fume to sacrifice.
With her choyse breath fell *Cupid* blowes his fire,
And after, burns himselfe in her desire.   315

Gentle, and noble are theyr tempers framde,
That can be quickned with perfumes and sounds,
And they are cripple-minded, Gowt-wit lamde,
That lye like fire-fit blocks, dead without wounds,
    Stird up with nought, but hell-descending gaine,   320
The soule of fooles that all theyr soules confounds,
    The art of Pessants and our Nobles staine,
The bane of vertue and the blisse of sinne.
Which none but fooles and Pessants glorie in.

Sweete sounds and Odors, are the heavens, on earth   325
Where vertues live, of vertuous men deceast,
Which in such like, receive theyr second birth
By smell and hearing endlesly encreast;

They were meere flesh were not with them delighted,
And every such is perisht like a beast 330
  As all they shall that are so foggye sprighted,
Odors feede love, and love cleare heaven discovers,
Lovers weare sweets then; sweetest mindes, be lovers.

Odor in heate and drynes is consite
Love then a fire is much thereto affected; 335
And as ill smells do kill his appetite
With thankfull savors it is still protected;
  Love lives in spyrits, and our spyrits be
Nourisht with Odors, therefore love refected;
  And ayre lesse corpulent in quallitie 340
Then Odors are, doth nourish vitall spyrits
Therefore may they be prov'd of equall merits;

O soveraigne Odors; not of force to give
Foode to a thing that lives nor let it dye,
But to ad life to that did never live; 345
Nor to ad life, but immortallitie.
  Since they pertake her heate that like the fire
Stolne from the wheeles of *Phœbus* waggonrie
  To lumps of earth, can manly lyfe inspire;
Else be these fumes the lives of sweetest dames 350
That (dead) attend on her for novell frames;

Rejoyce blest Clime, thy ayre is so refinde
That while shee lives no hungry pestilence
Can feede her poysoned stomack with thy kynde;
But as the Unicorns pregredience 355
  To venomd Pooles, doth purdge them with his horne,
And after him the desarts Residence
  May safely drinke, so in the holesome morne
After her walke, who there attends her eye,
Is sure that day to tast no maladye. 360

Thus was his course of Odors sweet and sleight,
Because he long'd to give his sight assaye,
And as in fervor of the summers height,
The sunne is so ambitious in his sway

He will not let the Night an howre be plast,   365
So in this *Cupids* Night (oft seene in day
  Now spred with tender clouds these Odors cast,)
Her sight, his sunne so wrought in his desires,
His savor vanisht in his visuale fires.

So vulture love on his encreasing liver,   370
And fruitfull entrails egerly did feede,
And with the goldnest Arrow in his Quiver,
Wounds him with longings, that like Torrents bleeds,
  To see the Myne of knowledge that enricht
His minde with povertie, and desperate neede   375
  A sight that with the thought of sight bewitcht,
A sight taught Magick his deepe misterie,
Quicker in danger then *Dianas* eye.

Stay therefore *Ovid*, venter not, a sight
May prove thy rudenes, more then shew thee loving,   380
And make thy Mistres thinke thou think'st her light:
Which thought with lightest Dames is nothing moving.
  The slender hope of favor thou hast yet
Should make thee feare, such grosse conclusions proving:
  Besides, the Thicket *Floras* hands hath set   385
To hide thy theft, is thinne and hollow harted,
Not meete to have so high a charge imparted.

And should it keepe thy secrets, thine owne eye
Would fill thy thoughts so full of lightenings,
That thou must passe through more extremitie.   390
Or stand content to burne beneath theyr wings,
  Her honor gainst thy love, in wager layde,
Thou would'st be prickt with other sences stings,
  To tast, and feele, and yet not there be staide:
These casts, he cast, and more, his wits more quick   395
Then can be cast, by wits Arithmetick.

Forward, and back, and forward went he thus,
Like wanton *Thamysis*, that hastes to greete
The brackish Court of old *Oceanus*;
And as by Londons bosome she doth fleet   400

Casts herselfe proudly through the Bridges twists,
Where (as she takes againe her Christall feete:)
 She curls her silver hayre like Amorists,
Smoothes her bright cheekes, adorns her browes with ships
And Empresse-like along the Coast she trips.   405

Till comming neere the Sea, she heares him rore,
Tumbling her churlish billowes in her face,
Then, more dismaid, then insolent before
Charg'd to rough battaile, for his smooth embrace,
 She crowcheth close within her winding bancks,   410
And creepes retreate into her peacefull Pallace;
 Yet straite high-flowing in her female prancks
Againe shee will bee wanton, and againe,
By no meanes stayde, nor able to containe.

So *Ovid* with his strong affections striving,   415
Maskt in a friendly Thicket neere her Bowre,
Rubbing his temples, fainting, and reviving,
Fitting his garments, praying to the howre,
 Backwards, and forwards went, and durst not venter,
To tempt the tempest of his Mistres lowre,   420
 Or let his eyes her beauties ocean enter,
At last, with prayer he pierceth *Junos* eare,
Great Goddesse of audacitie and feare,

Great Goddesse of audacitie, and feare,
Queene of Olympus, *Saturns* eldest seede,   425
That doost the scepter over *Samos* beare,
And rul'st all Nuptiale rites with power, and meede,
 Since thou in nature art the meane to mix
Still sulphure humors, and canst therefore speede
 Such as in Cyprian sports theyr pleasures fix   430
Venus herselfe, and *Mars* by thee embracing,
Assist my hopes, me and my purpose gracing.

Make love within me not too kinde but pleasing,
Exiling Aspen feare out of his forces,
My inward sight, with outward seeing, easing,   435
And if he please further to stretch his courses,

Arme me with courage to make good his charges,
Too much desire to please, pleasure divorces,
    Attemps, and not entreats get Ladies larges,
Wit is with boldnes prompt, with terror danted,   440
And grace is sooner got of Dames then graunted.

This sayde, he charg'd the Arbor with his eye,   *Visus.*
Which pierst it through, and at her brests reflected,
Striking him to the hart with exstasie:
As doe the sun-beames gainst the earth prorected,   445
    With their reverberate vigor mount in flames,
And burne much more then where they were directed,
    He saw th'extraction of all fayrest Dames:
The fayre of Beauty, as whole Countries come
And shew theyr riches in a little Roome.   450

Heere *Ovid* sold his freedome for a looke,
And with that looke was ten tymes more enthralde,
He blusht, lookt pale, and like a fevour shooke,
And as a burning vapor being exhalde
    Promist by *Phœbus* eye to be a star,   455
Heavens walles denying to be further scalde
    The force dissolves that drewe it up so far:
And then it lightens gainst his death and fals,
So *Ovids* powre, this powrefull sight appals.

This beauties fayre is an enchantment made   460
By natures witchcraft, tempting men to buy
With endles showes, what endlesly will fade
Yet promise chapmen all eternitie:
    But like to goods ill got a fate it hath,
Brings men enricht therewith to beggerie   465
    Unlesse th'enricher be as rich in fayth,
Enamourd (like good selfe-love) with her owne,
Seene in another, then tis heaven alone.

For sacred beautie, is the fruite of sight,
The curtesie that speakes before the tongue,   470
The feast of soules, the glory of the light,
Envy of age, and everlasting young,

Pitties Commander, *Cupids* richest throne,
Musick intransed, never duely sung,
　　The summe and court of all proportion:　　　475
And that I may dull speeches best afforde,
All Rethoricks flowers in lesse then in a worde.

Then in the truest wisdome can be thought,
Spight of the publique *Axiom* worldlings hold,
That nothing wisdome is, that getteth nought,　　480
This all-things-nothing, since it is no gold.
　　Beautie enchasing love, love gracing beautie,
To such as constant simpathies enfold,
　　To perfect riches dooth a sounder duetie
Then all endevours, for by all consent　　　485
All wealth and wisdome rests in true Content.

Contentment is our heaven, and all our deedes
Bend in that circle, seld or never closde,
More then the letter in the word preceedes,
And to conduce that compasse is reposde.　　　490
　　More force and art in beautie joynd with love,
Then thrones with wisdome, joyes of them composde
　　Are armes more proofe gainst any griefe we prove,
Then all their vertue-scorning miserie
Or judgments graven in Stoick gravitie,　　　495

But as weake colour alwayes is allowde
The proper object of a humaine eye,
Though light be with a farre more force endowde
In stirring up the visuale facultie,
　　This colour being but of vertuous light　　　500
A feeble Image; and the cause dooth lye
　　In th'imperfection of a humaine sight,
So this for love, and beautie, loves cold fire
May serve for my praise, though it merit higher.

With this digression, wee will now returne　　　505
To *Ovids* prospect in his fancies storme:
Hee thought hee sawe the Arbors bosome burne,
Blaz'd with a fire wrought in a Ladyes forme:

F

Where silver past the least: and Natures vant
Did such a precious miracle performe,   510
   Shee lay, and seemd a flood of Diamant
Bounded in flesh: as still as *Vespers* hayre,
When not an Aspen leafe is styrrd with ayre.

Shee lay at length, like an immortall soule
At endlesse rest in blest *Elisium*:   515
And then did true felicitie enroule
So fayre a Lady, figure of her kingdome.
   Now *Ovids* Muse as in her tropicke shinde,
And hee (strooke dead) was meere heaven-borne become,
   So his quick verse in equall height was shrinde: 520
Or els blame mee as his submitted debter,
That never Mistresse had to make mee better.

Now as shee lay, attirde in nakednes,
His eye did carve him on that feast of feasts:
Sweet fields of life which Deaths foote dare not presse,
Flowrd with th'unbroken waves of my Loves brests,   526
   Unbroke by depth of those her beauties floods:
See where with bent of Gold curld into Nests
   In her heads Grove, the Spring-bird Lameate broods:
Her body doth present those fields of peace   530
Where soules are feasted with the soule of ease.

To prove which Parradise that nurseth these,
See see the golden Rivers that renowne it:
Rich *Gehon, Tigris, Phison, Euphrates,*
Two from her bright Pelopian shoulders crowne it,   535
   And two out of her snowye Hills doe glide,
That with a Deluge of delights doe drowne it:
   The highest two, theyr precious streames divide
To tenne pure floods, that doe the body dutie
Bounding themselves in length, but not in beautie.   540

These winde theyr courses through the painted bowres,
And raise such sounds in theyr inflection,
As ceaseles start from Earth fresh sorts of flowers,
And bound that booke of life with every section.

In these the Muses dare not swim for drowning, 545
Theyr sweetnes poisons with such blest infection,
 And leaves the onely lookers on them swouning,
These forms so decks, and colour makes so shine,
That Gods for them would cease to be divine.

Thus though my love be no *Elisium* 550
That cannot move, from her prefixed place;
Yet have her feete no powre from thence to come,
For where she is, is all *Elisian* grace:
 And as those happy men are sure of blisse
That can performe so excellent a race 555
 As that Olympiad where her favor is,
So shee can meete them, blessing them the rather
And give her sweetes, as well as let men gather.

Ah how should I be so most happy then
T'aspire that place, or make it come to mee? 560
To gather, or be given, the flowre of women?
Elisium must with vertue gotten bee,
 With labors of the soule and continence,
And these can yeeld no joy with such as she,
 Shee is a sweet *Elisium* for the sence 565
And Nature dooth not sensuall gifts infuse
But that with sence, shee still intends their use.

The sence is given us to excite the minde,
And that can never be by sence exited
But first the sence must her contentment finde, 570
We therefore must procure the sence delighted,
 That so the soule may use her facultie;
Mine Eye then to this feast hath her invited;
 That she might serve the soveraigne of mine Eye,
Shee shall bid Time, and Time so feasted never 575
Shall grow in strength of her renowne for ever.

Betwixt mine Eye and object, certayne lynes,
Move in the figure of a Pyramis,
Whose chapter in mine eyes gray apple shines,
The base within my sacred object is: 580

On this will I inscribe in golden verse
The mervailes raigning in my soveraigns blisse,
   The arcks of sight, and how her arrowes pierse:
This in the Region of the ayre shall stand
In Fames brasse Court, and all her Trumps commaund.

Rich Beautie, that ech Lover labors for,   586
Tempting as heapes of new-coynd-glowing Gold,
(Rackt of some miserable Treasurer)
Draw his desires, and them in chaynes enfold
   Urging him still to tell it, and conceale it,   590
But Beauties treasure never can be told
   None can peculier joy, yet all must steale it,
O Beautie, this same bloody siedge of thine
Starves me that yeeld, and feedes mee till I pine.

And as a Taper burning in the darke   595
(As if it threatned every watchfull eye
That viewing burns it,) makes that eye his marke,
And hurls guilt Darts at it continually,
   Or as it envied, any eye but it
Should see in darknes, so my Mistres beautie   600
   From foorth her secret stand my hart doth hit:
And like the Dart of *Cephalus* dooth kill
Her perfect Lover, though shee meane no ill.

Thus, as the innocence of one betraide
Carries an *Argus* with it, though unknowne,   605
And Fate to wreake the trecherie bewraide;
Such vengeance hath my Mistres Beautie showne
   On me the Traitor to her modestie,
So unassailde, I quite am overthrowne,
   And in my tryumph bound in slaverie,   610
O Beauty, still thy Empire swims in blood,
And in thy peace, Warre stores himselfe with foode.

O Beautie, how attractive is thy powre?
For as the lives heate clings about the hart,
So all Mens hungrie eyes do haunt thy Bowre,   615
Raigning in Greece, Troy swum to thee in Art;

Remov'd to Troy, Greece follow'd thee in feares;
Thou drewst each Syreles sworde, each childles Dart
   And pulld'st the towres of Troy about thine eares:
Shall I then muse that thus thou drawest me? 620
No, but admire, I stand thus farre from thee.

Heerewith shee rose like the Autumnale Starre
Fresh burnisht in the loftie Ocean floode,
That darts his glorious influence more farre
Then any Lampe of bright *Olympus* broode; 625
   Shee lifts her lightning arms above her head,
And stretcheth a Meridian from her blood,
     That slept awake in her *Elisian* bed:
Then knit shee up, lest loose, her glowing hayre
Should scorch the Center and incense the ayre. 630

Thus when her fayre hart-binding hands had tied
Those liberall Tresses, her high frontier part,
Shee shrunk in curls, and curiously plied
Into the figure of a swelling hart:
   And then with Jewels of devise, it graced: 635
One was a Sunne graven at his Eevens depart,
   And under that a Mans huge shaddow placed,
Wherein was writ, in sable Charectry,
Decrescente nobilitate, crescunt obscuri.

An other was an Eye in Saphire set, 640
And close upon it a fresh Lawrell spray,
The skilfull Posie was, *Medio caret,*
To showe not eyes, but meanes must truth display.
   The third was an *Apollo* with his Teme
About a Diall and a worlde in way, 645
   The Motto was, *Teipsum et orbem,*
Graven in the Diall; those exceeding rare
And other like accomplements she ware.

Not *Tygris, Nilus,* nor swift *Euphrates,*
Quoth *Ovid* now, can more subdue my flame, 650
I must through hell adventure to displease,
To tast and touch, one kisse may worke the same:

If more will come, more then much more I will;
Each naturall agent doth his action frame,
    To render that he works on like him styll: 655
The fire on water working doth induce
Like qualitie unto his owne in use.

But Heaven in her a sparckling temper blewe
(As love in mee) and so will soone be wrought,
    Good wits will bite at baits most strang and new,   660
And words well plac'd, move things were never thought;
    What Goddesse is it *Ovids* wits shall dare
And he disgrace them with attempting nought?
    My words shall carry spirits to ensnare
The subtelst harts affecting sutes importune,   665
'Best loves are lost for wit when men blame Fortune.'

With this, as she was looking in her Glasse,   NARRATIO
She saw therein a mans face looking on her:
Whereat she started from the frighted Grasse,
As if some monstrous Serpent had been shown her: 670
    Rising as when (the sunne in *Leos* signe)
Auriga with the heavenly Goate upon her,
    Shows her horn'd forehead with her Kids divine,
Whose rise, kils Vines, Heavens face with storms disguising;
No man is safe at sea, the Hædy rising.   675

So straight wrapt shee her body in a Clowde,
And threatned tempests for her high disgrace,
Shame from a Bowre of Roses did unshrowde
And spread her crimson wings upon her face;
    When running out, poore *Ovid* humbly kneeling   680
Full in the Arbors mouth, did stay her race
    And saide; faire Nimph, great Goddesse have some feeling
Of *Ovids* paines; but heare: and your dishonor
Vainely surmisde, shall vanish with my horror.

Traytor to Ladies modesties (said shee)   685
What savage boldnes hardned thee to this?
Or what base reckoning of my modestie?
What should I thinke thy facts proude reason is?

Love (sacred Madam) love exhaling mee
(Wrapt in his Sulphure,) to this clowde of his   690
   Made my affections his artillerie,
Shot me at you his proper Cytadell,
And loosing all my forces, heere I fell.

This Glosse is common, as thy rudenes strange
Not to forbeare these private times, (quoth she)   695
Whose fixed Rites, none shoulde presume to change
Not where there is adjudg'd inchastitie;
   Our nakednes should be as much conceald
As our accomplishments desire the eye:
   It is a secrete not to be revealde,   700
But as Virginitie, and Nuptialls clothed,
And to our honour all to be betrothed.

It is a want, where our aboundance lyes,
Given a sole dowre t'enrich chast *Hymens* Bed,
A perfect Image of our purities,   705
And glasse by which our actions should be dressed.
   That tells us honor is as soone defild
And should be kept as pure, and incompressed,
   But sight attainteth it: for Thought Sights childe
Begetteth sinne; and Nature bides defame,   710
When light and lawles eyes bewray our shame.

Deere Mistresse (answerd *Ovid*,) to direct
Our actions, by the straitest rule that is,
We must in matters Morrall, quite reject
Vulgar Opinion, ever led amisse   715
   And let autentique Reason be our guide,
The wife of Truth, and Wisdoms Governisse:
   The nature of all actions must be waide,
And as they then appeare, breede love or loathing,
Use makes things nothing huge, and huge things nothing.   720

As in your sight, how can sight simply beeing
A Sence receiving essence to his flame
Sent from his object, give it harme by seeing
Whose action in the Seer hath his frame?

All excellence of shape is made for sight,   725
Else, to be like a Beast were no defame;
  Hid Beauties lose theyr ends, and wrong theyr right:
And can kinde love, (where no harms kinde can be)
Disgrace with seeing that is given to see?

Tis I (alas) and my hart-burning Eye   730
Doe all the harme, and feele the harme wee doo:
I am no Basiliske, yet harmles I
Poyson with sight, and mine owne bosome too;
  So am I to my selfe a Sorceresse
Bewitcht with my conceites in her I woo: 735
  But you unwrongd, and all dishonorlesse
No ill dares touch, affliction, sorcerie,
One kisse of yours can quickly remedie.

I could not times observe, as others might
Of cold affects, and watry tempers framde,   740
Yet well assurde the wounder of your sight
Was so farre of from seeing you defamde,
  That ever in the Phane of Memorie
Your love shall shine by it, in mee enflamde.
  Then let your powre be clad in lenitie,   745
Doe not (as others would) of custome storme,
But prove your wit as pregnant as your forme.

Nor is my love so suddaine, since my hart
Was long loves *Vulcan*, with his pants unrest
Ham'ring the shafts bred this delightsome smart: 750
And as when *Jove* at once from East and West
  Cast off two Eagles, to discerne the sight
Of this world Center, both his Byrds joynd brest
  In Cynthian *Delphos*, since *Earths navill* hight:
So casting off my ceaseles thoughts to see   755
My harts true Center, all doe meete in thee.

Cupid that acts in you, suffers in mee
To make himselfe one tryumph-place of twaine,
Into your tunes and odors turned hee,
And through my sences flew into my braine   760

Where rules the Prince of sence, whose Throne hee takes,
And of my Motions engines framd a chaine
   To leade mee where hee list; and heere hee makes
Nature (my fate) enforce mee: and resignes
The raines of all, to you, in whom hee shines.   765

For yeelding love then, doe not hate impart,
Nor let mine Eye, your carefull Harbengere
That hath purvaide your Chamber in my hart,
Be blamde for seeing who it lodged there;
   The freer service merrits greater meede,   770
Princes are serv'd with unexpected chere,
   And must have things in store before they neede:
Thus should faire Dames be wise and confident,
Not blushing to be noted excellent.

Now, as when Heaven is muffled with the vapors   775
His long since just divorced wife the Earth,
In envie breath's, to maske his spurrie Tapers
From the unrich aboundance of her birth,
   When straight the westerne issue of the Ayre
Beates with his flowrie wings those Brats of dearth,   780
   And gives *Olympus* leave to shew his fayre,
So fled th'offended shaddowes of her cheere,
And showd her pleased count'nance full as cleare.

Which for his fourth course made our Poet court her, &c.

This motion of my soule, my fantasie   *Gustus*
Created by three sences put in act,   785
Let justice nourish with thy simpathie,
Putting my other sences into fact,
   If now thou grant not, now changde that offence;
To suffer change, doth perfect sence compact:
   Change then, and suffer for the use of sence,   790
Wee live not for our selves, the Eare, and Eye,
And every sence, must serve societie.

To furnish then, this Banquet where the tast
Is never usde, and yet the cheere divine,

The neerest meane deare Mistres that thou hast   795
To blesse me with it, is a kysse of thine,
   Which grace shall borrow organs of my touch
T'advance it to that inward taste of mine
   Which makes all sence, and shall delight as much
Then with a kisse (deare life) adorne thy feast   800
And let (as Banquets should) the last be best.

I see unbidden Guests are boldest still,   *Corynna*
And well you showe how weake in soule you are
That let rude sence subdue your reasons skill
And feede so spoilefully on sacred fare;   805
   In temper of such needles feasts as this
We show more bounty still the more we spare,
   Chiefly where birth and state so different is:
Ayre too much rarefied breakes forth in fire,
And favors too farre urg'd do end in ire.   810

The difference of our births (imperiall Dame)   *Ovid*
Is heerein noted with too triviall eyes
For your rare wits; that should your choices frame
To state of parts, that most doth royalize,
   Not to commend mine owne; but that in yours   815
Beyond your birth, are perrils soveraignties
   Which (urgd) your words had strook with sharper powers;
Tis for mere looke-like Ladies, and for men
To boast of birth that still be childeren.

Running to Father straight to helpe theyr needs,   820
True dignities and rites of reverence,
Are sowne in mindes, and reapt in lively deedes,
And onely pollicie makes difference
   Twixt States, since vertue wants due imperance
Vertue makes honor, as the soule doth sence,   825
   And merit farre exceedes inheritance,
The Graces fill loves cup, his feasts adorning,
Who seekes your service now, the Graces scorning.

Pure love (said she) the purest grace pursues,
And there is contact, not by application   830

Of lips or bodies, but of bodies vertues,
As in our elementale Nation
  Stars by theyr powers, which are theyr heat and light
Do heavenly works, and that which hath probation
    By vertuall contact hath the noblest plight,   835
Both for the lasting and affinitie
It hath with naturall divinitie.

Ovid replied; in thys thy vertuall presence
(Most fayre *Corynna*) thou canst not effuse
The true and solid parts of thy pure essence   840
But doost the superficiall beames produce
  Of thy rich substance; which because they flow
Rather from forme then from the matters use
    Resemblance onely of thy body showe
Whereof they are thy wondrous species,   845
And t'is thy substance must my longings ease.

Speake then sweet ayre, that giv'st our speech event
And teach my Mistres tractabilitie,
That art to motion most obedient,
And though thy nature, swelling be and high   850
  And occupiest so infinite a space,
Yet yeeldst to words, and art condeust thereby
    Past nature prest into a little place
Deare soveraigne then, make ayre thy rule in this,
And me thy worthy servant with a kisse.   855

Ovid (sayd shee) I am well pleasd to yeeld:
Bountie by vertue cannot be abusde:
Nor will I coylie lyft *Minervas* shielde
Against *Minerva*, honor is not brusde
  With such a tender pressure as a kisse,   860
Nor yeelding soone to words, though seldome usde,
  Nicenes in civill favours, folly is:
Long sutes make never good a bad detection,
Nor yeelding soone, makes bad, a good affection.

To some I know, (and know it for a fault)   865
Order and reverence, are repulst in skaling,

When pryde and rudenes, enter with assault,
Consents to fall, are worse to get then falling:
 Willing resistance, takes away the will,
And too much weakenes tis to come with calling: 870
 Force in these frayes, is better man then skyll,
Yet I like skill, and *Ovid* if a kis
May doe thee so much pleasure, heere it is.

Her mooving towards him, made *Ovids* eye
Beleeve the Firmament was comming downe 875
To take him quick to immortalitie,
And that th'Ambrosian kisse set on the Crowne:
 Shee spake in kissing, and her breath infusde
Restoring syrrop to his tast, in swoune:
 And hee imaginde *Hebes* hands had brusde 880
A banquet of the Gods into his sence,
Which fild him with this furious influence.

The motion of the Heavens that did beget
The golden age, and by whose harmonie
Heaven is preservd, in mee on worke is set, 885
All instruments of deepest melodie
 Set sweet in my desires to my loves liking
With this sweet kisse in mee theyr tunes apply,
 As if the best Musitians hands were striking:
This kisse in mee hath endlesse Musicke closed, 890
Like *Phœbus* Lute, on *Nisus* Towrs imposed.

And as a Pible cast into a Spring,
Wee see a sort of trembling cirkles rise,
One forming other in theyr issuing
Till over all the Fount they circulize, 895
 So this perpetuall-motion-making kisse,
Is propagate through all my faculties,
 And makes my breast an endlesse Fount of blisse,
Of which, if Gods could drink, theyr matchlesse fare
Would make them much more blessed then they are. 900

But as when sounds doe hollow bodies beate,
Ayre gatherd there, comprest, and thickned,

The selfe same way shee came doth make retreate,
And so effects the sounde reecchoed
   Onely in part, because shee weaker is   905
In that redition, then when first shee fled:
   So I alas, faint eccho of this kisse,
Onely reiterate a slender part
Of that high joy it worketh in my hart.

And thus with feasting, love is famisht more,   910
Without my touch are all things turnd to gold,
And till I touch, I cannot joy my store:
To purchase others, I my selfe have sold,
   Love is a wanton famine, rich in foode,
But with a richer appetite controld,   915
   An argument in figure and in Moode,
Yet hates all arguments: disputing still
For Sence, gainst Reason, with a sencelesse will.

Then sacred Madam, since my other sences   *Tactus*
Have in your graces tasted such content,   920
Let wealth not to be spent, feare no expences,
But give thy bountie true eternizement:
   Making my sences ground-worke, which is, Feeling,
Effect the other, endlesse excellent,
   Their substance with flint-softning softnes steeling: 925
Then let mee feele, for know sweet beauties Queene,
Dames may be felt, as well as heard or seene.

For if wee be allowd to serve the Eare
With pleasing tunes, and to delight the Eye
With gracious showes, the Taste with daintie cheere, 930
The Smell with Odors, ist immodestie
   To serve the sences Emperor, sweet Feeling
With those delights that fit his Emperie?
   Shall Subjects free themselves, and bind theyr King?
Mindes taint no more with bodies touch or tyre,   935
Then bodies nourish with the mindes desire.

The minde then cleere, the body may be usde,
Which perfectly your touch can spritualize;

As by the great elixer is trans-fusde
Copper to Golde, then grant that deede of prise: 940
  Such as trans-forme into corrupt effects
What they receave from Natures purities,
  Should not wrong them that hold her due respects:
To touch your quickning side then give mee leave,
Th'abuse of things, must not the use bereave.   945

Heere-with, even glad his arguments to heare,
Worthily willing to have lawfull grounds
To make the wondrous power of Heaven appeare,
In nothing more then her perfections found,
  Close to her navill shee her Mantle wrests,   950
Slacking it upwards, and the foulds unwound,
  Showing *Latonas* Twinns, her plenteous brests
The Sunne and *Cynthia* in theyr tryumph-robes
Of Lady-skin; more rich then both theyr Globes

Whereto shee bad, blest *Ovid* put his hand: 955
Hee, well acknowledging it much too base
For such an action, did a little stand,
Enobling it with tytles full of grace,
  And conjures it with charge of reverend verse,
To use with pietie that sacred place,   960
  And through his Feelings organ to disperse
Worth to his spirits, amply to supply
The porenes of his fleshes facultie.

And thus hee sayd: King of the King of Sences,
Engine of all the engines under heaven,   965
To health, and life, defence of all defences,
Bountie by which our nourishment is given,
  Beauties bewtifier, kinde acquaintance maker,
Proportions odnes that makes all things even,
  Wealth of the laborer, wrongs revengement taker,   970
Patterne of concord, Lord of exercise,
And figure of that power the world did guise:

Deere Hand, most dulie honored in this
And therefore worthy to be well employde:

Yet know, that all that honor nothing is,   975
Compard with that which now must be enjoyd:
  So thinke in all the pleasures these have showne
(Likened to this) thou wert but meere anoyde,
    That all hands merits in thy selfe alone
With this one touch, have more then recompence,   980
And therefore feele, with feare and reverence.

See *Cupids* Alps which now thou must goe over,
Where snowe that thawes the Sunne doth ever lye:
Where thou maist plaine and feelingly discover
The worlds fore-past, that flow'd with Milke and Honny:
  Where, (like an Empresse seeing nothing wanting   986
That may her glorious child-bed bewtifie)
  Pleasure her selfe lyes big with issue panting:
Ever deliverd, yet with childe still growing,
Full of all blessings, yet all blisse bestowing.   990

This sayd, hee layde his hand upon her side,
Which made her start like sparckles from a fire,
Or like *Saturnia* from th'Ambrosian pride
Of her morns slumber, frighted with admire
  When *Jove* layd young *Alcydes* to her brest,   995
So startled shee, not with a coy retire,
  But with the tender temper shee was blest,
Proving her sharpe, unduld with handling yet,
Which keener edge on *Ovids* longings set.

And feeling still, he sigh'd out this effect;   1000
Alas why lent not heaven the soule a tongue?
Nor language, nor peculier dialect,
To make her high conceits as highly sung,
  But that a fleshlie engine must unfold
A spirituall notion; birth from Princes sprung   1005
  Pessants must nurse, free vertue waite on gold
And a profest though flattering enemie,
Must pleade my honor, and my libertie.

O nature how doost thou defame in this
Our humane honors? yoking men with beasts   1010

And noblest mindes with slaves? thus beauties blisse,
Love and all vertues that quick spirit feasts
     Surfet on flesh; and thou that banquests mindes
Most bounteous Mistresse, of thy dull-tongu'd guests
     Reapst not due thanks; thus rude frailetie bindes   1015
What thou giv'st wings; thus joyes I feele in thee
Hang on my lips and will not uttered be.

Sweete touch the engine that loves bow doth bend,
The sence wherewith he feeles him deified,
The object whereto all his actions tend,   1020
In all his blindenes his most pleasing guide,
     For thy sake will I write the Art of love,
Since thou doost blow his fire and feede his pride
     Since in thy sphere his health and life doth move,
For thee I hate who hate societie   1025
And such as selfe-love makes his slaverie.

In these dog-dayes how this contagion smoothers
The purest bloods with vertues diet fined
Nothing theyr owne, unlesse they be some others
Spite of themselves, are in themselves confined   1030
     And live so poore they are of all despised,
Theyr gifts, held down with scorne should be divined,
     And they like Mummers mask, unknowne, unprised:
A thousand mervailes mourne in some such brest
Would make a kinde and worthy Patrone blest.   1035

To mee (deere Soveraigne) thou art Patronesse,
And I, with that thy graces have infused,
Will make all fat and foggy braines confesse,
Riches may from a poore verse be deduced:
     And that Golds love shall leave them groveling heere,
When thy perfections shall to heaven be Mused,   1041
     Deckt in bright verse, where Angels shall appeare
The praise of vertue, love, and beauty singing,
Honor to Noblesse, shame to Avarice bringing.

Heere *Ovid* interupted with the view   1045
Of other Dames, who then the Garden painted,

Shrowded himselfe, and did as death eschew
All note by which his loves fame might be tainted:
   And as when mighty *Macedon* had wun
The Monarchie of Earth, yet when hee fainted,   1050
   Griev'd that no greater action could be doone,
And that there were no more worlds to subdue,
So loves defects, loves Conqueror did rue.

But as when expert Painters have displaid,
To quickest life a Monarchs royall hand   1055
Holding a Scepter, there is yet bewraide
But halfe his fingers; when we understand
   The rest not to be seene; and never blame
The Painters Art, in nicest censures skand:
   So in the compasse of this curious frame,   1060
Ovid well knew there was much more intended,
With whose omition none must be offended.

INTENTIO, ANIMI ACTIO.
EXPLICIT CONVIVIUM.

Salmacis and Hermaphroditus

FRANCIS BEAUMONT (1602)

The Author to the Reader

I sing the fortunes of a lucklesse payre,
Whose spotlesse soules now in one body be:
For beauty still is *Prodromus* to care,
Crost by the sad starres of nativitie;
And of the strange inchauntment of a well
Gi'n by the gods my sportive Muse doth write,
Which sweet-lipt *Ovid* long agoe did tell,
Wherein who bathes, strait turnes *Hermaphrodite*.
   I hope my Poeme is so lively writ,
    That thou wilt turne halfe-mayd with reading it.

My wanton lines doe treate of amorous love,
Such as would bow the hearts of gods above:
Then *Venus*, thou great Citherean Queene,
That hourely tripst on the Idalian greene,
Thou laughing *Erycina*, daygne to see   5
The verses wholly consecrate to thee;
Temper them so within thy Paphian shrine,
That every Lovers eye may melt a line;
Commaund the god of Love that little King,
To give each verse a sleight touch with his wing,   10
That as I write, one line may draw the tother,
And every word skip nimbly o're another.
There was a lovely boy the Nymphs had kept,
That on the Idane mountaines oft had slept,
Begot and borne by powers that dwelt above,   15
By learned *Mercury* of the Queene of love:
A face he had that shew'd his parents fame,
And from them both conjoynd, he drew his name:

So wondrous fayre he was, that (as they say)
Diana being hunting on a day, 20
Shee saw the boy upon a greene banke lay him,
And there the virgin-huntresse meant to slay him,
Because no Nymphes did now pursue the chase:
For all were strooke blind with the wantons face.
But when that beauteous face *Diana* saw, 25
Her armes were nummed, and shee could not draw;
Yet did she strive to shoot, but all in vaine,
Shee bent her bow, and loos'd it streight againe.
Then she began to chide her wanton eye,
And fayne would shoot, but durst not see him die. 30
She turnd and shot, and did of purpose misse him,
Shee turnd againe, and did of purpose kisse him.
Then the boy ran: for (some say) had he stayd,
Diana had no longer bene a mayd.
Phoebus so doted on this rosiat face, 35
That he hath oft stole closely from his place,
When he did lie by fayre *Leucothoes* side,
To dally with him in the vales of Ide:
And ever since this lovely boy did die,
Phoebus each day about the world doth flie, 40
And on the earth he seekes him all the day,
And every night he seekes him in the sea:
His cheeke was sanguine, and his lip as red
As are the blushing leaves of the Rose spred:
And I have heard, that till this boy was borne, 45
Roses grew white upon the virgin thorne,
Till one day walking to a pleasant spring,
To heare how cunningly the birds could sing,
Laying him downe upon a flowry bed,
The Roses blush'd and turnd themselves to red. 50
The Rose that blush'd not, for his great offence,
The gods did punish, and for impudence
They gave this doome that was agreed by all;
The smell of the white Rose should be but small.
His haire was bushie, but it was not long, 55
The Nymphs had done his tresses mighty wrong:
For as it grew, they puld away his haire,
And made abilliments of gold to weare.

His eyes were *Cupids*: for untill his birth,
Cupid had eyes, and liv'd upon the earth,   60
Till on a day, when the great Queene of love
Was by her white doves drawn from heaven above,
Unto the top of the Idalian hill,
To see how well the Nymphs their charge fulfill,
And whether they had done the goddesse right,   65
In nursing of her sweet *Hermaphrodite*:
Whom when she saw, although complete and full,
Yet she complaynd, his eyes were somewhat dull:
And therefore, more the wanton boy to grace,
She puld the sparkling eyes from *Cupids* face,   70
Fayning a cause to take away his sight,
Because the Ape would sometimes shoot for spight.
But *Venus* set those eyes in such a place,
As grac't those cleare eyes with a clearer face.
For his white hand each goddesse did him woo: 75
For it was whiter then the driven snow:
His legge was straighter then the thigh of *Jove*:
And he farre fairer then the god of love.
When first this wel-shapt boy, beauties chiefe king,
Had seene the labour of the fifteenth spring,   80
How curiously it paynted all the earth,
He 'gan to travaile from his place of birth,
Leaving the stately hils where he was nurst,
And where the Nymphs had brought him up at first:
He lov'd to travaile to the coasts unknowne,   85
To see the regions farre beyond his owne,
Seeking cleare watry springs to bathe him in:
(For he did love to wash his ivory skinne)
The lovely Nymphes have oft times seene him swimme,
And closely stole his clothes from off the brim,   90
Because the wanton wenches would so fayne
See him come nak'd to aske his clothes againe.
He lov'd besides to see the Lycian grounds,
And know the wealthy Carians utmost bounds.
Using to travaile thus, one day he found   95
A cristall brooke, that tril'd along the ground,
A brooke, that in reflection did surpasse
The cleare reflection of the clearest glasse.

About the side there grew no foggy reedes,
Nor was the fount compast with barren weedes: 100
But living turfe grew all along the side,
And grasse that ever flourisht in his pride.
Within this brook a beauteous Nymph did dwell,
Who for her comely feature did excell;
So faire she was, of such a pleasing grace,   105
So straight a body, and so sweet a face,
So soft a belly, such a lustie thigh,
So large a forehead, such a cristall eye,
So soft and moyst a hand, so smooth a brest,
So faire a cheeke, so well in all the rest,   110
That *Jupiter* would revell in her bowre,
Were he to spend againe his golden showre:
Her teeth were whiter then the mornings milke,
Her lip was softer then the softest silke,
Her haire as farre surpast the burnisht gold,   115
As silver doth excell the basest mold:
Jove courted her for her translucent eye,
And told her, he would place her in the skye,
Promising her, if she would be his love,
He would ingrave her in the heaven above,   120
Telling this lovely Nymph, that if he would,
He could deceive her in a showre of gold,
Or like a Swanne come to her naked bed,
And so deceive her of her maiden-head:
But yet, because he thought that pleasure best,   125
Where each consenting joynes each loving brest,
He would put off that all-commaunding crowne,
Whose terrour strooke th'aspiring Giants downe,
That glittering crown, whose radiant sight did tosse
Great *Pelion* from the top of mighty *Osse*,   130
He would depose from his world-swaying head,
To taste the amorous pleasures of her bed:
This added he besides, the more to grace her,
Like a bright starre he would in heavens vault place her.
By this the proud lascivious Nymph was mov'd,   135
Perceiving by great *Jove* shee was belov'd,
And hoping as a starre she should ere long
Be sterne or gracious to the Sea-mans song,

(For mortals still are subject to their eye,
And what it sees, they strive to get as hie:)   140
Shee was contented that almighty *Jove*
Should have the first and best fruits of her love:
(For women may be likened to the yeere,
Whose first fruites still do make the dayntiest cheere)
But yet *Astræa* first should plight her troth,   145
For the performance of *Joves* sacred oth.
(Just times decline, and all good dayes are dead,
When heavenly othes had need be warranted)
This heard great *Jupiter* and lik'd it well,
And hastily he seekes *Astræas* cell,   150
About the massie earth searching her towre:
But she had long since left this earthly bowre,
And flew to heaven above, lothing to see
The sinfull actions of humanitie.
Which when *Jove* did perceive, he left the earth,   155
And flew up to the place of his owne birth,
The burning heavenly throne, where he did spy
Astræas palace in the glittering skie.
This stately towre was builded up on hie,
Farre from the reach of any mortall eye;   160
And from the palace side there did distill
A little water, through a little quill,
The dewe of justice, which did seldome fall,
And when it dropt, the drops were very small.
Glad was great *Jove* when he beheld her towre,   165
Meaning a while to rest him in her bowre;
And therefore sought to enter at her dore:
But there was such a busie rout before;
Some serving men, and some promooters bee,
That he could passe no foote without a fee: 170
But as he goes, he reaches out his hands,
And payes each one in order as he stands;
And still, as he was paying those before,
Some slipt againe betwixt him and the dore.
At length (with much adoo) he past them all,   175
And entred straight into a spacious hall,
Full of darke angles and of hidden wayes,
Crooked Mæanders, infinite delayes;

All which delayes and entries he must passe,
Ere he could come where just *Astræa* was.   180
All these being past by his immortall wit,
Without her doore he saw a porter sit,
An aged man, that long time there had beene,
Who us'd to search all those that entred in,
And still to every one he gave this curse,   185
None must see Justice but with emptie purse.
This man searcht *Jove* for his owne private gaine,
To have the money which did yet remaine,
Which was but small: for much was spent before
On the tumultuous rout that kept the dore.   190
When he had done, he brought him to the place
Where he should see divine *Astræas* face.
Then the great King of gods and men in went,
And saw his daughter *Venus* there lament,
And crying lowd for justice, whom *Jove* found   195
Kneeling before *Astræa* on the ground,
And still she cry'd and beg'd for a just doome
Against blacke *Vulcan*, that unseemely groome,
Whome she had chosen for her onely love,
Though she was daughter to great thundring *Jove*:   200
And though the fairest goddesse, yet content
To marrie him, though weake and impotent;
But for all this they alwayes were at strife:
For evermore he rayld at her his wife,
Telling her still, Thou art no wife of mine,   205
Anothers strumpet, *Mars* his concubine.
By this *Astræa* spyde almighty *Jove*,
And bow'd her finger to the Queene of love,
To cease her sute, which she would heare anon,
When the great King of all the world was gone.   210
Then she descended from her stately throne,
Which seat was builded all of Jasper stone,
And o're the seat was paynted all above,
The wanton unseene stealths of amorous *Jove*;
There might a man behold the naked pride   215
Of lovely *Venus* in the vale of Ide,
When *Pallas*, and *Joves* beauteous wife and she
Strove for the prise of beauties raritie:

And there lame *Vulcan* and his *Cyclops* strove
To make the thunderbolts for mighty *Jove*:   220
From this same stately throne she down descended,
And sayd, The griefs of *Jove* should be amended,
Asking the King of gods what lucklesse cause,
What great contempt of state, what breach of lawes
(For sure she thought, some uncouth cause befell,   225
That made him visit poore *Astræas* cell)
Troubled his thought: and if she might decide it,
Who vext great *Jove*, he dearely should abide it.
Jove onely thankt her, and beganne to show
His cause of comming (for each one doth know   230
The longing words of Lovers are not many,
If they desire to be injoyd of any)
Telling *Astræa*, It might now befall,
That she might make him blest, that blesseth all:
For as he walk'd upon the flowry earth,   235
To which his owne hands whilome gave a birth,
To see how streight he held it and how just
He rold this massy pondrous heape of dust,
He laid him downe by a coole river side,
Whose pleasant water did so gently slide   240
With such soft whispering: for the brook was deepe,
That it had lul'd him in a heavenly sleepe.
When first he laid him downe, there was none neere him:
(For he did call before, but none could heare him)
But a faire Nymph was bathing when he wak'd,   245
(Here sigh'd great *Jove*, and after brought forth) nak'd,
He seeing lov'd, the Nymph yet here did rest,
Where just *Astræa* might make *Jove* be blest,
If she would passe her faithfull word so farre,
As that great *Jove* should make the mayd a starre.   250
Astræa yeelded: at which *Jove* was pleas'd,
And all his longing hopes and feares were eas'd.
Jove tooke his leave, and parted from her sight,
Whose thoughts were ful of lovers sweet delight,
And she ascended to her throne above,   255
To heare the griefes of the great Queene of love:
But she was satisfide, and would no more
Rayle at her husband as she did before:

But forth she tript apace, because she strove,
With her swift feet to overtake great Jove;   260
She skipt so nimbly as she went to looke him,
That at the palace doore she overtooke him,
Which way was plaine and broad as they went out,
And now they could see no tumultuous rout.
Here *Venus* fearing, lest the love of *Jove*   265
Should make this mayd be plac'd in heaven above,
Because she thought this Nymph so wondrous bright,
That she would dazel her accustom'd light:
And fearing now she should not first be seene
Of all the glittring starres as shee had beene,   270
But that the wanton Nymph would ev'ry night
Be first that should salute eche mortall sight,
Began to tell great *Jove*, she griev'd to see
The heaven so full of his iniquity,
Complayning that eche strumpet now was grac'd,   275
And with immortall goddesses was plac'd,
Intreating him to place in heaven no more
Eche wanton strumpet and lascivious whore.
Jove mad with love, harkned not what she sayd,
His thoughts were so intangled with the mayd,   280
But furiously he to his Palace lept,
Being minded there till morning to have slept:
For the next morne, as soone as *Phoebus* rayes
Should yet shine coole, by reason of the seas,
And ere the parting teares of *Thætis* bed,   285
Should be quite shak't from off his glittring head,
Astræa promis'd to attend great *Jove*,
At his owne Palace in the heaven above,
And at that Palace she would set her hand
To what the love-sick god should her command: 290
But to descend to earth she did deny,
She loath'd the sight of any mortall eye;
And for the compasse of the earthly round,
She would not set one foot upon the ground.
Therefore *Jove* meant to rise but with the sunne,   295
Yet thought it long untill the night was done.
In the meane space *Venus* was drawne along
By her white Doves unto the sweating throng

Of hammering Black-smithes, at the lofty hill
Of stately *Etna*, whose top burneth still: 300
(For at that burning mountaynes glittring top,
Her cripple husband *Vulcan* kept his shop)
To him she went, and so collogues that night
With the best straines of pleasures sweet delight,
That ere they parted, she made *Vulcan* sweare   305
By dreadfull *Stix*, an othe the gods do feare,
If *Jove* would make the mortall mayd a starre,
Himselfe should frame his instruments of warre,
And tooke his othe by blacke *Cocitus* Lake,
He never more a thunder-bolt would make: 310
For *Venus* so this night his sences pleas'd,
That now he thought his former griefs were eas'd.
She with her hands the black-smiths body bound,
And with her Iv'ry armes she twyn'd him round,
And still the faire Queene with a pretty grace,   315
Disperst her sweet breath o're his swarty face:
Her snowy armes so well she did display,
That *Vulcan* thought they melted as they lay.
Untill the morne in this delight they lay:
Then up they got, and hasted fast away   320
In the white Chariot of the Queene of love,
Towards the Palace of great thundring *Jove*,
Where they did see divine *Astræa* stand,
To passe her word for what *Jove* should command.
In limpt the Blacke-smith; after stept his Queene,   325
Whose light arrayment was of lovely greene.
When they were in, *Vulcan* began to sweare
By othes that *Jupiter* himselfe doth feare,
If any whore in heavens bright vault were seene,
To dimme the shining of his beauteous Queene,   330
Each mortall man should the great gods disgrace,
And mocke almightie *Jove* unto his face,
And Giants should enforce bright heaven to fall,
Ere he would frame one thunderbolt at all.
Jove did intreat him that he would forbeare.   335
The more he spoke, the more did *Vulcan* sweare.
Jove heard his words, and 'gan to make his mone,
That mortall men would plucke him from his throne,

Or else he must incurre this plague, he said,
Quite to forgoe the pleasure of the mayd:　　　340
And once he thought, rather then lose her blisses,
Her heavenly sweets, her most delicious kisses,
Her soft embraces, and the amorous nights,
That he should often spend in her delights,
He would be quite thrown down by mortal hands,　　345
From the blest place where his bright palace stands.
But afterwards hee saw with better sight,
He should be scorn'd by every mortall wight,
If he should want his thunderbolts, to beate
Aspiring mortals from his glittering seate:　　　350
Therefore the god no more did woo or prove her,
But left to seeke her love, though not to love her.
Yet he forgot not that he woo'd the lasse,
But made her twise as beauteous as she was,
Because his wonted love he needs would shew.　　355
This have I heard, but yet scarce thought it true.
And whether her cleare beautie was so bright,
That it could dazel the immortall sight
Of gods, and make them for her love despaire,
I do not know; but sure the maid was faire.　　　360
Yet the faire Nymph was never seene resort
Unto the savage and the bloudy sport
Of chaste *Diana*, nor was ever wont
To bend a bow, nor ever did she hunt,
Nor did she ever strive with pretie cunning,　　　365
To overgoe her fellow Nymphs in running:
For she was the faire water-Nymph alone,
That unto chaste *Diana* was unknowne.
It is reported, that her fellowes us'd
To bid her (though the beauteous Nymph refus'd)　　370
To take, or painted quivers or a dart,
And put her lazy idlenesse apart.
Nor tooke she painted quivers, nor a dart,
Nor put her lazy idlenesse apart,
But in her cristall fountaine oft she swimmes,　　　375
And oft she washes o're her snowy limmes:
Sometimes she comb'd her soft dischevel'd hayre,
Which with a fillet tide she oft did weare:

But sometimes loose she did it hang behind,
When she was pleas'd to grace the Easterne wind: 380
For up and downe it would her tresses hurle,
And as she went, it made her loose hayre curle:
Oft in the water did she looke her face,
And oft she us'd to practise what quaint grace
Might well become her, and what comely feature   385
Might be best fitting so divine a creature.
Her skinne was with a thinne vaile overthrowne,
Through which her naked beauty clearely shone.
She us'd in this light rayment as she was,
To spread her body on the dewy grasse: 390
Sometimes by her owne fountaine as she walkes,
She nips the flowres from off the fertile stalkes,
And with a garland of the sweating vine,
Sometimes she doth her beauteous front in-twine:
But she was gathring flowres with her white hand,   395
When she beheld *Hermaphroditus* stand
By her cleare fountaine, wondring at the sight,
That there was any brooke could be so bright:
For this was the bright river where the boy
Did dye himselfe, that he could not enjoy   400
Himselfe in pleasure, nor could taste the blisses
Of his owne melting and delicious kisses.
Here did she see him, and by *Venus* law,
She did desire to have him as she saw:
But the fayre Nymph had never seene the place,   405
Where the boy was, nor his inchanting face,
But by an uncouth accident of love
Betwixt great *Phoebus* and the sonne of *Jove*,
Light-headed *Bacchus*: for upon a day,
As the boy-god was keeping on his way,   410
Bearing his Vine leaves and his Ivie bands,
To *Naxos*, where his house and temple stands,
He saw the Nymph; and seeing, he did stay,
And threw his leaves and Ivie bands away,
Thinking at first she was of heavenly birth,   415
Some goddesse that did live upon the earth,
Virgin *Diana* that so lively shone,
When she did court her sweet *Endimion*:

But he a god, at last did plainely see,
She had no marke of immortalitie.　　　　　　　　420
Unto the Nymph went the yong god of wine,
Whose head was chaf'd so with the bleeding vine,
That now, or feare or terrour had he none,
But 'gan to court her as she sate alone:
Fayrer then fayrest (thus began his speech)　　　425
Would but your radiant eye please to inrich
My eye with looking, or one glaunce to give,
Whereby my other parts might feede and live,
Or with one sight my sences to inspire,
Far livelier then the stole *Promethean* fire;　　　430
Then might I live, then by the sunny light
That should proceed from thy thrise-radiant sight,
I might survive to ages; but that missing,
(At that same word he would have faine bin kissing)
I pine, fayre Nymph: O never let me dye　　　435
For one poore glaunce from thy translucent eye,
Farre more transparent then the clearest brooke.
The Nymph was taken with his golden hooke:
Yet she turn'd backe, and would have tript away;
But *Bacchus* forc't the lovely mayd to stay,　　　440
Asking her why she struggled to be gone,
Why such a Nymph should wish to be alone?
Heaven never made her faire, that she should vaunt
She kept all beautie, it would never graunt
She should be borne so beauteous from her mother,　　445
But to reflect her beauty on another:
Then with a sweet kisse cast thy beames on mee,
And Ile reflect them backe againe on thee.
At *Naxos* stands my Temple and my Shrine,
Where I do presse the lusty swelling Vine,　　　450
There with greene Ivie shall thy head be bound,
And with the red Grape be incircled round;
There shall *Silenus* sing unto thy praise,
His drunken reeling songs and tickling layes.
Come hither, gentle Nymph. Here blusht the maid,　　455
And faine she would have gone, but yet she staid.
Bacchus perceiv'd he had o'recome the lasse,
And downe he throwes her in the dewy grasse,

And kist the helplesse Nymph upon the ground,
And would have stray'd beyond that lawful bound.   460
This saw bright *Phoebus*: for his glittering eye
Sees all that lies below the starry skye;
And for an old affection that he bore
Unto this lovely Nymph long time before,
(For he would ofttimes in his circle stand,   465
To sport himselfe upon her snowy hand)
He kept her from the sweets of *Bacchus* bed,
And 'gainst her wil he sav'd her maiden-head.
Bacchus perceiving this, apace did hie
Unto the Palace of swift *Mercury*:   470
But he did find him farre below his birth,
Drinking with theeves and catch-poles on the earth;
And they were drinking what they stole to day,
In consultation for to morrowes prey.
To him went youthfull *Bacchus*, and begun   475
To shew his cause of griefe against the Sunne,
How he bereft him of his heavenly blisses,
His sweet delights, his Nectar-flowing kisses,
And other sweeter sweetes that he had wonne,
But for the malice of the bright-fac't Sunne,   480
Intreating *Mercury* by all the love,
That had bene borne amongst the sonnes of *Jove*,
Of which they two were part, to stand his friend,
Against the god that did him so offend:
The quaint-tongu'd issue of great *Atlas* race,   485
Swift *Mercury*, that with delightfull grace,
And pleasing accents of his fayned tongue,
Hath oft reform'd a rude uncivill throng
Of mortals; that great messenger of *Jove*,
And all the meaner gods that dwell above: 490
He whose acute wit was so quicke and sharpe
In the invention of the crooked Harpe:
He that's so cunning with his jesting slights,
To steale from heavenly gods or earthly wights,
Bearing a great hate in his grieved brest,   495
Against that great commaunder of the West,
Bright-fac't *Apollo*: for upon a day,
Yong *Mercury* did steale his beasts away:

Which the great god perceiving, streight did shew
The pearcing arrowes and the fearefull bow   500
That kild great *Pithon*, and with that did threat him,
To bring his beasts againe, or he would beat him.
Which *Mercury* perceiving, unespide,
Did closely steale his arrowes from his side.
For this old grudge, he was the easlyer wonne   505
To helpe young *Bacchus* 'gainst the fierie Sunne.
And now the Sunne was in the middle way,
And had o'recome the one halfe of the day,
Scorching so hot upon the reeking sand,
That lies upon the neere *Egyptian* land,   510
That the hot people burnt e'ne from their birth,
Do creepe againe into their mother earth,
When *Mercury* did take his powerfull wand,
His charming *Cadusæus* in his hand,
And a thicke Bever which he us'd to weare,   515
When ought from *Jove* he to the *Sunne* did beare,
That did protect him from the piercing light,
Which did proceed from *Phoebus* glittring sight.
Clad in these powerfull ornaments he flies,
With out-stretcht wings up to the azure skies: 520
Where seeing *Phoebus* in his orient shrine,
He did so well revenge the god of wine,
That whil'st the Sun wonders his Chariot reeles,
The craftie god had stole away his wheeles.
Which when he did perceive, he downe did slide,   525
(Laying his glittring Coronet aside)
From the bright spangled firmament above,
To seeke the Nymph that *Bacchus* so did love,
And found her looking in her watry glasse,
To see how cleare her radiant beauty was: 530
And, for he had but little time to stay,
Because he meant to finish out his day,
At the first sight he 'gan to make his mone,
Telling her how his fiery wheeles were gone;
Promising her, if she would but obtaine   535
The wheeles, that *Mercury* had stolne, againe,
That he might end his day, she should enjoy
The heavenly sight of the most beauteous boy

That ever was. The Nymph was pleas'd with this,
Hoping to reape some unaccustom'd blisse   540
By the sweet pleasure that she should enjoy,
In the blest sight of such a melting boy.
Therefore at his request she did obtaine
The burning wheeles, that he had lost, againe:
Which when he had receiv'd, he left the land,   545
And brought them thither where his Coach did stand,
And there he set them on: for all this space,
The horses had not stirr'd from out their place.
Which when he saw, he wept and 'gan to say,
Would *Mercury* had stole my wheeles away,   550
When *Phaeton* my hare-brain'd issue tride,
What a laborious thing it was to guide
My burning chariot, then he might have pleas'd me,
And of one fathers griefe he might have eas'd me:
For then the Steeds would have obayd his will,   555
Or else at least they would have rested still.
When he had done, he tooke his whip of steele,
Whose bitter smart he made his horses feele:
For he did lash so hard, to end the day,
That he was quickly at the Westerne sea,   560
And there with *Thætis* did he rest a space:
For he did never rest in any place
Before that time: but ever since his wheeles
Were stole away, his burning chariot reeles
Tow'rds the declining of the parting day: 565
Therefore he lights and mends them in the sea.
And though the Poets fayne, that *Jove* did make
A treble night for faire *Alcmena's* sake,
That he might sleepe securely with his love;
Yet sure the long night was unknowne to *Jove*:   570
But the Sunnes wheeles one day disordred more,
Were thrise as long amending as before.
Now was the Sunne inviron'd with the Sea,
Cooling his watrie tresses as he lay,
And in dread *Neptunes* kingdome while he sleeps,   575
Faire *Thætis* clips him in the watry deeps,
The *Mayre-maids* and the *Tritons* of the West,
Strayning their voyces, to make *Titan* rest.

And while the blacke night with her pitchie hand,
Tooke just possession of the swarfie land: 580
He spent the darkesome howres in this delight,
Giving his power up to the gladsome night:
For ne're before he was so truely blest,
To take an houre or one poore minutes rest.
But now the burning god this pleasure feeles,   585
By reason of his newly crazed wheeles,
There must he stay untill lame *Vulcan* send
The fierie wheeles which he had tooke to mend.
Now al the night the Smith so hard had wrought,
That ere the Sunne could wake, his wheeles were brought.
Titan being pleas'd with rest, and not to rise,   591
And loth to open yet his slumbring eyes:
And yet perceiving how the longing sight
Of mortals wayted for his glittring light,
He sent *Aurora* from him to the skie,   595
To give a glimsing to each mortall eye.
Aurora much asham'd of that same place
That great *Apollos* light was wont to grace,
Finding no place to hide her shamefull head,
Paynted her chaste cheeks with a blushing red,   600
Which ever since remain'd upon her face,
In token of her new receiv'd disgrace:
Therefore she not so white as she had beene,
Lothing of ev'ry mortall to be seene,
No sooner can the rosie fingred morne   605
Kisse ev'ry flowre that by her dew is borne,
But from her golden window she doth peepe,
When the most part of earthly creatures sleepe.
By this, bright *Titan* opened had his eyes,
And 'gan to jerke his horses through the skies,   610
And taking in his hand his fierie whip,
He made *Æous* and swift *Æthon* skip
So fast, that straight he dazled had the sight
Of faire *Aurora*, glad to see his light.
And now the Sunne in all his fierie haste,   615
Did call to mind his promise lately past,
And all the vowes and othes that he did passe
Unto faire *Salmacis*, the beauteous lasse:

G

For he had promis'd her she should enjoy
So lovely faire, and such a well shap't boy,   620
As ne're before his owne all-seeing eye
Saw from his bright seate in the starry skye:
Remembring this, he sent the boy that way,
Where the cleare fountain of the fayre Nymph lay.
There was he comne to seeke some pleasing brooke.   625
No sooner came he, but the Nymph was strooke:
And though she hasted to imbrace the boy,
Yet did the Nymph awhile deferre her joy,
Till she had bound up her loose flagging haire,
And ordred well the garments she did weare,   630
Fayning her count'nance with a lovers care,
And did deserve to be accounted fayre.
And thus much spake she while the boy abode:
O boy, most worthy to be thought a god,
Thou mayst inhabit in the glorious place   635
Of gods, or maist proceed from humane race:
Thou mayst be *Cupid*, or the god of wine,
That lately woo'd me with the swelling vine:
But whosoe're thou art, O happy he,
That was so blest, to be a sire to thee;   640
Thy happy mother is most blest of many,
Blessed thy sisters, if her wombe bare any,
Both fortunate, and O thrise happy shee,
Whose too much blessed brests gave suck to thee:
If any wife with thy sweet bed be blest,   645
O, she is farre more happy then the rest;
If thou hast any, let my sport be sto'ne,
Or else let me be she, if thou hast none.
Here did she pause awhile, and then she sayd,
Be not obdurate to a silly mayd.   650
A flinty heart within a snowy brest,
Is like base mold lockt in a golden chest:
They say the eye's the Index of the heart,
And shewes th'affection of eche inward part:
There love playes lively, there the little god   655
Hath a cleare cristall Palace of abode.
O barre him not from playing in thy heart,
That sports himselfe upon eche outward part.

Thus much she spake, and then her tongue was husht.
At her loose speach *Hermaphroditus* blusht: 660
He knew not what love was, yet love did shame him,
Making him blush, and yet his blush became him:
Then might a man his shamefast colour see,
Like the ripe apple on the sunny tree,
Or Ivory dide o're with a pleasing red,   665
Or like the pale Moone being shadowed.
By this, the Nymph recover'd had her tongue,
That to her thinking lay in silence long,
And sayd, Thy cheeke is milde, O be thou so,
Thy cheeke, saith I, then do not answere no,   670
Thy cheeke doth shame, then doe thou shame, she sayd,
It is a mans shame to deny a mayd.
Thou look'st to sport with *Venus* in her towre,
And be belov'd of every heavenly powre.
Men are but mortals, so are women too,   675
Why should your thoughts aspire more then ours doo?
For sure they doe aspire: Else could a youth,
Whose count'nance is so full of spotlesse truth,
Be so relentlesse to a virgins tongue?
Let me be woo'd by thee but halfe so long,   680
With halfe those tearmes doe but my love require,
And I will easly graunt thee thy desire.
Ages are bad, when men become so slow,
That poore unskilfull mayds are forc't to woo.
Her radiant beauty and her subtill arte   685
So deepely strooke *Hermaphroditus* heart,
That she had wonne his love, but that the light
Of her translucent eyes did shine too bright:
For long he look'd upon the lovely mayd,
And at the last *Hermaphroditus* sayd,   690
How should I love thee, when I doe espie
A farre more beauteous Nymph hid in thy eye?
When thou doost love, let not that Nymph be nie thee;
Nor when thou woo'st, let that same Nymph be by thee:
Or quite obscure her from thy lovers face,   695
Or hide her beauty in a darker place.
By this, the Nymph perceiv'd he did espie
None but himselfe reflected in her eye,

And, for himselfe no more she meant to shew him,
She shut her eyes and blind-fold thus did woo him: 700
Fayre boy, thinke not thy beauty can dispence
With any payne due to a bad offence;
Remember how the gods punisht that boy
That scorn'd to let a beauteous Nymph enjoy
Her long wisht pleasure; for the peevish elfe,   705
Lov'd of all others, needs would love himselfe.
So mayst thou love, perhaps thou mayst be blest,
By graunting to a lucklesse Nymphs request:
Then rest awhile with me amid these weeds.
The Sunne that sees all, sees not lovers deeds;   710
Phoebus is blind when love-sports are begun,
And never sees untill their sports be done:
Beleeve me, boy, thy blood is very stayd,
That art so loth to kisse a youthfull mayd.
Wert thou a mayd, and I a man, Ile show thee,   715
With what a manly boldnesse I could woo thee:
Fayrer then loves Queene, thus I would begin,
Might not my over-boldnesse be a sinne,
I would intreat this favour, if I could,
Thy rosiat cheeke a little to behold: 720
Then would I beg a touch, and then a kisse,
And then a lower; yet a higher blisse:
Then would I aske what *Jove* and *Læda* did,
When like a Swan the craftie god was hid?
What came he for? why did he there abide?   725
Surely I thinke hee did not come to chide:
He came to see her face, to talke, and chat,
To touch, to kisse: came he for nought but that?
Yes, something else: what was it he would have?
That which all men of maydens ought to crave.   730
This sayd, her eye-lids wide she did display:
But in this space the boy was runne away:
The wanton speeches of the lovely lasse
Forc't him for shame to hide him in the grasse.
When she perceiv'd she could not see him neere her,   735
When she had cal'd, and yet he could not heare her,
Looke how when *Autumne* comes, a little space
Paleth the red blush of the Summers face,

Tearing the leaves the Summers covering,
Three months in weaving by the curious spring,   740
Making the grasse his greene locks go to wracke,
Tearing each ornament from off his backe;
So did she spoyle the garments she did weare,
Tearing whole ounces of her golden hayre:
She thus deluded of her longed blisse,   745
With much adoo at last she uttred this:
Why wert thou bashfull, boy? Thou hast no part
Shewes thee to be of such a female heart.
His eye is gray, so is the mornings eye,
That blusheth alwayes when the day is nye.   750
Then his gray eye's the cause: that cannot be:
The grey-ey'd morne is farre more bold then he:
For with a gentle dew from heavens bright towre,
It gets the mayden-head of ev'ry flowre.
I would to God, he were the rosiat morne,   755
And I a flowre from out the earth new borne!
His face is smooth; *Narcissus* face was so,
And he was carelesse of a sad Nymphs woe.
Then that's the cause; and yet that cannot be:
Youthfull *Narcissus* was more bold then he,   760
Because he dide for love, though of his shade:
This boy nor loves himselfe, nor yet a mayd.
Besides, his glorious eye is wondrous bright;
So is the fierie and all-seeing light
Of *Phoebus*, who at ev'ry mornings birth   765
Blusheth for shame upon the sullen earth.
Then that's the cause; and yet that cannot be:
The fierie Sunne is farre more bold then he;
He nightly kisseth *Thætis* in the sea:
All know the story of *Leucothoë*.   770
His cheeke is red; so is the fragrant Rose,
Whose ruddie cheeke with over-blushing gloes:
Then that's the cause; and yet that cannot bee:
Eche blushing Rose is farre more bold then he,
Whose boldnesse may be plainely seene in this,   775
The ruddy Rose is not asham'd to kisse;
For alwayes when the day is new begun,
The spreading Rose will kisse the morning Sun.

This sayd, hid in the grasse she did espie him,
And stumbling with her will, she fel down by him,　　780
And with her wanton talke, because he woo'd not,
Beg'd that, which he poore novice understood not:
And, for she could not get a greater blisse,
She did intreat at least a sisters kisse;
But still the more she did the boy beseech,　　785
The more he powted at her wanton speech.
At last the Nymph began to touch his skin,
Whiter then mountaine snow hath ever bin,
And did in purenesse that cleare spring surpasse,
Wherein *Actæon* saw th'Arcadian lasse.　　790
Thus did she dally long, till at the last,
In her moyst palme she lockt his white hand fast:
Then in her hand his wrest she 'gan to close,
When through his pulses strait the warme bloud gloes,
Whose youthfull musike fanning *Cupids* fire,　　795
In her warme brest kindled a fresh desire.
Then did she lift her hand unto his brest,
A part as white and youthfull as the rest,
Where, as his flowry breath still comes and goes,
She felt his gentle heart pant through his clothes.　　800
At last she tooke her hand from off that part,
And sayd, It panted like anothers heart.
Why should it be more feeble, and lesse bold?
Why should the bloud about it be more cold?
Nay sure, that yeelds, onely thy tongue denyes,　　805
And the true fancy of thy heart belyes.
Then did she lift her hand unto his chin,
And prays'd the prety dimpling of his skin:
But straight his chin she 'gan to overslip,
When she beheld the rednesse of his lip;　　810
And sayd, thy lips are soft, presse them to mine,
And thou shalt see they are as soft as thine.
Then would she faine have gone unto his eye,
But still his ruddy lip standing so nie,
Drew her hand backe, therefore his eye she mist,　　815
'Ginning to claspe his neck, and would have kist;
But then the boy did struggle to be gone,
Vowing to leave her and that place alone.

But then bright *Salmacis* began to feare,
And sayd, Fayre stranger, I wil leave thee here	820
Amid these pleasant places all alone.
So turning back, she fayned to be gone;
But from his sight she had no power to passe,
Therefore she turn'd, and hid her in the grasse,
When to the ground bending her snow-white knee,	825
The glad earth gave new coates to every tree.
He then supposing he was all alone,
(Like a young boy that is espy'd of none)
Runnes here, and there, then on the bankes doth looke,
Then on the cristall current of the brooke,	830
Then with his foote he toucht the silver streames,
Whose drowzy waves made musike in their dreames,
And, for he was not wholy in, did weepe,
Talking alowd and babbling in their sleepe:
Whose pleasant coolenesse when the boy did feele,	835
He thrust his foote downe lower to the heele:
O'recome with whose sweet noyse, he did begin
To strip his soft clothes from his tender skin,
When strait the scorching Sun wept teares of brine,
Because he durst not touch him with his shine,	840
For feare of spoyling that same Iv'ry skin,
Whose whitenesse he so much delighted in;
And then the Moone, mother of mortall ease,
Would fayne have come from the *Antipodes*,
To have beheld him naked as he stood,	845
Ready to leape into the silver flood;
But might not: for the lawes of heaven deny,
To shew mens secrets to a womans eye:
And therefore was her sad and gloomy light
Confin'd unto the secret-keeping night.	850
When beauteous *Salmacis* awhile had gaz'd
Upon his naked corps, she stood amaz'd,
And both her sparkling eyes burnt in her face,
Like the bright Sunne reflected in a glasse:
Scarce can she stay from running to the boy,	855
Scarce can she now deferre her hoped joy;
So fast her youthfull bloud playes in her vaynes,
That almost mad, she scarce her selfe contaynes.

When young *Hermaphroditus* as he stands,
Clapping his white side with his hollow hands, 860
Leapt lively from the land, whereon he stood,
Into the mayne part of the cristall flood.
Like Iv'ry then his snowy body was,
Or a white Lilly in a cristall glasse.
Then rose the water-Nymph from where she lay, 865
As having wonne the glory of the day,
And her light garments cast from off her skin.
Hee's mine, she cry'd; and so leapt spritely in.
The flattering Ivy who did ever see
Inclaspe the huge trunke of an aged tree, 870
Let him behold the young boy as he stands,
Inclaspt in wanton *Salmacis's* hands,
Betwixt those Iv'ry armes she lockt him fast,
Striving to get away, till at the last,
Fondling, she sayd, why striv'st thou to be gone? 875
Why shouldst thou so desire to be alone?
Thy cheeke is never fayre, when none is by:
For what is red and white, but to the eye?
And for that cause the heavens are darke at night,
Because all creatures close their weary sight; 880
For there's no mortall can so earely rise,
But still the morning waytes upon his eyes.
The earely-rising and soone-singing Larke
Can never chaunt her sweete notes in the darke;
For sleepe she ne're so little or so long, 885
Yet still the morning will attend her song.
All creatures that beneath bright *Cinthia* be,
Have appetite unto society;
The overflowing waves would have a bound
Within the confines of the spacious ground, 890
And all their shady currents would be plaste
In hollow of the solitary vaste,
But that they lothe to let their soft streames sing,
Where none can heare their gentle murmuring.
Yet still the boy regardlesse what she sayd, 895
Struggled apace to overswimme the mayd.
Which when the Nymph perceiv'd, she 'gan to say,
Struggle thou mayst, but never get away.

So graunt, just gods, that never day may see
The separation twixt this boy and mee.   900
The gods did heare her pray'r and feele her woe;
And in one body they began to grow.
She felt his youthfull bloud in every vaine;
And he felt hers warme his cold brest againe.
And ever since was womans love so blest,   905
That it will draw bloud from the strongest brest.
Nor man nor mayd now could they be esteem'd:
Neither, and either, might they well be deem'd,
When the young boy *Hermaphroditus* sayd,
With the set voyce of neither man nor mayd,   910
Swift *Mercury*, thou author of my life,
And thou my mother *Vulcans* lovely wife,
Let your poore offsprings latest breath be blest,
In but obtayning this his last request,
Grant that who e're heated by *Phoebus* beames,   915
Shall come to coole him in these silver streames,
May nevermore a manly shape retaine,
But halfe a virgine may returne againe.
His parents hark'ned to his last request,
And with that great power they the fountaine blest.   920
And since that time who in that fountaine swimmes,
A mayden smoothnesse seyzeth halfe his limmes.

FINIS

Willobie His Avisa,

or

The true picture of a modest Maide,
and of a chast and constant
wife

HENRY WILLOBY (1594)

CANTO I

Let martiall men, of Mars his praise,
Sound warlike trumpe: let lust-led youth,
Of wicked love, write wanton layes;
Let sheepeheards sing, their sheepe coates ruth:
   The wiser sort, confesse it plaine,   5
   That these have spent good time in vaine.

My sleepie Muse that wakes but now,
Nor now had wak't if one had slept,
To vertues praise hath past her vow,
To paint the Rose which grace hath kept,   10
   Of sweetest Rose, that still doth spring,
   Of vertues birde my Muse must sing.

The birde that doth resemble right,
The Turtles faith in constant love,
The faith that first her promise plight;   15
No change, nor chance could once remove:
   This have I tri'd; This dare I trust,
   And sing the truth, I will, I must.

Afflicted *Susans* spotlesse thought,
Intis't by lust to sinfull crime,   20
To lasting fame her name hath brought,
Whose praise incounters endlesse time:

I sing of one whose beauties warre,
For trials passe *Susanna's* farre.

The wandring Greekes renowmed mate,   25
That still withstoode such hote assayes,
Of raging lust whose doubtfull state,
Sought strong refuge, from strange delayes,
   For fierce assaults and tryals rare,
   With this my Nimph may not compare.   30

Hote tryals try where Golde be pure,
The Diamond daunts the sharpest edge,
Light chaffe, fierce flames may not indure,
All quickly leape the lowly hedge,
   The object of my Muse hath past   35
   Both force and flame, yet stands she fast.

Though Egle-eyde this bird appeare,
Not blusht at beames of Phœbus raies:
Though Faulkcon wing'd to pearce the aire,
Whose high-pla'st hart no feare dismaies: 40
   Yet sprang she not from Egles nest,
   But Turtle-bred, loves Turtle best.

At wester side of Albions Ile,
Where Austine pitcht his Monkish tent,
Where Sheapheards sing, where Muses smile,   45
The graces met with one consent,
   To frame each one in sundry parte,
   Some cunning worke to shew their arte.

First *Venus* fram'd a luring eye,
A sweete aspect, and comly grace;   50
There did the Rose and Lillie lie,
That bravely deckt a smiling face,
   Here Cupids mother bent her wil,
   In this to shew her utmost skill.

Then *Pallas* gave a reaching head,   55
With deepe conceites, and passing wit,

A setled mind, not fancie-led,
Abhorring Cupids frantique fit,
  With modest lookes, and blushing cheekes,
  A filed tongue which none mislikes.   60

Diana deckt the remnant partes
With fewture brave, that nothing lacke,
A quiver full of pearcing Darts,
She gave her hanging at her backe;
  And in her hand a Golden shaft,   65
  To conquer Cupids creeping craft.

This done they come to take the view,
Of novell worke, of perelesse frame;
Amongst them three, contention grew,
But yet *Diana* gave the name,   70
  Avisa shall she called be,
  The chiefe attendant still on me.

When *Juno* view'd her luring grace,
Olde *Juno* blusht to see a new,
She fear'd least Jove would like this face,   75
And so perhaps might play untrew,
  They all admir'd so sweete a sight,
  They all envide so rare a wight.

When *Juno* came to give her wealth,
(Which wanting beautie, wants her life)   80
She cryde, this face needes not my pelffe,
Great riches sow the seedes of strife:
  I doubt not, some Olympian power
  Will fill her lap, with Golden shower.

This jealous *Juno* faintly said,   85
As halfe misdeeming wanton Jove,
But chast *Diana* tooke the maide,
Such new-bred qualmes quite to remove:
  O jealous envie, filthie beast,
  For envie *Juno* gave her least.   90

In lew of *Juno's* Golden parte,
Diana gave her double grace;
A chast desire, a constant heart,
Disdaine of love in fawning face,
    A face, and eye, that should intice   95
    A smile, that should deceive the wise.

A sober tongue that should allure,
And draw great numbers to the fielde;
A flintie hart, that should indure
All fierce assaults, and never yeelde,   100
    And seeming oft as though she would;
    Yet fardest off when that she should.

Can filthy sinke yeelde holsome aire,
Or vertue from a vice proceede?
Can envious hart, or jealous feare   105
Repell the things that are decreed?
    By envie though she lost her thrift,
    She got by grace a better gift.

Not farre from thence there lyes a vale,
A rosie vale in pleasant plaine;   110
The Nimphes frequent this happie dale,
Olde Helicon revives againe;
    Here Muses sing, here Satyres play,
    Here mirth resounds both night and day.

At East of this, a Castle stands,   115
By auncient sheepheards built of olde,
And lately was in sheepheards hands,
Though now by brothers bought and solde,
    At west side springs a Christall well;
    There doth this chast *Avisa* dwell.   120

And there she dwels in publique eye,
Shut up from none that list to see;
She answeres all that list to try,
Both high and low of each degree:
    But few that come, but feele her dart,   125
    And try her well ere they depart.

They try'd her hard in hope to gaine,
Her milde behaviour breeds their hope,
Their hope assures them to obtaine,
Till having runne their witlesse scope;   130
   They find their vice by vertue crost,
   Their foolish words, and labour lost.

This strange effect, that all should crave,
Yet none obtaine their wrong desire,
A secret gift, that nature gave,   135
To feele the frost, amidst the fire:
   Blame not this Dians Nimphe too much,
   Sith God by nature made her such.

Let all the graces now be glad,
That fram'd a grace that past them all,   140
Let *Juno* be no longer sad;
Her wanton Jove hath had a fall;
   Ten yeares have tryde this constant dame,
   And yet she holds a spotles fame.

Along this plaine there lyes a downe,   145
Where sheepheards feed their frisking flocke;
Her Sire the Maior of the towne,
A lovely shout of auncient stocke,
   Full twentie yeares she lived a maide,
   And never was by man betrayde.   150

At length by *Juno's* great request,
Diana loth, yet gave her leave,
Of flowring yeares, to spend the rest
In wed-locke band; but yet receive,
   Quod she, this gift; Thou virgin pure,   155
   Chast wife in wed-locke shalt indure.

O happie man that shall enjoy
A blessing of so rare a price;
That frees the hart from such annoy;
As often doth torment the wise,   160
   A loving wife unto her death,
   With full assurance of her faith.

When flying fame began to tell,
How beauties wonder was returnd,
From countrie hils, in towne to dwell,   165
With special gifts and grace adornd,
 Of sutors store there might you see;
 And some were men, of high degree.

But wisdom wild her chuse her mate,
If that she lov'd a happy life,   170
That might be equall to her state,
To crop the sprigges of future strife;
 Where rich in grace, wher sound in health,
 Most men do wed, but for the wealth.

Though jealous *Juno* had denyde   175
This happy wench, great store of pelffe:
Yet is she now in wedlocke tyde,
To one that loves her as himselfe,
 So thus they live, and thus they love;
 And God doth blesse them from above.   180

This rare seene bird, this Phœnix sage
Yeelds matter to my drowsie pen,
The mirror of this sinneful age,
That gives us beasts in shapes of men,
 Such beasts as still continue sinne,   185
 Where age doth leave, there youths begin.

Our English soile, to Sodoms sinke
Excessive sinne transformd of late,
Of foule deceite the lothsome linke,
Hath worne all faith cleane out of date,   190
 The greatest sinnes mongst greatest sort,
 Are counted now but for a sport.

Old Asues grandame is restor'd;
Her grovie Caves are new refinde:
The monster Idoll is ador'd   195
By lustie dames of Macha's kinde:
 They may not let this worship fall,
 Although they leese their honours all.

Our Moab Cozbies cast no feare,
To Jet in view of every eye,   200
Their gainelesse games they holde so deere,
They follow must, although they dye.
   For why? the sword that Phineas wore,
   Is broken now, and cuts no more.

My tender Muse, that never try'd   205
Her joynted wings till present time,
At first the perelesse bird espy'd,
That mounts aloft, devoide of crime;
   Though high she sore, yet will I trie,
   Where I her passage can discry.   210

Her high conceites, her constant minde;
Her sober talke, her stout denies;
Her chast advise, here shall you find;
Her fierce assaults, her milde replies,
   Her dayly fight with great and small,   215
   Yet constant vertue conquers all.

The first that saies to plucke the Rose,
That scarce appear'd without the bud,
With Gorgeous shewes of Golden glose,
To sow the seeds that were not good: 220
   Suppose it were some noble man
   That tride her thus, and thus began.

The first triall of AVISA, before she was married, by a Noble man: under which is represented a warning to all young maids of every degree, that they beware of the alluring intisements of great men.

CANT. II

Now is the time, if thou be wise,   NOB.
Thou happie maide, if thou canst see,
Thy happiest time, take good advise,
Good fortune laughs, be rulde by me:
   Be rulde by me, and her's my faith,   5
   No Golde shall want thee till thy death.

Thou knowest my power, thou seest my might,
Thou knowest I can maintaine thee well,
And helpe thy friends unto their right;
Thou shalt with me for ever dwell,   10
   My secret friend thou shalt remaine,
   And all shall turne to thy great gaine.

Thou seest thy parents meane estate,
That barres the hope of greater chance;
And if thou prove not wise too late,   15
Thou maist thy selfe, and thine advance:
   Repulse not fondly this good hap,
   That now lies offred in thy lap.

Abandon feare that bars consent,
Repel the shame that feares a blot,   20
Let wisdome way what faith is ment,
That all may praise thy happie lot;
   Thinke not I seeke thy lives disgrace;
   For thou shalt have a Ladies place.

Thou art the first my fancie chose,   25
I know thy friends will like it well:
This friendly fault to none disclose,
And what thou thinkst, blush not to tell,
   Thou seest my love, thou know'st my mind,
   Now let me feele, what grace I find.   30

CANT. III

Your Honours place, your riper yeares,   AVISA
Might better frame some graver talkes:
Midst sunnie rayes, this cloud appeares;
Sweete Roses grow on prickly stalkes:
   If I conceive, what you request,   5
   You aime at that I most detest.

My tender age that wants advice,
And craves the aide of sager guides,
Should rather learne for to be wise,
To stay my steps from slipperie slides;   10

Then thus to sucke, then thus to tast
The poys'ned sap, that kils at last.

I wonder what your wisdome ment,
Thus to assault a silly maide:
Some simple wench, might chance consent,   15
By false resembling shewes betraide:
  I have by grace a native shield,
  To lewd assaults that cannot yeeld,

I am too base to be your wife,
You choose me for your secret frend;   20
That is to lead a filthy life,
Whereon attends a fearefull end:
  Though I be poore, I tell you plaine,
  To be your whore, I flat disdaine.

Your high estate, your silver shrines,   25
Repleate with wind and filthy stinke;
Your glittering gifts, your golden mynes,
May force some fooles perhaps to shrinke:
  But I have learnd that sweetest bayt,
  Oft shrowds the hooke of most desayt.   30

What great good hap, what happie time,
Your proffer brings, let yeelding maids
Of former age, which thought to clime,
To highest tops of earthly aids,
  Come backe a while, and let them tell,   35
  Where wicked lives have ended well.

Shores wife, a Princes secret frend,
Faire *Rosomond*, a Kings delight:
Yet both have found a gastly end,
And fortunes friends, felt fortunes spight: 40
  What greater joyes, could fancie frame,
  Yet now we see, their lasting shame.

If princely pallace have no power,
To shade the shame of secret sinne,

If blacke reproch such names devoure, 45
What gaine, or glory can they winne,
    That tracing tracts of shamelesse trade,
    A hate of God, and man are made?

This onely vertue must advaunce
My meane estate to joyfull blisse: 50
For she that swaies dame vertues launce,
Of happie state can never misse,
    But they that hope to gaine by vice,
    Shall surely prove too late unwise.

The roote of woe is fond desire, 55
That never feeles her selfe content:
But wanton wing'd, will needes aspire,
To finde the thing, she may lament,
    A courtly state, a Ladies place,
    My former life will quite deface. 60

Such strange conceites may hap prevaile,
With such as love such strong desayts,
But I am taught such qualmes to quaile,
And flee such sweete alluring bayts,
    The witlesse Flie playes with the flame, 65
    Till she be scorched with the same.

You long to know what grace you find,
In me, perchance, more then you would,
Except you quickly change your mind,
I find in you, lesse then I should, 70
    Move this no more, use no reply,
    I'le keepe mine honour till I die.

CANT. IIII

Alas, good soule, and will yee so?   NOB.
You will be chast *Diana's* mate;
Till time have wove the web of woe,
Then to repent wil be too late,
    You shew your selfe so foole-precise, 5
    That I can hardly thinke you wise,

You sprang belike from Noble stocke,
That stand so much upon your fame,
You hope to stay upon the rocke,
That will preserve a faultlesse name,   10
    But while you hunt for needelesse praise,
    You loose the Prime of sweetest daies.

A merry time, when countrie maides
Shall stand (forsooth) upon their garde;
And dare controll the Courtiers deedes,   15
At honours gate that watch and warde;
    When Milke maids shal their pleasures flie,
    And on their credits must relie.

Ah silly wench, take not a pride,
Though thou my raging fancie move,   20
Thy betters far, if they were try'd,
Would faine accept my proffered love;
    T'was for thy good, if thou hadst wist,
    For I may have whome ere I list.

But here thy folly may appeare,   25
Art thou preciser then a Queene:
Queene *Joane* of Naples did not feare,
To quite mens love, with love againe:
    And *Messalina*, t'is no newes,
    Was dayly seene to haunt the stewes.   30

And *Cleopatra*, prince of Nile,
With more then one was wont to play:
And yet she keepes her glorious stile,
And fame that never shall decaie,
    What need'st thou then to feare of shame,   35
    When Queenes and Nobles use the same?

CANT. V

Needs must the sheepe strake all awrie,   AVISA
Whose sheepheards wander from their way:
Needes must the sickly patient die,
Whose Doctor seekes his lives decay:

Needs must the people well be taught,   5
Whose chiefest leaders all are naught.

Such lawlesse guides Gods people found,
When Moab maides allur'd their fall;
They sought no salve to cure this wound,
Till God commaunds, to hange them all;   10
    For wicked life, a shamefull end
    To wretched men, the Lord doth send.

Was earth consumde with wreakfull waves?
Did Sodom burne and after sinke?
What sinne is that, which vengaunce craves;   15
If wicked lust no sinne we thinke?
    O blind conceites! O filthy breath!
    That drawes us headlong to our death.

If death be due to every sinne,
How can I then be too precise?   20
Where pleasures end, if paine beginne,
What neede have we, then to be wise?
    They weave indeed the web of woe,
    That from the Lord doe yeeld to goe.

I will remember whence I came,   25
I hunt not for this worldly praise,
I long to keepe a blamelesse fame,
And constant hart gainst hard assaies:
    If this be folly, want of skill,
    I will remaine thus foolish still.   30

The blindfold rage of Heathen Queenes,
Or rather queanes that know not God,
Gods heavie judgements tried since,
And felt the waight of angry rod;
    God save me from that Sodomes crie,   35
    Whose deadly sting shall never die.

CANT. VI

Forgive me wench, I did mistake,   NOB.
I little thought, that you could preach,
All worldly joyes, you must forsake:
For so your great Divines doe teach,
    But yet beware, be not too bold,   5
    A yongling Saint, a Devill old.

Well wanton well, thou art but yong,
This is the error of thy youth,
Thou wilt repent this faith ere long,
And see too late (perhaps) the truth;   10
    And they that seeme so pure at first,
    Are often found in proofe the worst.

Thy youth and beautie will not last,
For sicknes one, the other age
May captive take, when both are past,   15
You may have leasure to be sage,
    The time will come, if these retire,
    The worst will scorne that I desire.

Of chast renowme, you seeke the praise,
You build your hope above the ayre,   20
When wonders last not twentie daies,
What need you rusticke rumors feare?
    Esteeme not words above thy wealth,
    Which must procure thy credits health.

And yet in truth I can not see,   25
From whence such great discredit growes,
To live in spight of every eye,
And swim in silkes, and bravest shewes,
    To take the choise of daintiest meate,
    And see thy betters stand and waite.   30

These grave respects breede pleasures bane,
Thy youthly yeares for joyes crave,
And fading credit hath his wane,
That none to thee doth shine so brave:

That smokie fame which likes thee best,   35
The wisest have esteemed least.

CANT. VII

Well now I see, why Christ commends,   AVISA
To loving mates the Serpents wit,
That stops his eares, and so defends
His hart, from luring sounds unfit,
    If you your madnes still bewraye,   5
    I'le stop my eares, or goe my way.

Ulisses wise, yet dar'd not stay
The tising sound of Syrens song:
What fancie then doth me betray,
That thinke my selfe, so wise and strong;   10
    That dare to heare, what you dare speake,
    And hope for strength, when you be weake?

My wisdome is the living Lord,
That gives me grace which nature wants,
That holds my feate from waies abhord,   15
And in my hart good motions plants:
    With him I dare to bide the field,
    Strive while you list, I can not yeeld.

Fond favour failes, the time will passe,
All earthly pleasures have their end,   20
We see not that, which sometime was,
Nor that which future times will send:
    You say the truth, remember this,
    And then confesse, you stray amisse.

The shorter time, the greater care,   25
Are pleasures vaine? the lesse delight,
Are daungers nye? why then beware,
From base affections take your flight,
    Thinke God a reckning will require,
    And strive to quaile this bad desire.   30

To swim in silkes, and brave aray,
Is that you thinke which women love,
That leads poore maides so oft astray,
That are not garded from above?
  But this I know, that know not all,   35
  Such wicked pride, will have a fall.

CANT. VIII

NOB.

Alas the feare, alas the fall,
And what's the fall, that you so feare?
To tosse good fortunes golden ball,
And gaine the goale I prize so deare,
  I doubt least these your needlesse feares, 5
  Will bar good hap, from witlesse yeares.

Thy age experience wants I see,
And lacking tryall art afraid,
Least ventring farre to credit me,
Our secret dealings might be wrayd;   10
  What then doth not my mightie name,
  Suffice to sheeld thy fact from shame?

Who dares to stirre, who dares to speake,
Who dares our dealings to reprove?
Though some suspect, yet none will creake, 15
Or once controll thy worthy love;
  My might will stand for thy defence,
  And quite thee cleare from great offence.

Who sees our face, knowes not our facts,
Though we our sport in secret use,   20
Thy cheekes will not bewray thy acts,
But rather blushing make excuse:
  If thou wilt yeeld, here is my faith,
  I'le keepe it secret till thy death.

To seeme as chast, let that suffice,   25
Although indeed thou be not so,

Thus deale our women that are wise,
And let thy godly Doctors go,
   Still faine as though thou godly art,
   It is inough, who knowes thy hart? 30

Let not the idle vulgar voice,
Of fained credit witch thee so,
To force thee leave this happie choise,
And flying pleasure live in woe;
   If thou refuse, assure thy mind, 35
   The like of this shalt never find.

CANT. IX

AVISA

Let that word stand, let that be true,
I doe refuse and so doe still,
God shield me from your cursed crew,
That thus are led by beastly will,
   It grieves my hart, that I doe find 5
   In Noble bloud so base a mind.

On worldly feare, you thinke I stand,
Or fame that may my shame resound,
No Sir, I feare his mightie hand,
That will both you and me confound, 10
   His feare it is that makes me stay
   My wandring steps from wicked way.

Who dares, say you, our facts unfold?
Ev'n he that mightie Kings can tame,
And he that Princes hath controld, 15
He dares provide a mightie shame,
   What fence have you for to withstand
   His firie plagues, and hevie hand?

Though *Samson* queld the Lyons rage,
Though *Solomon*, a mightie King, 20
Yet when to sinne their harts they gage,
On both doth God confusion bring,

How can you then his wrath avoid,
That you and yours be not destroid?

He sees our facts, he viewes our deeds,   25
Although we sinne in secret place,
A guiltie conscience alwaies bleeds:
My faults will shew upon my face,
   My cheekes will blush, when I doe sin;
   Let all men know, when I begin.   30

To seeme as chast, and not to be,
To beare a shew, and yet to faine,
Is this the love, you beare to me,
To damne my soule in lasting paine?
   If this the best you have to say,   35
   Pray give me leave, to goe my way.

CANT. X

NOB.

Well then I see, you have decreed,
And this decree must light on mee:
Unhappie Lillie loves a weed,
That gives no sent, that yeelds no glee,
   Thou art the first I ever tride,   5
   Shall I at first be thus denide?

My haplesse hap, fell much awrie,
To fix my fancies prime delight,
In haggard Hauke that mounts so hie,
That checkes the lure, and Fawkners sight;   10
   But sore you hie, or flie you low,
   Stoupe needs you must, before you goe.

Your modest speech is not amisse,
Your maidens blush becomes you well;
Now will I see how sweete you kisse,   15
And so my purpose farder tell;
   Your coye lookes and trickes are vaine,
   I will no nay, and that is plaine.

Thou must perforce be well content,
To let me win thee with thy will;   20
Thy chiefest friends have giv'n consent,
And therefore thinke, it is not ill,
  Abandon all thy fond delay;
  And marke this well, that I shall say.

My house, my hart, my land, my life,   25
My credit to thy care I give:
And if thou list to be a wife,
In shew of honest fame to live;
  I'le fit thee one, shall beare the cloke,
  And be a chimnie for the smoke.   30

But say the word, it shall be don,
And what thou list, or what thou crave,
What so be lost, what ever won,
Shall nothing want, that thou wilt have,
  Thou shalt have all, what wilt thou more,   35
  Which never woman had before.

Here's fortie Angels to begin;
A little pledge of great good will,
To buy thee lace, to buy a pin;
I will be carefull of thee still: 40
  If youth be quaild, if I be old,
  I can supply that with my gold.

Silke gownes and velvet shalt thou have,
With hoods and cauls, fit for thy head;
Of goldsmithes worke a border brave,   45
A chaine of golde ten double spread;
  And all the rest shall answere this,
  My purse shall see that nothing misse.

Two wayting maides, attendant still,
Two serving men, foure geldings prest,   50
Go where you list, ride where you will,
No jealous thought shal me molest;
  Two hundreth pounds I doe intend,
  To give thee yearely for to spend.

Of this I will assurance make,   55
To some good friend, whom thou wilt chuse
That this in trust from me shall take,
Whiie thou dost live, unto thy use;
    A thousand markes, to thee give I,
    And all my Jewels when I die.   60

This will I doe, what ever chance,
I'le shortly send, and fetch thee hence;
Thy chiefest friends I will advance,
And leave them cause of no offence,
    For all this same, I onely crave   65
    But thy good-will, that let me have.

A modest maide is loth to say,
In open words, she doth consent,
Till gentle force doe breake the stay,
Come on mine owne, and be content,   70
    Possesse me of my loves desire,
    And let me tast that I require.

CANT. XI

AVISA

Hand off my Lord, this will not serve,
Your wisdome wanders much awrie,
From reasons rule thus farre to swarve,
I'le never yeeld, I'le rather die,
    Except you leave, and so depart,   5
    This knife shall sticke within your hart.

Is this the love, your franticke fit
Did so pretend in glosing shew?
Are these your waies, is this your wit,
To tice and force poore maidens so?   10
    You strive in vaine, by raging lust,
    To gaine consent, or make me trust.

For who can trust your flattering stile,
Your painted words, your brave pretence,

When you will strive, by trayned will   15
To force consent to lewd offence,
    Then thus to yeeld by chaunted charmes,
    I'le rather die within your armes.

Your golden Angels I repell,
Your lawlesse lust I here defie   20
These Angels are the posts of hell,
That often lead poore soules awrie,
    Shame on them all, your eyes shall see,
    These Angels have no power of me.

Your gownes of silke, your golden chaines,   25
Your men, your maides, your hundreth pounds,
Are nothing else but divelish traines,
That fill fond eares with tickling sounds,
    A bladder full of traiterous wind,
    And fardest off from filthy mind.   30

Well, sith your meaning now is plaine,
And lust would give no longer leave,
To faithlesse hart, to lie and faine,
Which might perchance in time deceive,
    By Jesus Christ I doe protest,   35
    I'le never graunt that you request.

CANT. XII

NOB. Furens

Thou beggers brat, thou dunghill mate,
Thou clownish spawne, thou country gill,
My love is turnd to wreakefull hate,
Go hang, and keepe thy credit still,
    Gad where thou list, aright or wrong,   5
    I hope to see thee begge, erre long.

Was this great offer well refus'd,
Or was this proffer all too base?
Am I fit man to be abus'd,
With such disgrace, by flattering gase?   10

On thee or thine, as I am man,
I will revenge this if I can.

Thou think'st thy selfe a pearelesse peice,
And peevish pride that doth possesse
Thy hart; perswades that thou art wise,   15
When God doth know ther's nothing lesse,
    T'was not thy beautie that did move
    This fond affect, but blinded love.

I hope to see some countrie clowne,
Possessor of that fleering face,   20
When need shall force thy pride come downe,
I'le laugh to see thy foolish case,
    For thou that think'st thy selfe so brave,
    Wilt take at last some paltrie knave,

Thou selfewill gig that dost detest   25
My faithfull love, looke to thy fame,
If thou offend, I doe protest,
I'le bring thee out to open shame,
    For sith thou fayn'st thy selfe so pure,
    Looke to thy leapes that they be sure.   30

I was thy friend, but now thy foe,
Thou hadst my hart, but now my hate,
Refusing wealth, God send thee woe,
Repentance now will come too late,
    That tongue that did protest my faith,   35
    Shall waile thy pride, and wish thy death.

CANT. XIII

AVISA

Yea so I thought, this is the end
Of wandring lust, resembling love,
Was't love or lust, that did intend
Such friendlesse force, as you did move?
    Though you may vaunt of happier fate,   5
    I am content with my estate.

I rather chuse a quiet mind,
A conscience cleare from bloudy sinnes,
Then short delights, and therein find
That gnawing worme, that never linnes,   10
   Your bitter speeches please me more,
   Then all your wealth, and all your store.

I love to live devoid of crime,
Although I begge, although I pine,
These fading joyes for little time,   15
Imbrace who list, I here resine,
   How poore I goe, how meane I fare,
   If God be pleas'd, I doe not care.

I rather beare your raging ire,
Although you sweare revengment deepe,   20
Then yeeld for gaine to lewd desire,
That you might laugh, when I should weepe,
   Your lust would like but for a space,
   But who could salve my foule disgrace?

Mine eares have heard your taunting words,   25
Of yeelding fooles by you betraid,
Amongst your mates at open bords,
Know'st such a wife? know'st such a maid?
   Then must you laugh, then must you winke,
   And leave the rest for them to thinke.   30

Nay yet welfare the happie life,
That need not blush at every view:
Although I be a poore mans wife,
Yet then I'le laugh as well as you,
   Then laugh as long, as you thinke best,   35
   My fact shall frame you no such jest.

If I doe hap to leape aside,
I must not come to you for aide,
Alas now that you be denide,
You thinke to make me sore afraide;   40
   Nay watch your worst, I doe not care,
   If I offend, pray doe not spare.

You were my friend, you were but dust,
The Lord is he, whome I doe love,
He hath my hart, in him I trust,
And he doth gard me from above,
    I waie not death, I feare not hell,
    This is enough, and so farewell.

45

The Complaint of Rosamond

SAMUEL DANIEL (1592)

Out from the horror of infernall deepes,
My poore afflicted ghost comes heere to plaine it:
Attended with my shame that never sleepes,
The spot wherewith my kinde, and youth did staine it:
My body found a grave where to containe it,   5
  A sheete could hide my face, but not my sin,
  For Fame finds never tombe t'inclose it in.

And which is worse, my soule is nowe denied,
Her transport to the sweet Elisean rest,
The joyfull blisse for ghosts repurified,   10
Th'ever springing Gardens of the blest,
Caron denies me waftage with the rest.
  And sayes my soule can never passe that River,
  Till Lovers sighes on earth shall it deliver.

So shall I never passe; for how should I   15
Procure this sacrifice amongst the living?
Time hath long since worne out the memorie,
Both of my life, and lives unjust depriving:
Sorrow for me is dead for aye reviving.
  Rosamond hath little left her but her name,   20
  And that disgrac'd, for time hath wrong'd the same.

No Muse suggests the pittie of my case,
Each penne dooth overpasse my just complaint,
Whilst others are preferd, though farre more base:
Shores wife is grac'd, and passes for a Saint;   25
Her Legend justifies her foule attaint;
  Her well-told tale did such compassion finde,
  That she is pass'd, and I am left behinde.

Which seene with griefe, my myserable ghost,
(*Whilome* invested in so faire a vaile,⁣   30
Which whilst it liv'd, was honoured of the most,
And being dead, gives matter to bewaile)
Comes to sollicit thee, since others faile,
   To take this taske, and in thy wofull Song
   To forme my case, and register my wrong.⁣   35

Although I knowe thy just lamenting Muse,
Toylde in th'affliction of thine owne distresse,
In others cares hath little time to use,
And therefore maist esteeme of mine the lesse:
Yet as thy hopes attend happie redresse,⁣   40
   Thy joyes depending on a womans grace,
   So move thy minde a wofull womans case.

Delia may happe to deygne to read our story,
And offer up her sigh among the rest,
Whose merit would suffice for both our glorie,⁣   45
Whereby thou might'st be grac'd, and I be blest,
That indulgence would profit me the best;
   Such powre she hath by whom thy youth is lead,
   To joy the living and to blesse the dead.

So I through beautie made the wofull'st wight,⁣   50
By beautie might have comfort after death:
That dying fayrest, by the fayrest might
Finde life above on earth, and rest beneath:
She that can blesse us with one happy breath,
   Give comfort to thy Muse to doe her best.⁣   55
   That thereby thou maist joy, and I might rest.

Thus saide: forthwith mov'd with a tender care
And pittie, which my selfe could never finde:
What she desir'd, my Muse deygn'd to declare,
And therefore will'd her boldly tell her minde:⁣   60
And I more willing tooke this charge assignd,
   Because her griefes were worthy to be knowne,
   And telling hers, might hap forget mine owne.

Then write quoth shee the ruine of my youth,
Report the downe-fall of my slippry state: 65
Of all my life reveale the simple truth,
To teach to others, what I learnt too late:
Exemplifie my frailtie, tell howe Fate
   Keepes in eternall darke our fortunes hidden,
   And ere they come, to know them tis forbidden.   70

For whilst the sunn-shine of my fortune lasted,
I joy'd the happiest warmth, the sweetest heat
That ever yet imperious beautie tasted,
I had what glory ever flesh could get:
But this faire morning had a shamefull set;   75
   Disgrace darkt honor, sinne did clowde my brow,
   As note the sequel, and Ile tell thee how.

The blood I staind was good and of the best,
My birth had honor, and my beautie fame:
Nature and Fortune joyn'd to make me blest,   80
Had I had grace t'have knowne to use the same:
My education shew'd from whence I came,
   And all concur'd to make me happy furst,
   That so great hap might make me more accurst.

Happie liv'd I whilst Parents eye did guide,   85
The indiscretion of my feeble wayes:
And Country home kept me from being eyde,
Where best unknowne I spent my sweetest dayes;
Till that my frindes mine honour sought to rayse,
   To higher place, which greater credite yeeldes,   90
   Deeming such beauty was unfit for feeldes.

From Country then to Court I was preferr'd,
From calme to stormes, from shore into the deepes:
There where I perish'd, where my youth first err'd;
There where I lost the Flowre which honour keepes;   95
There where the worser thrives, the better weepes;
   Ah me poore wench, on this unhappy shelfe
   I grounded me, and cast away my selfe.

For thither com'd, when yeeres had arm'd my youth
With rarest proofe of beautie ever seene: 100
When my reviving eye had learnt the truth,
That it had powre to make the winter greene,
And flowre affections whereas none had beene:
    Soone could I teach my browe to tyrannize,
    And make the world do homage to mine eyes.   105

For age I saw, though yeeres with cold conceit,
Congeald theyr thoughts against a warme desire:
Yet sigh their want, and looke at such a baite,
I saw how youth was waxe before the fire:
I saw by stealth, I fram'd my looke a lire,   110
    Yet well perceiv'd how Fortune made me then,
    The envy of my sexe, and wonder unto men.

Looke how a Comet at the first appearing,
Drawes all mens eyes with wonder to behold it:
Or as the saddest tale at suddaine hearing,   115
Makes silent listning unto him that told it:
So did my speech when rubies did unfold it;
    So did the blasing of my blush appeere,
    T'amaze the world, that holds such sights so deere.

Ah beauty Syren, fayre enchaunting good,   120
Sweet silent rethorique of perswading eyes:
Dombe eloquence, whose powre doth move the blood,
More then the words, or wisedome of the wise:
Still harmonie, whose diapason lyes
    Within a brow, the key which passions move,   125
    To ravish sence, and play a world in love.

What might I then not doe whose powre was such?
What cannot women doe that know theyr powre?
What women knowes it not I feare too much,
How blisse or bale lyes in theyr laugh or lowre?   130
Whilst they enjoy their happy blooming flowre,
    Whilst nature decks her with her proper fayre
Which cheeres the worlde, joyes each sight, sweetens th'ayre.

Such one was I, my beautie was mine owne,
No borrowed blush which banck-rot beauties seeke: 135
The newfound-shame, a sinne to us unknowne,
Th'adulterate beauty of a falsed cheeke:
Vild staine to honor and to women eeke,
   Seeing that time our fading must detect,
   Thus with defect to cover our defect.   140

Impiety of times, chastities abator,
Falshod, wherein thy selfe, thy selfe deniest:
Treason, to counterfeit the seale of nature,
The stampe of heaven, impressed by the hiest.
Disgrace unto the world, to whom thou lyest,   145
   Idol unto thy selfe, shame to the wise,
   And all that honors thee idolatrise.

Farre was that sinne from us whose age was pure,
When simple beautie was accounted best,
The time when women had no other lure   150
But modestie, pure cheekes, a vertuous brest:
This was the pompe wherewith my youth was blest;
   These were the weapons which mine honour wunne
   In all the conflicts that mine eyes begunne.

Which were not small, I wrought on no meane object;
A Crowne was at my feete, Scepters obaide mee: 156
Whom Fortune made my King, Love made my Subject,
Who did commaund the Land, most humbly praid mee:
Henry the second, that so highly weigh'd mee,
   Founde well by proofe the priviledge of Beautie,   160
   That it hath powre to counter-maund all duetie.

For after all his victories in *Fraunce,*
Tryumphing in the honour of his deedes:
Unmatch'd by sword, was vanquisht by a glaunce,
And hotter warres within his bosome breedes: 165
Warres whom whole Legions of desires feedes,
   Against all which my chastity opposes,
   The fielde of honour, vertue never loses.

No armour might bee founde that coulde defend,
Transpearcing rayes of Christall-pointed eyes: 170
No Stratagem, no reason could amend,
No not his age; yet olde men should be wise:
But shewes deceive, outward appearance lyes;
  Let none for seeming so, thinke Saints of others,
  For all are men, and all have suckt their Mothers.   175

Who would have thought, a Monarch would have ever
Obayed his handmaide, of so meane a state;
Vultur ambition feeding on his lyver,
Age having worne his pleasures out of date:
But happe comes never or it comes too late,   180
  For such a daintie which his youth found not,
  Unto his feeble age did chaunce allot.

Ah Fortune never absolutely good,
For that some crosse still counterchecks our luck:
As heere beholde th'incompatible blood,   185
Of age and youth was that whereon we stuck:
Whose loathing, we from natures brests do suck,
  As opposit to what our blood requires;
  For equall age doth equall like desires.

But mightie men in highest honor sitting,   190
Nought but applause and pleasure can behold:
Sooth'd in their liking, carelesse what is fitting,
May not be suffred once to thinke the'are old:
Not trusting what they see, but what is told.
  Miserable fortune to forget so farre,   195
  The state of flesh, and what our frailties are.

Yet must I needes excuse so great defect,
For drinking of the *Lethe* of myne eyes:
H'is forc'd forget himselfe, and all respect
Of majestie whereon his state relyes: 200
And now of loves, and pleasures must devise.
  For thus reviv'd againe, he serves and su'th,
  And seekes all meanes to undermine my youth.

Which never by assault he could recover,
So well incamp'd in strength of chaste desires: 205
My cleane-arm'd thoughts repell'd an unchast lover,
The Crowne that could commaund what it requires,
I lesser priz'd then chastities attires,
    Th'unstained vaile, which innocents adornes,
    Th'ungathred Rose, defended with the thornes.   210

And safe mine honor stoode till that in truth,
One of my Sexe, of place, and nature bad:
Was set in ambush to intrap my youth,
One in the habit of like frailtie clad,
One who the liv'ry of like weakenes had.   215
    A seeming Matrone, yet a sinfull monster,
    As by her words the chaster sort may conster.

Shee set upon me with the smoothest speech,
That Court and age could cunningly devise:
Th'one autentique made her fit to teach,   220
The other learnt her how to subtelise:
Both were enough to circumvent the wise.
    A document that well may teach the sage,
    That there's no trust in youth, nor hope in age.

Daughter (saith she) behold thy happy chaunce,   225
That hast the lot cast downe into thy lap,
Whereby thou maist thy honor great advaunce,
Whilst thou (unhappy) wilt not see thy hap:
Such fond respect thy youth doth so inwrap,
    T'oppose thy selfe against thine owne good fortune,   230
    That points thee out, and seemes thee to importune.

Doost thou not see how that thy King thy *Jove*,
Lightens foorth glory on thy darke estate:
And showres downe golde and treasure from above,
Whilst thou doost shutte thy lappe against thy fate: 235
Fye fondling fye, thou wilt repent too late
    The error of thy youth; that canst not see
    What is the fortune that dooth followe thee.

Thou must not thinke thy flowre can always florish,
And that thy beautie will be still admired: 240
But that those rayes which all these flames doe nourish,
Canceld with Time, will have their date expyred,
And men will scorne what now is so desired:
   Our frailtyes doome is written in the flowers,
   Which florish now and fade ere many howers.   245

Reade in my face the ruines of my youth,
The wracke of yeeres upon my aged brow:
I have beene faire, I must confesse the trueth,
And stoode uppon as nice respects as thow;
I lost my time, and I repent it now;   250
   But were I to beginne my youth againe,
   I would redeeme the time I spent in vayne.

But thou hast yeeres and priviledge to use them,
Thy priviledge doth beare beauties great seale:
Besides, the law of nature doth excuse them,   255
To whom thy youth may have a just appeale:
Esteeme not fame more then thou doost thy weale,
   Fame, wherof the world seemes to make such choyce:
   Is but an Eccho, and an idle voyce.

Then why should thys respect of honor bound us,   260
In th'imaginary lists of reputation?
Titles which cold severitie hath found us,
Breath of the vulgar, foe to recreation:
Melancholies opinion, customs relation;
   Pleasures plague, beauties scourge, hell to the fayre,
   To leave the sweete for Castles in the ayre.   266

Pleasure is felt, opinion but conceav'd,
Honor, a thing without us, not our owne:
Whereof we see how many are bereav'd,
Which should have rep'd the glory they had sowne,   270
And many have it, yet unworthy knowne.
   So breathes his blasts this many-headed beast,
   Whereof the wisest have esteemed least.

The subtile Citty-women better learned,
Esteeme them chast ynough that best seeme so: 275
Who though they sport, it shall not be discerned,
Their face bewraies not what their bodies doe;
Tis warie walking that doth safliest goe.
　　With shew of vertue, as the cunning knowes,
　　Babes are beguild with sweetes, and men with showes.

Then use thy tallent, youth shall be thy warrant,   281
And let not honor from thy sports detract:
Thou must not fondly thinke thy selfe transparent,
That those who see thy face can judge the fact;
Let her have shame that cannot closely act.   285
　　And seeme the chast, which is the cheefest arte,
　　For what we seeme each sees, none knowes our harte.

The mightie who can with such sinnes dispence,
In steed of shame doe honors great bestow:
A worthie author doth redeeme th'offence,   290
And makes the scarelet sinne as white as snow.
The Majestie that doth descend so low,
　　Is not defilde, but pure remaines therein:
　　And being sacred, sanctifies the sin.

What, doost thou stand on thys, that he is olde,   295
Thy beauty hath the more to worke uppon:
Thy pleasures want shal be supply'd with gold,
Cold age dotes most when heate of youth is gone:
Enticing words prevaile with such a one,
　　Alluring shewes most deepe impression strikes,   300
　　For age is prone to credite what it likes.

Heere interupt she leaves me in a doubt,
When loe began the combat in my blood:
Seeing my youth invirond round about,
The ground uncertaine where my reasons stood;   305
Small my defence to make my party good,
　　Against such powers which were so surely layde,
　　To overthrow a poore unskilful mayde.

Treason was in my bones my selfe conspyring,
To sell my selfe to lust, my soule to sinne: 310
Pure-blushing shame was even in retiring,
Leaving the sacred hold it glory'd in.
Honor lay prostrate for my flesh to win,
  When cleaner thoughts my weakenes gan upbray
  Against my selfe, and shame did force me say. 315

Ah *Rosamond*, what doth thy flesh prepare,
Destruction to thy dayes, death to thy fame:
Wilt thou betray that honor held with care,
T'intombe with blacke reproch a spotted name,
Leaving thy blush the collours of thy shame. 320
  Opening thy feete to sinne, thy soule to lust,
  Gracelesse to lay thy glorie in the dust.

Nay first let th'earth gape wide to swallow thee,
And shut thee up in bosome with her dead:
Ere Serpent tempt thee taste forbidden tree, 325
Or feele the warmth of an unlawfull bed:
Suffring thy selfe by lust to be misled;
  So to disgrace thy selfe and grieve thine heires,
  That *Cliffords* race should scorne thee one of theyrs.

Never wish longer to injoy the ayre,   330
Then that thou breath'st the breath of chastitie:
Longer then thou preserv'st thy soule as faire
As is thy face, free from impuritie:
Thy face that makes th'admired in every eye:
  Where natures care such rarities inroule, 335
  Which us'd amisse, may serve to damne thy soule.

But what? he is my King and may constraine me,
Whether I yeelde or not I live defamed:
The world will thinke authority did gaine me,
I shal be judg'd hys love, and so be shamed: 340
We see the fayre condemn'd, that never gamed.
  And if I yeeld, tis honorable shame,
  If not, I live disgrac'd, yet thought the same.

What way is left thee then unhappy mayde,
Whereby thy spotlesse foote may wander out   345
Thys dreadfull danger, which thou seest is layd,
Wherein thy shame doth compasse thee about?
Thy simple yeeres cannot resolve this doubt.
   Thy youth can never guide thy foote so even,
   But in despight some scandall will be given.   350

Thus stood I ballanc'd equallie precize,
Till my fraile flesh did weigh me downe to sinne:
Till world and pleasure made me partialize,
And glittering pompe my vanitie did winne;
When to excuse my fault my lusts beginne,   355
   And impious thoughts alledg'd this wanton clause,
   That though I sinn'd, my sinne had honest cause.

So well the golden balles cast downe before me,
Could entertaine my course, hinder my way:
Whereat my rechlesse youth stooping to store me,   360
Lost me the gole, the glory, and the day.
Pleasure had set my wel-skoold thoughts to play,
   And bade me use the vertue of mine eyes,
   For sweetly it fits the fayre to wantonise.

Thus wrought to sinne, soone was I traind from Court,
To a solitarie Grange there to attend   366
The time the King should thether make resort,
Where he loves long desired-work should end.
Thether he daily messages doth send,
   With costly jewels orators of love: 370
   Which (ah too well men know) doe women move.

The day before the night of my defeature,
He greets me with a Casket richly wrought:
So rare, that arte did seeme to strive with nature,
T'expresse the cunning work-mans curious thought;   375
The mistery whereof I prying sought.
   And found engraven on the lidde above,
   Amymone how she with *Neptune* strove.

Amymone old *Danaus* fayrest daughter,
As she was fetching water all alone   380
At *Lerna*: whereas *Neptune* came and caught her,
From whom she striv'd and strugled to be gone,
Beating the ayre with cryes and pittious mone.
    But all in vaine, with him sh'is forc'd to goe:
    Tis shame that men should use poore maydens so. 385

There might I see described how she lay,
At those proude feete, not satisfied with prayer:
Wailing her heavie hap, cursing the day,
In act so pittious to expresse dispaire:
And by how much more greev'd, so much more fayre; 390
    Her teares upon her cheekes poore carefull gerle,
    Did seeme against the sunne cristall and perle.

Whose pure cleere streames, which loe so faire appeares,
Wrought hotter flames, O myracle of love,
That kindles fire in water, heate in teares,   395
And makes neglected beautie mightier prove:
Teaching afflicted eyes affects to move;
    To shew that nothing ill becomes the fayre,
    But crueltie, that yeeldes unto no prayer.

This having viewd and therewith something moved,   400
Figured I found within the other squares:
Transformed *Io, Joves* deerely loved,
In her affliction how she strangely fares,
Strangelie distress'd, (O beautie borne to cares)
    Turn'd to a Heiffer, kept with jealous eyes,   405
    Alwaies in danger of her hatefull spyes.

These presidents presented to my view,
Wherein the presage of my fall was showne:
Might have fore-warn'd me well what would ensue,
And others harmes have made me shunne mine owne; 410
But fate is not prevented though fore-knowne.
    For that must hap decreed by heavenly powers,
    Who worke our fall, yet make the fault still ours.

Witnes the world, wherein is nothing rifer,
Then miseries unkend before they come: 415
Who can the characters of chaunce discipher,
Written in clowdes of our concealed dome?
Which though perhaps have beene reveald to some,
    Yet that so doubtfull as successe did prove them,
    That men must know they have the heavens above them.

I sawe the sinne wherein my foote was entring,   421
I sawe how that dishonour did attend it,
I sawe the shame whereon my flesh was ventring,
Yet had I not the powre for to defende it;
So weake is sence when error hath condemn'd it: 425
    We see what's good, and thereto we consent us;
    But yet we choose the worst, and soone repent us.

And now I come to tell the worst of ilnes,
Now drawes the date of mine affliction neere:
Now when the darke had wrapt up all in stilnes,   430
And dreadfull blacke, had dispossess'd the cleere:
Com'd was the night, mother of sleepe and feare,
    Who with her sable mantle friendly covers,
    The sweet-stolne sports, of joyfull meeting Lovers.

When loe I joyde my Lover not my Love,   435
And felt the hand of lust most undesired:
Enforc'd th'unprooved bitter sweete to prove,
Which yeeldes no mutuall pleasure when tis hired.
Love's not constrain'd, nor yet of due required,
    Judge they who are unfortunately wed,   440
    What tis to come unto a loathed bed.

But soone his age receiv'd his short contenting,
And sleepe seald up his languishing desires:
When he turnes to his rest, I to repenting,
Into my selfe my waking thought retires: 445
My nakednes had prov'd my sences liers.
    Now opned were mine eyes to looke therein,
    For first we taste the fruite, then see our sin.

Now did I find my selfe unparadis'd,
From those pure fieldes of my so cleane beginning: 450
Now I perceiv'd how ill I was advis'd,
My flesh gan loathe the new-felt touch of sinning:
Shame leaves us by degrees, not at first winning.
    For nature checks a new offence with lothing:
    But use of sinne doth make it seeme as nothing.   455

And use of sinne did worke in me a boldnes,
And love in him, incorporates such zeale:
That jealosie increas'd with ages coldnes,
Fearing to loose the joy of all his weale.
Or doubting time his stealth might els reveale,   460
    H'is driven to devise some subtile way,
    How he might safeliest keepe so rich a pray.

A stately Pallace he foorthwith did buylde,
Whose intricate innumerable wayes,
With such confused errors so beguil'd   465
Th'unguided entrers with uncertaine strayes,
And doubtfull turnings kept them in delayes,
    With bootlesse labor leading them about,
    Able to finde no way, nor in, nor out.

Within the closed bosome of which frame,   470
That serv'd a Center to that goodly round:
Were lodgings, with a garden to the same,
With sweetest flowers that ev'r adorn'd the ground.
And all the pleasures that delight hath found,
    T'entertaine the sence of wanton eyes,   475
    Fuell of love, from whence lusts flames arise.

Heere I inclos'd from all the world a sunder,
The Minotaure of shame kept for disgrace:
The monster of fortune, and the worlds wonder,
Liv'd cloystred in so desolate a case: 480
None but the King might come into the place.
    With certaine maides that did attend my neede,
    And he himselfe came guided by a threed.

O Jealousie, daughter of envy' and love
Most wayward issue of a gentle Syer;   485
Fostred with feares, thy Fathers joyes t'improve,
Myrth-marring Monster, borne a subtile lyer;
Hatefull unto thy selfe, flying thine owne desier:
    Feeding upon suspect that dooth renue thee,
    Happie were Lovers if they never knewe thee.   490

Thou hast a thousand gates thou enterest by,
Conducting trembling passions to our hart:
Hundred eyed *Argus*, ever waking Spye,
Pale hagge, infernall fury, pleasures smart,
Envious Observer, prying in every part;   495
    Suspicious, fearefull, gazing still about thee,
    O would to God that love could be without thee.

Thou didst deprive (through false suggesting feare)
Him of content, and me of libertie:
The onely good that women holde so deare,   500
And turnst my freedome to captivitie,
First made a Prisoner, ere an enemy:
    Enjoynd the raunsome of my bodies shame,
    Which though I paide could not redeeme the same.

What greater torment ever could have beene,   505
Then to inforce the fayre to live retired?
For what is Beautie if it be not seene,
Or what is't to be seene unlesse admired?
And though admyred, unlesse in love desired?
    Never were cheekes of Roses, locks of Amber,   510
Ordayn'd to live imprisond in a Chamber.

Nature created Beautie for the view,
Like as the fire for heate, the Sunne for light:
The Faire doe holde this priviledge as due,
By auncient Charter, to live most in sight,   515
And she that is debarr'd it, hath not right.
    In vaine our friends in this use their dehorting,
    For Beautie will be where is most resorting.

Witnes the fayrest streetes that Thames doth visit,
The wondrous concourse of the glittering Faire: 520
For what rare women deckt with Beautie is it,
That thither covets not to make repaire.
The solitary Country may not stay her,
 Heere is the center of all beauties best,
 Excepting *Delia*, left to adorne the West.   525

Heere doth the curious with judiciall eyes,
Contemplate beauty gloriously attired:
And heerein all our cheefest glory lyes,
To live where we are prais'd and most desired.
O how we joy to see our selves admired,   530
 Whilst niggardly our favours we discover,
 We love to be belov'd, yet scorne the Lover.

Yet would to God my foote had never moved
From Countrey safety, from the fields of rest:
To know the danger to be highly loved,   535
And lyve in pompe to brave among the best,
Happy for me, better had I beene blest;
 If I unluckely had never strayde:
 But liv'd at home a happy Country mayde.

Whose unaffected innocencie thinks   540
No guilefull fraude, as doth the Courtly liver:
She's deckt with trueth, the River where she drinks
Doth serve her for her glasse, her counsell giver:
She loves sincerely, and is loved ever.
 Her dayes are peace, and so she ends her breath,   545
 True life that knowes not what's to die till death.

So should I never have beene registred,
In the blacke booke of the unfortunate:
Nor had my name enrold with Maydes misled,
Which bought theyr pleasures at so hie a rate.   550
Nor had I taught through my unhappy fate,
 This lesson which my selfe learnt with expence,
 How most it hurts that most delights the sence.

Shame followes sinne, disgrace is duly given,
Impietie will out, never so closely doone: 555
No walles can hide us from the eyes of heaven,
For shame must end what wickednesse begun:
Forth breakes reproch when we least thinke thereon.
    And thys is ever propper unto Courts:
    That nothing can be doone but Fame reports. 560

Fame doth explore what lyes most secrete hidden,
Entring the closet of the Pallace dweller:
Abroade revealing what is most forbidden,
Of trueth and falshood both an equall teller:
Tis not a guarde can serve for to expell her, 565
    The sword of justice cannot cutte her wings,
    Nor stop her mouth from utt'ring secrete things.

And this our stealth she could not long conceale,
From her whom such a forfeit most concerned:
The wronged Queene, who could so closely deale: 570
That she the whole of all our practise learned,
And watcht a time when least it was discerned,
    In absence of the King, to wreake her wrong,
    With such revenge as she desired long.

The Laberinth she entred by that threed 575
That serv'd a conduct to my absent Lord:
Left there by chaunce, reserv'd for such a deede,
Where she surpriz'd me whom she so abhord.
Enrag'd with madnes, scarce she speakes a word,
    But flyes with eger fury to my face, 580
    Offring me most unwomanly disgrace.

Looke how a Tygresse that hath lost her whelpe,
Runs fearcely raging through the woods astray:
And seeing her selfe depriv'd of hope or helpe,
Furiously assaults what's in her way, 585
To satisfie her wrath, not for a pray:
    So fell she on me in outragious wise,
    As could Disdaine and Jealousie devise.

And after all her vile reproches used,
She forc'd me take the poyson she had brought: 590
To end the lyfe that had her so abused,
And free her feares, and ease her jealous thought.
No crueltie her wrath would leave unwrought,
    No spightfull act that to revenge is common:
    For no beast fearcer then a jealous woman.   595

Those handes that beauties ministers had bin,
Must now gyve death, that me adorn'd of late:
That mouth that newly gave consent to sin,
Must now receive destruction in there-at.
That body which my lusts did violate,   600
    Must sacrifice it selfe t'appease the wrong,
    So short is pleasure, glory lasts not long.

The poyson soone disperc'd through all my vaines,
Had dispossess'd my living sences quite:
When naught respecting, death the last of paines,   605
Plac'd his pale collours, th'ensigne of his might,
Upon his new-got spoyle before his right;
    Thence chac'd my soule, setting my day ere noone,
    When I least thought my joyes could end so soone.

And as convaid t'untimely funerals,   610
My scarce colde corse not suffred longer stay:
Behold the King (by chance) returning, falls
T'incounter with the same upon the way,
As he repaird to see his deerest joy.
    Not thinking such a meeting could have beene,   615
    To see his love, and seeing beene unseene.

Judge those whom chaunce deprives of sweetest treasure,
What tis to lose a thing we hold so deare:
The best delight, wherein our soule takes pleasure,
The sweet of life, that penetrates so neare.   620
What passions feeles that hart, inforc'd to beare
    The deepe impression of so strange a sight?
    Tongue, pen, nor art, can never shew a right.

Amaz'd he standes, nor voyce nor body steares,
Words had no passage, teares no issue found:⠀⠀⠀⠀625
For sorrow shut up words, wrath kept in teares,
Confus'd affects each other doe confounde:
Oppress'd with griefe his passions had no bounde:
⠀⠀Striving to tell his woes, wordes would not come;
⠀⠀For light cares speake, when mightie griefes are dombe.

At length extremitie breakes out away,⠀⠀⠀⠀631
Through which th'imprisoned voice with teares attended,
Wayles out a sound that sorrowes doe bewray:
With armes a crosse and eyes to heaven bended,
Vauporing out sighes that to the skyes ascended.⠀635
⠀⠀Sighes, the poore ease calamitie affords,
⠀⠀Which serve for speech when sorrow wanteth words.

O heavens (quoth he) why doe myne eyes behold,
The hatefull rayes of this unhappy sonne?
Why have I light to see my sinnes controld,⠀⠀640
With blood of mine owne shame thus vildly donne?
How can my sight endure to looke thereon?
⠀⠀Why doth not blacke eternall darknes hide,
⠀⠀That from myne eyes my hart cannot abide?

What saw my life, wherein my soule might joy?⠀645
What had my dayes, whom troubles still afflicted?
But onely this, to counterpoize annoy,
This joy, this hope, which death hath interdicted:
This sweete, whose losse hath all distresse afflicted.
⠀⠀This that did season all my sowre of life,⠀⠀650
⠀⠀Vext still at home with broyles, abroade in strife.

Vext styll at home with broyles, abrode in strife,
Dissention in my blood, jarres in my bed:
Distrust at boord, suspecting still my life,
Spending the night in horror, dayes in dred;⠀⠀655
Such life hath tyrants, and thys lyfe I led.
⠀⠀These myseries goe mask'd in glittering showes,
⠀⠀Which wisemen see, the vulgar little knowes.

Thus as these passions doe him over-whelme,
He drawes him neere my bodie to behold it: 660
And as the Vine maried unto the Elme
With strict imbraces, so doth he infold it;
And as he in hys carefull armes doth hold it,
   Viewing the face that even death commends,
   On sencelesse lips, millions of kysses spends.   665

Pittifull mouth (quoth he) that living gavest
The sweetest comfort that my soule could wish:
O be it lawfull now, that dead thou havest,
Thys sorrowing farewell of a dying kisse.
And you fayre eyes, containers of my blisse,   670
   Motives of love, borne to be matched never:
   Entomb'd in your sweet circles sleepe for ever.

Ah how me thinks I see death dallying seekes,
To entertaine it selfe in loves sweet place:
Decayed Roses of discoloured cheekes,   675
Doe yet retaine deere notes of former grace:
And ougly death sits faire within her face;
   Sweet remnants resting of vermilion red,
   That death it selfe, doubts whether she be dead.

Wonder of beautie, oh receive these plaints,   680
The obsequies, the last that I shall make thee:
For loe my soule that now already faints,
(That lov'd thee lyving, dead will not forsake thee,)
Hastens her speedy course to over-take thee.
   Ile meete my death, and free my selfe thereby,   685
   For ah what can he doe that cannot die?

Yet ere I die, thus much my soule doth vow,
Revenge shall sweeten death with ease of minde:
And I will cause posterity shall know,
How faire thou wert above all women kind.   690
And after ages monuments shall find,
   Shewing thy beauties title not thy name,
   Rose of the world that sweetned so the same.

This said, though more desirous yet to say,
(For sorrow is unwilling to give over)   695
He doth represse what griefe would els bewray,
Least that too much his passions might discover:
And yet respect scarce bridles such a Lover.
    So farre transported that he knowes not whether,
    For love and Majestie dwell ill together.   700

Then were my funerals not long deferred,
But doone with all the rites pompe could devise:
At *Godstow*, where my body was interred,
And richly tomb'd in honorable wise.
Where yet as now scarce any note descries   705
    Unto these times, the memory of me,
    Marble and Brasse so little lasting be.

For those walles which the credulous devout,
And apt-beleeving ignorant did found:
With willing zeale that never call'd in doubt,   710
That time theyr works should ever so confound,
Lye like confused heapes as under-ground.
    And what their ignorance esteem'd so holy,
    The wiser ages doe account as folly.

And were it not thy favourable lynes,   715
Re-edified the wracke of my decayes:
And that thy accents willingly assignes,
Some farther date, and give me longer daies,
Fewe in this age had knowne my beauties praise.
    But thus renewd, my fame redeemes some time,   720
    Till other ages shall neglect thy rime.

Then when confusion in her course shall bring,
Sad desolation on the times to come:
When myrth-lesse Thames shall have no Swan to sing,
All Musique silent, and the Muses dombe.   725
And yet even then it must be known to some,
    That once they florisht, though not cherisht so,
    And Thames had Swannes as well as ever Po.

But heere an end, I may no longer stay thee,
I must returne t'attend at *Stigian* flood: 730
Yet ere I goe, thys one word more I pray thee,
Tell *Delia* now her sigh may doe me good,
And will her note the frailtie of our blood.
 And if I passe unto those happy banks,
 Then she must have her praise, thy pen her thanks. 735

So vanisht shee, and left me to returne,
To prosecute the tenor of my woes:
Eternall matter for my Muse to mourne,
But ah the worlde hath heard too much of those,
My youth such errors must no more disclose.   740
 Ile hide the rest, and greeve for what hath beene,
 Who made me knowne, must make me live unseene.

FINIS

Englands Heroicall Epistles

MICHAEL DRAYTON (1597)

The Epistle of Rosamond to King Henrie the Second

The Argument

Henrie the second of that name, King of England, the sonne of
Geffrey Plantaginet, Earle of Anjou, and Maude the Empresse, having
by long sute and princely gifts, wonne (to his unlawfull desire) faire
Rosamond, the daughter of the Lord Walter Clyfford, and to avoyde
the danger of Ellinor his jealous Queene, had caused a Labyrinth to
be made within his pallace at Woodstocke; in the center whereof, hee
had lodged his beautious paramore. Whilst the King is absent in his
warres in Normandy, this poore distressed Lady, inclosed in this
solitarie place, tucht with remorse of conscience, writes unto the King
of her distresse and miserable estate, urging him by all meanes and
perswasions, to cleere himselfe of this infamie, and her of the griefe of
minde by taking away her wretched lyfe.

If yet thine eyes (great *Henry*) may endure
These tainted lynes, drawne with a hand impure,
Which faine would blush, but feare keeps blushes back,
And therefore suted in dispayring blacke,
This in loves name, ô that these lypps might crave,   5
But that sweete name (vile I) prophaned have;
Punish my fault, or pittie mine estate,
Reade it for love, if not for love, for hate.
If with my shame thine eyes thou faine would'st feede,
Heere let them surfeit, on my shame to reede;   10
This scribled paper which I send to thee,
If noted rightly, dooth resemble mee:
As this pure ground, wheron these letters stand,
So pure was I, ere stayned by thy hand;

Ere I was blotted with this foule offence,   15
So cleere and spotlesse was mine innocence:
Now like these marks, which taint this hatefull scroule,
Such the black sinnes, which spotte my leprous soule.
O *Henry* why, by losse thus shouldst thou winne?
To get by conquest? to enrich with sinne?   20
Why on my name this slaunder doost thou bring,
To make my fault renowned by a King?
Fame never stoopes to things but meane and poore
The more our greatnes, makes our fault the more.
Lights on the ground, themselves doe lessen farre,   25
But in the ayre, each small sparke seemes a starre.
Why on a womans frailetie wouldst thou lay
This subtile plot, mine honour to betray?
Or thy unlawfull pleasure should'st thou buy
With vile expence of kinglie majestie?   30
T'was not my minde consented to this ill
Then had I beene transported by my will,
For what my body was enforst to doe,
(Heaven knowes) my soule did not consent unto;
For through mine eyes, had shee her liking seene,   35
Such as my love, such had my lover beene.
True love is simple, like his mother Truth,
Kindlie affection, youth to love with youth;
No sharper corsive to our blooming yeares,
Then the cold badge of winter-blasted haires.   40
Thy kinglie power makes to withstand thy foes,
But canst not keepe back age, with time it growes;
Though honour our ambitious sexe doth please,
Yet in that honour, age a foule disease.
Nature hath her free course in all, and then,   45
Age is alike in Kings, and other men,
Which all the world will to my shame impute
That I my selfe did basely prostitute;
And say, that gold was fuell to the fire,
Gray haires in youth not kindling greene desire.   50
O no; that wicked woman wrought by thee,
My temptor was to that forbidden tree;
That subtile serpent, that seducing devill,
Which bad mee taste the fruit of good and evill:

That *Circe*, by whose magicke I was charm'd,   55
And to this monstrous shape am thus transform'd;
That viperous hagge, the foe to her owne kind,
That wicked spirit, unto the weaker minde:
Our frailties plague, our natures onely curse,
Hells deep'st damnation, the worst evills worse.   60
But *Henry*, how canst thou affect me thus,
T'whom thy remembrance now is odious?
My haplesse name, with *Henries* name I found
Cut in the glasse with *Henries* Diamond:
That glasse from thence faine would I take away,   65
But then I feare the ayre would me betray
Then doe I strive to wash it out with teares,
But then the same more evident appeares.
Then doe I cover it with my guiltie hand,
Which that names witnes doth against mee stand: 70
Once did I sinne, which memory doth cherrish
Once I offended, but I ever perrish.
What griefe can be, but time dooth make it lesse?
But infamy tyme never can suppresse.
Some-times to passe the tedious irkesome howres,   75
I clymbe the top of Woodstocks mounting towers,
Where in a Turret secretly I lye
To viewe from farre such as doe travaile by,
Whether (mee thinks) all cast theyr eyes at mee,
As through the stones my shame did make them see,   80
And with such hate the harmles walls doe view,
As unto death theyr eyes would mee pursue.
The married women curse my hatefull life,
Which wrong a lawfull bed, a Queene, a wife;
The maydens wish I buried quicke may die   85
The lothsome staine to their virginitie.
Well knew'st thou what a monster I would bee,
When thou didst builde this Labyrinth for mee.
Whose strange *Meanders* turning every way,
Be like the course wherein my youth did stray: 90
Onely a Clue to guide mee out and in,
But yet still walke I, circuler in sinne.
As in the Tarras heere this other day
My maide and I did passe the time away,

Mongst manie pictures which we passed by,   95
The silly girle at length hapt to espie
Chast *Lucrece* picture, and desires to know
What shee should be herselfe that murdred so?
Why girle (quoth I) this is that Romaine dame:
Not able then to tell the rest for shame,   100
My tongue doth mine owne guiltines betray;
With that I send the pratling girle away,
Least when my lisping guiltie tongue should hault,
My lookes should be the Index to my fault.

As that life blood which from the hart is sent,   105
In beauties fielde pitching his Crimson Tent,
In lovely sanguine sutes the Lilly cheeke,
Whilst it but for a resting place dooth seeke;
And changing often-times with sweet delight,
Converts the white to red, the red to white.   110
The lovely blush, the palenes dooth distaine,
The palenes makes the blush more faire againe;
Thus in my breast a thousand thoughts I carry,
Which in my passion diversly doe varry.

When as the sunne hales towards the westerne slade   115
And the trees shadowes three times greater made,
Foorth goe I to a little Current neere,
Which like a wanton trayle creepes heere and there,
Where with mine angle casting in my baite,
The little fishes (dreading the deceit)   120
With fearefull nibbling flie th'inticing gin,
By nature taught what danger lyes therein.
Things reasonlesse thus warnd by nature bee,
Yet I devourd the baite was layd for mee;
Thinking thereon, and breaking into grones,   125
The bubling spring which trypps uppon the stones
Chides mee away, least sitting but too nie,
I should pollute that native puritie.
Rose of the World, so dooth import my name,
Shame of the Worlde, my life hath made the same;   130
And to th'unchast thys name shall given bee,
Of *Rosamond*, deriv'd from sinne and mee.
The *Clyffords* take from mee that name of theirs,
Famous for vertue many hundred yeeres.

They blot my birth with hatefull bastardie, 135
That I sprang not from their Nobilitie;
They my alliance utterly refuse,
Nor will a strumpet shall their name abuse.
Heere in the Garden, wrought by curious hands,
Naked *Diana* in the fountaine standes, 140
With all her Nimphs got round about to hide her,
As when *Acteon* had by chaunce espyde her:
This sacred image I no sooner view'd
But as that metamorphosd man pursu'd
By his owne hounds: so by my thoughts am I, 145
Which chase mee still, which way so ere I flie.
Touching the grasse, the honny-dropping dew,
Which falls in teares before my limber shue,
Upon my foote consumes in weeping still,
As it would say, Why went'st thou unto ill? 150
Thus to no place in safetie can I goe
But every thing doth give mee cause of woe.
In that faire Casket of such wondrous cost
Thou sent'st the night before mine honour lost,
Amimone was wrought, a harmelesse maide, 155
By *Neptune* that adulterous God betrayd;
Shee prostrate at his feete begging with prayers,
Wringing her hands, her eyes swolne up with teares:
This was not the entrapping baite of men,
But by thy vertue gentlie warning then; 160
To shew to mee for what intent it came,
Least I therein should ever keepe my shame.
And in this Casket (ill I see it now)
Was *Joves*-love *I-o* turnd into a Cowe.
Yet was shee kept with *Argus* hundred eyes, 165
So wakefull still be *Junos* jealousies;
By this I well might have fore-warned beene,
T'have cleerd my selfe to thy suspecting Queene,
Who with more hundred eyes attendeth mee
Then had poore *Argus* single eyes to see. 170
In this thou rightlie imitatest *Jove*,
Into a beast thou hast transformd thy love.
Nay worser farre; (degenerate from kinde)
A monster, both in body and in minde.

The waxen Taper which I burne by night,
With his dull vapory dimnes mocks my sight;
As though the dampe which hinders his cleere flame,
Came from my breath, in that night of my shame,
When it did burne as darknesse uglie eye
When shot the starre of my virginitie.　　　　　　　180
And if a starre but by the glasse appeare,
I straight intreate it not to looke in heere;
I am already hatefull to the light,
It is enough, betray mee not to night.
Then sith my shame so much belongs to thee,　　　　　　　185
Rid mee of that, by onelie murdring mee;
And let it justly to my charge be layd
Thy roiall person I would have betrayd:
Thou shalt not neede by circumstance t'accuse mee,
If I denie it, let the heavens refuse mee.　　　　　　　190
My lifes a blemish which dooth cloude thy name,
Take it away, and cleere shall shine thy fame:
Yeeld to my sute, if ever pitty moov'd thee,
In this shewe mercie, as I ever lov'd thee.

Henry to Rosamond

When first the Post arrived in my Tent,
And brought the letters *Rosamond* had sent,
Think from his lips, but what sweet comfort came,
When in mine eare he softly breath'd thy name,
Straight I enjoyne him of thy health to tell,　　　　　　　5
Longing to heare my *Rosamond* did well;
With newe enquiries then I cut him short
When of the same he gladly would report,
That with the earnest hast my tongue oft tryps,
Catching the words halfe spoke out of his lyps:　　　　　　　10
This told, yet more I urge him to reveale,
To loose no time whilst I unript the seale.
The more I read, still doe I erre the more,
As though mistaking some-what said before.
Missing the poynt, the doubtfull sence is broken,　　　　　　　15
Speaking againe, what I before had spoken;

Still in a swound, my hart revives, and faints,
Twixt hopes, dispaires, twixt smiles, and deepe complaints.
As these sad accents sort in my desires,
Smooth calmes, rough stormes, sharpe frosts, and raging fiers,
Put on with boldnesse, and put backe with feares, 21
My tongue with curses, when mine eyes with teares.
O how my hart at that black line did tremble,
That blotted paper should thy selfe resemble;
O were there paper but neere halfe so white, 25
The Gods thereon their sacred Lawes would write
With pennes of Angels wings, and for theyr inck,
That heavenly Nectar, their immortall drinke.
Majestick courage strives to have supprest
This fearefull passion stirr'd up in my brest, 30
But still in vaine the same I goe about,
My hart must breake within, or woes breake out.
Am I at home pursu'd with private hate,
And warre comes raging to my Pallace gate?
Is meager Envie stabbing at my throne, 35
Treason attending when I walke alone?
And am I branded with the curse of Rome,
And stand condemn'd by dreadfull counsells dombe?
And by the pride of my rebellious sonne,
Rich Normandy with Armies over-runne? 40
Fatall my birth, unfortunate my life,
Unkind my children, most unkinde my wife.
Griefe, cares, old age, suspition to torment mee,
Nothing on earth to quiet or content mee;
So manie woes, so many plagues to finde, 45
Sicknes of body, discontent of minde;
Hopes left, helps reft, life wrong'd, joy interdicted,
Banisht, distress'd, forsaken, and afflicted:
Of all releefe hath Fortune quite bereft mee?
Onely my love unto my comfort left mee. 50
And is one beautie thought so great a thing?
To mittigate the sorrowes of a King?
Barr'd of that choyce the vulgar often prove,
Have wee (then they) lesse priviledge in love?
Is it a King, the wofull widdow heares? 55
Is it a King, dryes up the Orphans teares?

Is it a King, regards the Clyants cry?
Gives life to him by justice domb'd to die?
Is it his care, the Common-wealth that keepes,
As doth the nurse her babie whilst it sleepes?   60
And that poore King, of all these hopes prevented,
Unhard, unhelp'd, unpittied, unlamented.
Yet let me be with povertie opprest,
Of earthly blessings rob'd, and dispossest,
Let me be scorn'd, rejected, and revild,   65
From kingdom, country, and from Court exild,
Let the worlds curse upon me still remaine,
And let the last bring on the first againe;
All miseries that wretched man may wound,
Leave for my comfort; onely *Rosamond*,   70
For thee swift Time her speedy course doth stay,
At thy commaund the Destinies obey;
Pitty is dead, that comes not from thine eyes,
And at thy feete, even mercy prostrate lyes;
If I were feeble, rhumaticke, or cold,   75
These were true signes that I were waxed old,
But I can march all day in massie steele,
Nor yet my armes unweeldie weight do feele,
Nor wak'd by night, with bruze or bloudy wound,
The Tent my bed, no pillow but the ground;   80
For very age had I layne bedrid long,
One smile of thine againe could make me yong.
Were there in Art a power but so divine
As is in that sweet Angell-tongue of thine,
That great Inchauntresse which once tooke such paines, 85
To force young blood in *Aesons* wither'd vaines,
And from groves, mountaines, medowes, marshe and fen,
Brought all the simples were ordained for men,
And of those plants, those hearbs, those flowers, those weeds,
Used the roots, the leaves, the juyce, the seeds,   90
And in this powerfull potion that shee makes,
Puts blood of men, of beasts, of birds, of snakes,
Never had needed to have gone so far,
To seeke the soyles where all those simples are,
One accent from thy lypps, the blood more warmes,   95
Then all her philtres, exorcismes, and charmes.

Thy presence hath repaired in one day,
What manie yeeres and sorrowes did decay,
And made fresh beauties fairest branches spring
From wrinckled furrowes of Times ruining.   100
Even as the hungry winter-starved earth
When shee by nature labours towards her birth;
Still as the day upon the darke world creepes,
One blossom foorth after another peepes,
Till the small flower whose roote is nowe unbound,   105
Gets from the frostie prison of the ground,
Spreading the leaves unto the powerfull noone,
Deck'd in fresh colours, smiles upon the sunne.
Never unquiet care lodg'd in that brest,
Where but one thought of *Rosamond* dyd rest;   110
Nor thirst, nor travaile, which on warre attend,
Ere brought the long day to desired end;
Nor yet did pale Feare, or leane Famine live,
Where hope of thee, did any comfort give.
Ah what injustice then is this of thee,   115
That thus the guiltlesse doost condemne for me?
When onely shee (by meanes of my offence)
Redeemes thy purenes, and thy innocence,
When to our wills perforce obey they must,
That just in them, what ere in us unjust;   120
Of what we doe, not them account we make,
Thys serves for all; they doe it for our sake,
And what to worke a Princes will may merit,
Hath deep'st impression on a gentle spirit:
Our powerfull wills drawne by attractive beautie,   125
They to our wills arm'd by subjective dutie.
And true affection doth no bound reteane,
For this is sure, firme love had never meane;
And whilst the cause by reason is disputed,
Reason it selfe, by love is most confuted.   130
Ift be my name that doth thee so offend,
No more my selfe shall be mine owne names friend;
And ift be that which thou doost onely hate
That name, in my name, lastly hath his date.
Say tis accurst, and fatall, and dispraise it,   135
If written blot it, if engraven, raze it.

Say that of all names tis a name of woe,
Once a Kings name, but now it is not so.
And when all this is done, I know twill grieve thee,
And therefore (sweet) why should I now beleeve thee?   140
Nor shouldst thou thinke those eyes with envie lower,
Which passing by thee, gaze up to thy tower,
But rather praise thine owne which be so cleere,
Which from the Turret like two starres appeare;
And in theyr moovings, like a Christall glasse,   145
Make such reflection unto all that passe,
Above the sunne doth shine, beneath thine eyes,
As though two sunnes at once, shin'd in two skyes.
The little streame which by thy tower doth glide,
Where oft thou spend'st the weary evening tide,   150
To view thee well his course would gladly stay,
As loth from thee to part so soone away;
And with salutes thy selfe would gladly greete,
And offer up those small drops at thy feete,
But finding that the envious bankes restraine it,   155
To 'xcuse it selfe doth in this sort complaine it,
And therefore this sad bubling murmur keepes,
And in this sort within the channell weepes.
And as thou doost into the water looke,
The fishe which see thy shadow in the brooke,   160
Forget to feede, and all amazed lye,
So daunted with the luster of thine eye.
And that sweet name which thou so much doost wrong,
In time shall be some famous Poets song;
And with the very sweetnes of that name   165
Lyons and Tygars, men shal learne to tame.
The carefull mother from her pensive brest
With *Rosamond* shall bring her babe to rest;
The little birds, (by mens continuall sound)
Shall learne to speake, and prattle *Rosamond*;   170
And when in Aprill they begin to sing,
With *Rosamond* shall welcome in the spring;
And she in whom all rarities are found,
Shall still be said to be a *Rosamond*.
The little flowers which dropping honied dew,   175
Which (as thou writ'st) doe weepe upon thy shue,

Not for thy fault (sweet *Rosamond*) doe mone,
But weep for griefe, that thou so soone art gone,
For if thy foote tuch Hemlocke as it goes,
That Hemlock's made more sweeter then the Rose,   180
Of *Jove* or *Neptune* how they did betray,
Nor speake of *I-o*, or *Amimone*,
When she for whom *Jove* once became a Bull,
Compar'd with thee, had been a tawny trull;
He a white Bull, and shee a whiter Cow,   185
Yet he, nor she, nere halfe so white as thou.
Long since (thou knowst) my care provided for
To lodge thee safe from jealious *Ellinor*;
The Labyrinths conveyance guides thee so,
(Which onely *Vahan* thou and I doe knowe)   190
If shee doe guard thee with a hundred eyes,
I have an hundred subtile *Mercuries*
To watch that *Argus*, which my love doth keep,
Untill eye, after eye, fall all to sleepe.
Those starrs looke in by night, looke in to see,   195
Wondring what starre heere on the earth should bee.
As oft the Moone amidst the silent night,
Hath come to joy us with her friendly light,
And by the Curtaine help'd mine eye to see
What envious night and darknes hid from mee;   200
When I have wish'd that shee might ever stay,
And other worlds might still enjoy the day.
What should I say? words, teares, and sighes be spent,
And want of time dooth further helps prevent;
My Campe resounds with fearefull shocks of war,   205
Yet in my breast the worser conflicts are;
Yet is my signall to the battailes sound,
The blessed name of beautious *Rosamond*.
Accursed be that hart, that tongue, that breath,
Should thinke, should speake, or whisper of thy death.   210
For in one smyle, or lower from thy sweet eye,
Consists my life, my hope, my victorie.
Sweet Woodstock, where my *Rosamond* doth rest,
Blessed in her; in whom thy King is blest;
For though in Fraunce a while my body bee,   215
(Sweet Paradice) my hart remaines in thee.

Christs Victorie and Triumph in Heaven, and Earth, over and after Death

GILES FLETCHER (1610)

Christs Victorie in Heaven

I

The birth of him that no beginning knewe,
Yet gives beginning to all that are borne,
And how the Infinite farre greater grewe,
By growing lesse, and how the rising Morne,
That shot from heav'n, did backe to heaven retourne,
 The obsequies of him that could not die,
 And death of life, ende of eternitie,
How worthily he died, that died unworthily;

The Argument propounded in generall: Our redemption by Christ.

2

How God, and Man did both embrace each other,
Met in one person, heav'n, and earth did kiss,
And how a Virgin did become a Mother,
And bare that Sonne, who the worlds Father is,
And Maker of his mother, and how Bliss
 Descended from the bosome of the High,
 To cloath himselfe in naked miserie,
Sayling at length to heav'n, in earth, triumphantly,

3

Is the first flame, wherewith my whiter Muse
Doth burne in heavenly love, such love to tell.
O thou that didst this holy fire infuse,
And taught'st this brest, but late the grave of hell,
Wherein a blind, and dead heart liv'd, to swell
 With better thoughts, send downe those lights that lend
 Knowledge, how to begin, and how to end
The love, that never was, nor ever can be pend.

The Authors Invocation, for the better handling of it.

248

4

Ye sacred writings in whose antique leaves
The memories of heav'n entreasur'd lie,
Say, what might be the cause that Mercie heaves
The dust of sinne above th'industrious skie;
And lets it not to dust, and ashes flie?
   Could Justice be of sinne so over-wooed,
   Or so great ill be cause of so great good,
That bloody man to save, mans Saviour shed his blood?

5

Or did the lips of Mercie droppe soft speech
For traytrous man, when at th'Eternalls throne
Incensed Nemesis did heav'n beseech
With thundring voice, that justice might be showne
Against the Rebells, that from God were flowne;
   O say, say how could Mercie plead for those
   That scarcely made, against their Maker rose?
Will any slay his friend, that he may spare his foes?

The Argument,
Mans redemption,
expounded from
the cause.
Mercie

6

There is a place beyond that flaming hill
From whence the starres their thin apparance shed,
A place, beyond all place, where never ill,
Nor impure thought was ever harboured,
But Sainctly Heroes are for ever s'ed
   To keepe an everlasting Sabbaoths rest,
   Still wishing that, of what th'ar still possest,
Enjoying but one joy, but one of all joyes best.

Dwelling in
heaven

7

Here, when the ruine of that beauteous frame,
Whose golden building shin'd with everie starre
Of excellence, deform'd with age became,
MERCY, remembring peace in midst of warre,
Lift up the musique of her voice, to barre
   Eternall fate, least it should quite erace
   That from the world, which was the first worlds grace,
And all againe into their, nothing, Chaos chase.

And pleading
for man now
guiltio.

8

For what had all this All, which Man in one
Did not unite; the earth, aire, water, fire,
Life, sense, and spirit, nay the powrefull throne
Of the divinest Essence, did retire,
And his owne Image into clay inspire:
   So that this Creature well might called be
   Of the great world, the small epitomie,
Of the dead world, the live, and quicke anatomie.

9

But Justice had no sooner Mercy seene   *with Justice,*
Smoothing the wrinkles of her Fathers browe,   *described*
But up she starts, and throwes her selfe betweene.
As when a vapour, from a moory slough,
Meeting with fresh Eous, that but now
   Open'd the world, which all in darkenesse lay,
   Doth heav'ns bright face of his rayes disaray,
And sads the smiling orient of the springing day.

10

She was a Virgin of austere regard,   *by her qualities.*
Not as the world esteemes her, deafe, and blind,
But as the Eagle, that hath oft compar'd
Her eye with heav'ns, so, and more brightly shin'd
Her lamping sight: for she the same could winde
   Into the solid heart, and with her eares,
   The silence of the thought loude speaking heares,
And in one hand a paire of even scoals she weares.

11

No riot of affection revell kept
Within her brest, but a still apathy
Possessed all her soule, which softly slept,
Securely, without tempest, no sad crie
Awakes her pittie, but wrong'd povertie,
   Sending his eyes to heav'n swimming in teares,
   With hideous clamours ever struck her eares,
Whetting the blazing sword, that in her hand she beares.

12

The winged Lightning is her Mercury, *Her Retinue.*
And round about her mightie thunders sound:
Impatient of himselfe lies pining by
Pale Sicknes, with his kercher'd head upwound,
And thousand noysome plagues attend her round,
  But if her clowdie browe but once growe foule,
  The flints doe melt, and rocks to water rowle,
And ayrie mountaines shake, and frighted shadowes howle.

13

Famine, and bloodles Care, and bloodie Warre,
Want, and the Want of knowledge how to use
Abundance, Age, and Feare, that runnes afarre
Before his fellowe Greefe, that aye pursues
His winged steps; for who would not refuse
  Greefes companie, a dull, and rawebon'd spright,
  That lankes the cheekes, and pales the freshest sight,
Unbosoming the cheerefull brest of all delight;

14

Before this cursed throng, goes Ignorance,
That needes will leade the way he cannot see:
And after all, Death doeth his flag advaunce,
And in the mid'st, Strife still would roaguing be,
Whose ragged flesh, and cloaths did well agree:
  And round about, amazed Horror flies,
  And over all, Shame veiles his guiltie eyes,
And underneth, Hells hungrie throat still yawning lies.

15

Upon two stonie tables, spread before her, *Her Subject.*
She lean'd her bosome, more then stonie hard,
There slept th'unpartiall judge, and strict restorer
Of wrong, or right, with paine, or with reward,
There hung the skore of all our debts, the card
  Whear good, and bad, and life, and death were painted:
  Was never heart of mortall so untainted,
But when that scroule was read, with thousand terrors fainted.

16

Witnes the thunder that mount Sinai heard,
When all the hill with firie clouds did flame,
And wandring Israel, with the sight afeard,
Blinded with seeing, durst not touch the same,
But like a wood of shaking leaves became.
 On this dead Justice, she, the Living Lawe,
 Bowing herselfe with a majestique awe,
All heav'n, to heare her speech, did into silence drawe.

17

Dread Lord of Spirits, well thou did'st devise
To fling the worlds rude dunghill, and the drosse
Of the ould Chaos, farthest from the skies,
And thine owne seate, that heare the child of losse,
Of all the lower heav'n the curse, and crosse,
 That wretch, beast, caytive, monster Man, might spend,
 (Proude of the mire, in which his soule is pend)
Clodded in lumps of clay, his wearie life to end.

*Her accusation
of Mans sinne.*

18

His bodie dust: whear grewe such cause of pride?
His soule thy Image: what could he envie?
Himselfe most happie: if he so would bide:
Now grow'n most wretched, who can remedie?
He slewe himselfe, himselfe the enemie.
 That his owne soule would her owne murder wreake,
 If I were silent, heav'n and earth would speake,
And if all fayl'd, these stones would into clamours breake.

*And 1. of
Adams first
sinne.*

19

How many darts made furrowes in his side,
When she, that out of his owne side was made,
Gave feathers to their flight? whear was the pride
Of their newe knowledge; whither did it fade,
When, running from thy voice into the shade,
 He fled thy sight, himselfe of sight bereav'd;
 And for his shield a leavie armour weav'd,
With which, vain man, he thought Gods eies to have deceav'd?

20

And well he might delude those eyes, that see,   *Then of his*
And judge by colours: for who ever sawe   *posterities,*
                                        in all kinde
A man of leaves, a reasonable tree?   *of Idolatrie.*
But those that from this stocke their life did drawe,
Soone made their Father godly, and by lawe
   Proclaimed Trees almightie: Gods of wood,
   Of stocks, and stones with crownes of laurell stood
Templed, and fed by fathers with their childrens blood.

21

The sparkling fanes, that burne in beaten gould,
And, like the starres of heav'n in mid'st of night,
Blacke Egypt, as her mirrhours, doth behould,
Are but the denns whear idoll-snakes delight
Againe to cover Satan from their sight:
   Yet these are all their gods, to whome they vie
   The Crocodile, the Cock, the Rat, the Flie.
Fit gods, indeede, for such men to be served by.

22

The Fire, the winde, the sea, the sunne, and moone,
The flitting Aire, and the swift-winged How'rs,
And all the watchmen, that so nimbly runne,
And centinel about the walled towers
Of the worlds citie, in their heav'nly bowr's.
   And, least their pleasant gods should want delight,
   Neptune spues out the Lady Aphrodite,
And but in heaven proude Junos peacocks skorne to lite.

23

The senselesse Earth, the Serpent, dog, and catte,
And woorse then all these, Man, and woorst of men
Usurping Jove, and swilling Bacchus fat,
And drunke with the vines purple blood, and then
The Fiend himselfe they conjure from his denne,
   Because he onely yet remain'd to be
   Woorse then the worst of men, they flie from thee,
And weare his altar-stones out with their pliant knee.

24

All that he speakes (and all he speakes are lies)
Are oracles, 'tis he (that wounded all)
Cures all their wounds, he (that put out their eyes)
That gives them light, he (that death first did call
Into the world) that with his orizall,
    Inspirits earth: he heav'ns al-seeing eye,
    He earths great Prophet, he, whom rest doth flie,
That on salt billowes doth, as pillowes, sleeping lie.

25

But let him in his cabin restles rest,
The dungeon of darke flames, and freezing fire,
Justice in heav'n against man makes request
To God, and of his Angels doth require
Sinnes punishment: if what I did desire,
    Or who, or against whome, or why, or whear,
    Of, or before whom ignorant I wear,
Then should my speech their sands of sins to mountaines rear.

How hopelesse any patronage of it.

26

Wear not the heav'ns pure, in whose courts I sue,
The Judge, to whom I sue, just to requite him,
The cause for sinne, the punishment most due,
Justice her selfe the plaintiffe to endite him,
The Angells holy, before whom I cite him,
    He against whom, wicked, unjust, impure;
    Then might he sinnefull live, and die secure,
Or triall might escape, or triall might endure,

27

The Judge might partiall be, and over-pray'd,
The place appeald from, in whose courts he sues,
The fault excus'd, or punishment delayd,
The parties selfe accus'd, that did accuse,
Angels for pardon might their praiers use:
    But now no starre can shine, no hope be got.
    Most wretched creature, if he knewe his lot,
And yet more wretched farre, because he knowes it not.

28

What should I tell how barren earth is growne,
All for to sterve her children, didst not thou
Water with heav'nly showers her wombe unsowne,
And drop downe cloudes of flow'rs, didst not thou bowe
Thine easie eare unto the plowmans vowe,
 Long might he looke, and looke, and long in vaine
 Might load his harvest in an emptie wayne,
And beat the woods, to finde the poore okes hungrie graine.

All the Creatures having disleagued themselves with him.

29

The swelling sea seethes in his angrie waves,
And smites the earth, that dares the traytors nourish,
Yet oft his thunder their light corke outbraves,
Mowing the mountaines, on whose temples flourish
Whole woods of garlands, and, their pride to cherish,
 Plowe through the seaes greene fields, and nets display
 To catch the flying winds, and steale away,
Coozning the greedie sea, prisning their nimble prey.

30

How often have I seene the waving pine,
Tost on a watrie mountaine, knocke his head
At heav'ns too patient gates, and with salt brine
Quench the Moones burning hornes, and safely fled
From heav'ns revenge, her passengers, all dead
 With stiffe astonishment, tumble to hell?
 How oft the sea all earth would overswell,
Did not thy sandie girdle binde the mightie well?

31

Would not the aire be fill'd with steames of death,
To poyson the quicke rivers of their blood,
Did not thy windes fan, with their panting breath,
The flitting region? would not the hastie flood
Emptie it selfe into the seas wide wood,
 Did'st not thou leade it wandring from his way,
 To give men drinke, and make his waters strey,
To fresh the flowrie medowes, through whose fields they play?

32

Who makes the sources of the silver fountaines
From the flints mouth, and rocky valleis slide,
Thickning the ayrie bowells of the mountaines?
Who hath the wilde heards of the forrest tide
In their cold denns, making them hungrie bide
   Till man to rest be laid? can beastly he,
    That should have most sense, onely senseles be,
And all things else, beside himselfe, so awefull see?

33

Wear he not wilder then the salvage beast,
Prowder then haughty hills, harder then rocks,
Colder then fountaines, from their springs releast,
Lighter then aire, blinder then senseles stocks,
More changing then the rivers curling locks,
   If reason would not, sense would soone reproove   *For his*
     him,   *extreame un-*
    And unto shame, if not to sorrow, moove him,   *gratefulnes.*
To see cold floods, wild beasts, dul stocks, hard stones out-love him.

34

Under the weight of sinne the earth did fall,
And swallowed Dathan; and the raging winde,
And stormie sea, and gaping Whale, did call
For Jonas; and the aire did bullets finde,
And shot from heav'n a stony showre, to grinde
   The five proud Kings, that for their idols fought,
    The Sunne it selfe stood still to fight it out,
And fire from heav'n flew downe, when sin to heav'n did shout.

35

Should any to himselfe for safety flie?   *So that beeing*
The way to save himselfe, if any were,   *destitute of*
                                       all hope, or
Wear to flie from himselfe: should he relie   *any remedie,*
Upon the promise of his wife? but there,
What can he see, but that he most may feare,
   A Syren, sweete to death: upon his friends?
   Who that he needs, or that he hath not lends?
Or wanting aide himselfe, ayde to another sends?

36

His strength? but dust: his pleasure? cause of paine:
His hope? false courtier: youth, or beawtie? brittle:
Intreatie? fond: repentance? late, and vaine:
Just recompence? the world wear all too little:
Thy love? he hath no title to a tittle:
 Hells force? in vaine her furies hell shall gather:
 His Servants, Kinsmen, or his children rather?
His child, if good, shall judge, if bad, shall curse his father.

37

His life? that brings him to his end, and leaves him:
His ende? that leaves him to beginne his woe:
His goods? what good in that, that so deceaves him?
His gods of wood? their feete, alas, are slowe
To goe to helpe, that must be help't to goe:
 Honour, great woorth? ah, little woorth they be
 Unto their owners: wit? that makes him see
He wanted wit, that thought he had it, wanting thee.

38

The sea to drinke him quicke? that casts his dead:
Angells to spare? they punish: night to hide?
The world shall burne in light: the heav'ns to spread
Their wings to save him? heav'n it selfe shall slide,
And rowle away like melting starres, that glide
 Along their oylie threads: his minde pursues him:
 His house to shrowde, or hills to fall, and bruse him?
As Seargeants both attache, and witnesses accuse him:

39

What need I urge, what they must needs confesse?
Sentence on them, condemn'd by their owne lust;
I crave no more, and thou canst give no lesse,   *He can look*
Then death to dead men, justice to unjust;   *for nothing,*
                    but a fearful
Shame to most shamefull, and most shameles dust: *sentence.*
 But if thy Mercie needs will spare her friends,
 Let Mercie there begin, where Justice endes.
Tis cruell Mercie, that the wrong from right defends.

40

She ended, and the heav'nly Hierarchies,
Burning in zeale, thickly imbranded weare:
Like to an armie, that allarum cries,
And every one shakes his ydraded speare,
And the Almighties selfe, as he would teare
    The earth, and her firme basis quite in sunder,
    Flam'd all in just revenge, and mightie thunder,
Heav'n stole it selfe from earth by clouds that moisterd under.

The effect of Justice her speech: the inflammation of the heavenly Powers,

41

As when the cheerfull Sunne, elamping wide,
Glads all the world with his uprising raye,
And wooes the widow'd earth afresh to pride,
And paint her bosome with the flowrie Maye,
His silent sister steales him quite away,
    Wrap't in a sable clowde, from mortall eyes,
    The hastie starres at noone begin to rise,
And headlong to his early roost the sparrowe flies.

Appeased by Mercie, who is described by her cherfulnes to defend Man.

42

But soone as he againe dishadowed is,
Restoring the blind world his blemish't sight,
As though another day wear newely ris,
The cooz'ned birds busily take their flight,
And wonder at the shortnesse of the night:
    So Mercie once againe her selfe displayes,
    Out from her sisters cloud, and open layes
Those sunshine lookes, whose beames would dim a thousand dayes.

43

How may a worme, that crawles along the dust,
Clamber the azure mountaines, thrown so high,
And fetch from thence thy faire Idea just,
That in those sunny courts doth hidden lie,
Cloath'd with such light, as blinds the Angels eye;
    How may weake mortall ever hope to file
    His unsmooth tongue, and his deprostrate stile?
O raise thou from his corse, thy now entomb'd exile.

Our inabilitie to describe her.

44

One touch would rouze me from my sluggish hearse,
One word would call me to my wished home,
One looke would polish my afflicted verse,
One thought would steale my soule from her thicke lome,
And force it wandring up to heav'n to come,
    Thear to importune, and to beg apace
    One happy favour of thy sacred grace,
To see, (what though it loose her eyes?) to see thy face.

45

If any aske why roses please the sight,   *Her beautie,*
Because their leaves upon thy cheekes doe bowre;   *resembled by*
                                       the creatures,
If any aske why lillies are so white,   *which are all*
Because their blossoms in thy hand doe flowre: *fraile shadows*
                                       of her essentiall
Or why sweet plants so gratefull odours shoure;   *perfection.*
    It is because thy breath so like they be:
    Or why the Orient Sunne so bright we see;
What reason can we give, but from thine eies, and thee?

46

Ros'd all in lively crimsin ar thy cheeks,
Whear beawties indeflourishing abide,
And, as to passe his fellowe either seekes,
Seemes both doe blush at one anothers pride:
And on thine eyelids, waiting thee beside,
    Ten thousand Graces sit, and when they moove   *Her Attendants.*
    To earth their amourous belgards from above,
They flie from heav'n, and on their wings convey thy love.

47

All of discolour'd plumes their wings ar made,
And with so wondrous art the quills ar wrought,
That whensoere they cut the ayrie glade,
The winde into their hollowe pipes is caught:
As seemes the spheres with them they down have brought:
    Like to the seaven-fold reede of Arcadie,
    Which Pan of Syrinx made, when she did flie
To Ladon sands, and at his sighs sung merily.

48

As melting hony, dropping from the combe,   *Her perswasive*
So still the words, that spring between thy lipps,   *power.*
Thy lippes, whear smiling sweetnesse keepes her home,
And heav'nly Eloquence pure manna sipps,
He that his pen but in that fountaine dipps,
    How nimbly will the golden phrases flie,
    And shed forth streames of choycest rhetorie,
Welling celestiall torrents out of poësie?

49

Like as the thirstie land, in summers heat,
Calls to the cloudes, and gapes at everie showre,
As though her hungry clifts all heav'n would eat,
Which if high God into her bosome powre,
Though much refresht, yet more she could devoure:
    So hang the greedie ears of Angels sweete,
    And every breath a thousand cupids meete,
Some flying in, some out, and all about her fleet.

50

Upon her breast, Delight doth softly sleepe,
And of eternall joy is brought abed,
Those snowie mountelets, through which doe creepe
The milkie rivers, that ar inly bred
In silver cesternes, and themselves doe shed
    To wearie Travailers, in heat of day,
    To quench their fierie thirst, and to allay
With dropping nectar floods, the furie of their way.

51

If any wander, thou doest call him backe,   *Her kind offices*
If any be not forward, thou incit'st him,   *to Man.*
Thou doest expect, if any should growe slacke,
If any seeme but willing, thou invit'st him,
Or if he doe offend thee, thou acquit'st him,
    Thou find'st the lost, and follow'st him that flies,
    Healing the sicke, and quickning him that dies,
Thou art the lame mans friendly staffe, the blind mans eyes.

52

So faire thou art that all would thee behold,
But none can thee behold, thou art so faire,
Pardon, O pardon then thy Vassall bold,
That with poore shadowes strives thee to compare,
And match the things, which he knowes matchlesse are;
   O thou vive mirrhour of celestiall grace,
   How can fraile colours pourtraict out thy face,
Or paint in flesh thy beawtie, in such semblance base?

53

Her upper garment was a silken lawne,   *Her Garments,*
With needle-woorke richly embroidered,   *wrought by her*
                                   owne hands,
Which she her selfe with her owne hand had drawne, *wherwith shee*
And all the world therein had pourtrayed,   *cloaths her selfe,*
                                   composd of all
With threads, so fresh, and lively coloured,   *the Creatures,*
   That seem'd the world she newe created thear,
   And the mistaken eye would rashly swear
The silken trees did growe, and the beasts living wear.

54

Low at her feet the Earth was cast alone,   *The Earth.*
(As though to kisse her foot it did aspire,
And gave it selfe for her to tread upon)
With so unlike, and different attire,
That every one that sawe it, did admire
   What it might be, was of so various hewe;
   For to it selfe it oft so diverse grewe,
That still it seem'd the same, and still it seem'd a newe.

55

And here, and there few men she scattered,
(That in their thought the world esteeme but small,
And themselves great) but she with one fine thread
So short, and small, and slender wove them all,
That like a sort of busie ants, that crawle
   About some molehill, so they wandered:
   And round about the waving Sea was shed,   *Sea,*
But, for the silver sands, small pearls were sprinkled.

56

So curiously the underworke did creepe,
And curling circlets so well shadowed lay,
That afar off the waters seem'd to sleepe,
But those that neere the margin pearle did play,
Hoarcely enwaved wear with hastie sway,
  As though they meant to rocke the gentle eare,
  And hush the former that enslumbred wear,
And here a dangerous rocke the flying ships did fear.

57

High in the ayrie element there hung   *Ayre,*
Another clowdy sea, that did disdaine
(As though his purer waves from heaven sprung)
To crawle on earth, as doth the sluggish maine:
But it the earth would water with his raine,
  That eb'd, and flow'd, as winde, and season would,
  And oft the Sun would cleave the limber mould
To alabaster rockes, that in the liquid rowl'd.

58

Beneath those sunny banks, a darker cloud,
Dropping with thicker deaw, did melt apace,
And bent it selfe into a hollowe shroude,
On which, if Mercy did but cast her face,
A thousand colours did the bowe enchace,
  That wonder was to see the silke distain'd
  With the resplendance from her beawtie gain'd,
And Iris paint her locks with beames, so lively feign'd.

59

About her head a cyprus heav'n she wore,   *The celestiall*
Spread like a veile, upheld with silver wire,   *bodies,*
In which the starres so burn't in golden ore,
As seem'd, the azure web was all on fire,
But hastily, to quench their sparkling ire,
  A flood of milke came rowling up the shore,
  That on his curded wave swift Argus bore,
And the immortall swan, that did her life deplore.

60

Yet strange it was, so many starres to see
Without a Sunne, to give their tapers light:
Yet strange it was not, that it so should be:
For, where the Sunne centers himselfe by right,
Her face, and locks did flame, that at the sight,
   The heavenly veile, that else should nimbly moove,
   Forgot his flight, and all incens'd with love,
With wonder, and amazement, did her beautie proove.

61

Over her hung a canopie of state,   *The third heaven.*
Not of rich tissew, nor of spangled gold,
But of a substance, though not animate,
Yet of a heav'nly, and spirituall mould,
That onely eyes of Spirits might behold:
   Such light as from maine rocks of diamound,
   Shooting their sparks at Phebus, would rebound,
And little Angels, holding hands, daunc't all around.

62

Seemed those little sprights, through nimbless bold,
The stately canopy bore on their wings,
But them it selfe, as pendants, did uphold,
Besides the crownes of many famous kings,
Among the rest, thear David ever sings,
   And now, with yeares growne young, renewes his layes
   Unto his golden harpe, and ditties playes,
Psalming aloud in well tun'd songs his Makers prayse.

63

Thou self-Idea of all joyes to come,
Whose love is such, would make the rudest speake,
Whose love is such, would make the wisest dumbe,
O when wilt thou thy too long silence breake,
And overcome the strong to save the weake!
   If thou no weapons hast, thine eyes will wound
   Th'Almighties selfe, that now sticke on the ground, *Her Objects.*
As though some blessed object thear did them empound.

64

Ah miserable Abject of disgrace,   *Repentance.*
What happines is in thy miserie?
I both must pittie, and envie thy case.
For she, that is the glorie of the skie,
Leaves heaven blind, to fix on thee her eye.
 Yet her (though Mercies selfe esteems not small)
 The world despis'd, they her Repentance call,
And she her selfe despises, and the world, and all.

65

Deepely, alas empassioned she stood,
To see a flaming brand, tost up from hell,
Boyling her heart in her owne lustfull blood,
That oft for torment she would loudely yell,
Now she would sighing sit, and nowe she fell
 Crouching upon the ground, in sackcloth trust,
 Early, and late she prayed, and fast she must,
And all her haire hung full of ashes, and of dust.

66

Of all most hated, yet hated most of all
Of her owne selfe she was; disconsolat
(As though her flesh did but infunerall
Her buried ghost) she in an arbour sat
Of thornie brier, weeping her cursed state,
 And her before a hastie river fled,
 Which her blind eyes with faithfull penance fed,
And all about, the grasse with tears hung downe his head.

67

Her eyes, though blind abroad, at home kept fast,
Inwards they turn'd, and look't into her head,
At which shee often started, as aghast,
To see so fearfull spectacles of dread,
And with one hand, her breast shee martyred,
 Wounding her heart, the same to mortifie,
 The other a faire damsell held her by,   *Faith.*
Which if but once let goe, shee sunke immediatly.

68

But Faith was quicke, and nimble as the heav'n,
As if of love, and life shee all had been,
And though of present sight her sense were reaven,
Yet shee could see the things could not be seen:
Beyond the starres, as nothing wear between,
  She fixt her sight, disdeigning things belowe,
  Into the sea she could a mountaine throwe,
And make the Sun to stande, and waters backewards flowe.

69

Such when as Mercie her beheld from high,
In a darke valley, drownd with her owne tears,
One of her graces she sent hastily,
Smiling Eirene, that a garland wears
Of guilded olive, on her fairer hears,
  To crowne the fainting soules true sacrifice,
  Whom when as sad Repentance comming spies,
The holy Desperado wip't her swollen eyes.

70

But Mercie felt a kinde remorse to runne   *Her deprecative*
Through her soft vaines, and therefore, hying fast   *spech for Man,*
To give an end to silence, thus begunne.   *in which*
Aye-honour'd Father, if no joy thou hast
But to reward desert, reward at last
  The Devils voice, spoke with a serpents tongue,
  Fit to hisse out the words so deadly stung,
And let him die, deaths bitter charmes so sweetely sung.

71

He was the father of that hopeles season,   *She translates*
That to serve other Gods, forgot their owne,   *the principal*
The reason was, thou wast above their reason: *fault unto the*
They would have any Gods, rather then none,   *Devill.*
A beastly serpent, or a senselesse stone:
  And these, as Justice hates, so I deplore:
  But the up-plowed heart, all rent, and tore,
Though wounded by it selfe, I gladly would restore.

72

He was but dust; why fear'd he not to fall?
And beeing fall'n, how can he hope to live?
Cannot the hand destroy him, that made all?
Could he not take away, as well as give?
Should man deprave, and should not God deprive?
    Was it not all the worlds deceiving spirit,
    (That, bladder'd up with pride of his owne merit,
Fell in his rise) that him of heav'n did disinherit?

And repeating
Justice her
aggravation of
mans sinne.

73

He was but dust: how could he stand before him?
And beeing fall'n, why should he feare to die?
Cannot the hand that made him first, restore him?
Deprav'd of sinne, should he deprived lie
Of grace? can he not hide infirmitie
    That gave him strength? unworthy the forsaking,
    He is, who ever weighs, without mistaking,
Or Maker of the man, or manner of his making.

Mittigates it
1. by a contrarie
inference.

74

Who shall thy temple incense any more;
Or to thy altar crowne the sacrifice;
Or strewe with idle flow'rs the hallow'd flore;
Or what should Prayer deck with hearbs, and spice,
Her vialls, breathing orisons of price?
    If all must paie that which all cannot paie?
    O first begin with mee, and Mercie slaie,
And thy thrice-honour'd Sonne, that now beneath doth strey.

2. By interessing
her selfe in the
cause, and Christ.

75

But if or he, or I may live, and speake,
And heav'n can joye to see a sinner weepe,
Oh let not Justice yron scepter breake
A heart alreadie broke, that lowe doth creep,
And with prone humblesse her feets dust doth sweep.
    Must all goe by desert? is nothing free?
    Ah, if but those that onely woorthy be,
None should thee ever see, none should thee ever see.

76

What hath man done, that man shall not undoe,
Since God to him is growne so neere a kin?
Did his foe slay him? he shall slay his foe:
Hath he lost all? he all againe shall win;
Is Sinne his Master? he shall master sinne:
    Too hardy soule, with sinne the field to trie:
    The onely way to conquer, was to flie,
But thus long death hath liv'd, and now deaths selfe shall die.

That is as sufficient to satisfie, as Man was impotent.

77

He is a path, if any be misled,
He is a robe, if any naked bee,
If any chaunce to hunger, he is bread,
If any be a bondman, he is free,
If any be but weake, howe strong is hee?
    To dead men life he is, to sicke men health,
    To blinde men sight, and to the needie wealth,
A pleasure without losse, a treasure without stealth.

78

Who can forget, never to be forgot,
The time, that all the world in slumber lies,
When, like the starres, the singing Angels shot
To earth, and heav'n awaked all his eyes,
To see another Sunne, at midnight rise,
    On earth? was never sight of pareil fame,
    For God before Man like himselfe did frame,
But God himselfe now like a mortall man became.

Whom shee celebrates from the time of his nativitie.

79

A Child he was, and had not learn't to speake,
That with his word the world before did make,
His Mothers armes him bore, he was so weake,
That with one hand the vaults of heav'n could shake,
See how small roome my infant Lord doth take,
    Whom all the world is not enough to hold.
    Who of his yeares, or of his age hath told?
Never such age so young, never a child so old.

From the effects of it in himselfe.

80

And yet but newely he was infanted,
And yet alreadie he was sought to die,
Yet scarcely borne, alreadie banished,
Not able yet to goe, and forc't to flie,
But scarcely fled away, when by and by,
    The Tyrans sword with blood is all defil'd,
    And Rachel, for her sonnes with furie wild,
Cries, O thou cruell King, and O my sweetest child.

81

Egypt his Nource became, whear Nilus springs,   *Egypt,*
Who streit, to entertaine the rising sunne,
The hasty harvest in his bosome brings;
But now for drieth the fields wear all undone,
And now with waters all is overrunne,
    So fast the Cynthian mountaines powr'd their snowe,
    When once they felt the sunne so neere them glowe,
That Nilus Egypt lost, and to a sea did growe.

82

The Angells caroll'd lowd their song of peace,   *The Angels,*
The cursed Oracles wear strucken dumb,
To see their Sheapheard, the poore Sheapheards   *Men,*
    press,
To see their King, the Kingly Sophies come,
And them to guide unto his Masters home,
    A Starre comes dauncing up the orient,
    That springs for joye over the strawy tent,
Whear gold, to make their Prince a crowne, they all present.

83

Young John, glad child, before he could be borne,
Leapt in the woombe, his joy to prophecie,
Old Anna though with age all spent, and worne,
Proclaimes her Saviour to posteritie,
And Simeon fast his dying notes doeth plie.
    Oh how the blessed soules about him trace.
    It is the fire of heav'n thou doest embrace,
Sing, Simeon, sing, sing Simeon, sing apace.

84

With that the mightie thunder dropt away
From Gods unwarie arme, now milder growne,
And melted into teares, as if to pray
For pardon, and for pittie, it had knowne,
That should have been for sacred vengeance throwne:
 Thereto the Armies Angelique devow'd
 Their former rage, and all to Mercie bow'd,
Their broken weapons at her feet they gladly strow'd.

The effect of Mercies speech.

85

Bring, bring ye Graces all your silver flaskets,
Painted with every choicest flowre that growes,
That I may soone unflow'r your fragrant baskets,
To strowe the fields with odours whear he goes,
Let what so e're he treads on be a rose.
 So downe shee let her eyelids fall, to shine
 Upon the rivers of bright Palestine,
Whose woods drop honie, and her rivers skip with wine.

A Transition to Christs second victorie.

Christs Victorie on Earth

I

Thear all alone she spi'd, alas the while;
In shadie darknes a poore Desolate,
That now had measur'd many a wearie mile,
Through a wast desert, whither heav'nly fate,
And his owne will him brought; he praying sate,
 And him to prey, as he to pray began,
 The Citizens of the wilde forrest ran,
And all with open throat would swallowe whole the man.

Christ brought into the place of combat, the wildernes, among the wilde beasts Mark 1. 13.

2

Soone did the Ladie to her Graces crie,
And on their wings her selfe did nimbly strowe,
After her coach a thousand Loves did flie,
So downe into the wildernesse they throwe,
Whear she, and all her trayne that with her flowe

Described by his proper Attribute. The Mercie of God

Thorough the ayrie wave, with sayles so gay,
Sinking into his brest that wearie lay,
Made shipwracke of themselves, and vanish't quite away.

3

Seemed that Man had them devoured all,
Whome to devoure the beasts did make pretence,
But him their salvage thirst did nought appall,
Though weapons none he had for his defence:
What armes for Innocence, but Innocence?
    For when they saw their Lords bright cognizance
    Shine in his face, soone did they disadvaunce,
And some unto him kneele, and some about him daunce.

4

Downe fell the Lordly Lions angrie mood,
And he himselfe fell downe, in congies lowe;
Bidding him welcome to his wastfull wood,
Sometime he kist the grasse whear he did goe,
And, as to wash his feete he well did knowe,
    With fauning tongue he lickt away the dust,
    And every one would neerest to him thrust,
And every one, with new, forgot his former lust.

*Whom the
creatures cannot
but adore.*

5

Unmindfull of himselfe, to minde his Lord,
The Lamb stood gazing by the Tygers side,
As though betweene them they had made accord,
And on the Lions back the goate did ride,
Forgetfull of the roughnes of the hide,
    If he stood still, their eyes upon him bayted,
    If walk't, they all in order on him wayted,
And when he slep't, they as his watch themselves conceited.

6

Wonder doeth call me up to see, O no,
I cannot see, and therefore sinke in woonder,
The man, that shines as bright as God, not so,
For God he is himselfe, that close lies under
That man, so close, that no time can dissunder

*By his unitie
with the Godhead.*

That band, yet not so close, but from him breake
Such beames, as mortall eyes are all too weake
Such sight to see, or it, if they should see, to speake.

7

Upon a grassie hillock he was laid, *His proper place.*
With woodie primroses befreckeled,
Over his head the wanton shadowes plaid
Of a wilde olive, that her bowgh's so spread,
As with her leav's she seem'd to crowne his head,
    And her greene armes t'embrace the Prince of peace,
    The Sunne so neere, needs must the winter cease,
The Sunne so neere, another Spring seem'd to increase.

8

His haire was blacke, and in small curls did twine, *The beutie of*
As though it wear the shadowe of some light, *his bodie.*
And underneath his face, as day, did shine, *Cant. 5. 11.*
But sure the day shined not halfe so bright, *Psalm 45. 2.*
Nor the Sunnes shadowe made so darke a night.
    Under his lovely locks, her head to shroude,
    Did make Humilitie her selfe growe proude,
Hither, to light their lamps, did all the Graces croude.

9

One of ten thousand soules I am, and more,
That of his eyes, and their sweete wounds complaine,
Sweete are the wounds of love, never so sore,
Ah might he often slaie mee so againe.
He never lives, that thus is never slaine.
    What boots it watch? those eyes, for all my art,
    Mine owne eyes looking on, have stole my heart,
In them Love bends his bowe, and dips his burning dart.

10

As when the Sunne, caught in an adverse clowde,
Flies crosse the world, and thear a new begets,
The watry picture of his beautie proude,
Throwes all abroad his sparkling spangelets,
And the whole world in dire amazement sets,

To see two dayes abroad at once, and all
Doubt whither nowe he rise, or nowe will fall:
So flam'd the Godly flesh, proude of his heav'nly thrall.

11

His cheekes as snowie apples, sop't in wine,   *Gen. 49. 12.*
Had their red roses quencht with lillies white,   *Cant. 5. 10.*
And like to garden strawberries did shine,
Wash't in a bowle of milke, or rose-buds bright
Unbosoming their brests against the light:
　　Here love-sicke soules did eat, thear dranke, and made
　　Sweete-smelling posies, that could never fade,
But worldly eyes him thought more like some living   *Isa. 53. 2.*
　　shade.

12

For laughter never look't upon his browe,
Though in his face all smiling joyes did bide,
No silken banners did about him flowe,
Fooles make their fetters ensignes of their pride:
He was best cloath'd when naked was his side,
　　A Lambe he was, and wollen fleece he bore,
　　Wove with one thread, his feete lowe sandalls wore,
But bared were his legges, so went the times of yore.

13

As two white marble pillars that uphold
Gods holy place whear he in glorie sets,
And rise with goodly grace and courage bold,
To beare his Temple on their ample jetts,
Vein'd every whear with azure rivulets,
　　Whom all the people on some holy morne,
　　With boughs and flowrie garlands doe adorne,
Of such, though fairer farre, this Temple was upborne.

14

Twice had Diana bent her golden bowe,   *By preparing*
And shot from heav'n her silver shafts, to rouse   *himself to the*
The sluggish salvages, that den belowe,   *combate*
And all the day in lazie covert drouze,

Since him the silent wildernesse did house,
  The heav'n his roofe, and arbour harbour was,
  The ground his bed, and his moist pillowe grasse.
But fruit thear none did growe, nor rivers none did passe.

15

At length an aged Syre farre off he sawe
Come slowely footing, everie step he guest
One of his feete he from the grave did drawe,
Three legges he had, the woodden was the best,
And all the waie he went, he ever blest
  With benedicities, and prayers store,
  But the bad ground was blessed n'er the more,
And all his head with snowe of Age was waxen hore.

*With his
Adversarie, that
seemd what he was
not,*

16

A good old Hermit he might seeme to be,
That for devotion had the world forsaken,
And now was travailing some Saint to see,
Since to his beads he had himselfe betaken,
Whear all his former sinnes he might awaken,
  And them might wash away with dropping brine,
  And almes, and fasts, and churches discipline,
And dead, might rest his bones under the holy shrine.

*Some devout
Essene.*

17

But when he neerer came, he lowted lowe
With prone obeysance, and with curt'sie kinde,
That at his feete his head he seemd to throwe;
What needs him now another Saint to finde?
Affections are the sailes, and faith the wind,
  That to this Saint a thousand soules conveigh
  Each hour: O happy Pilgrims thither strey!
What caren they for beasts, or for the wearie way?

18

Soone the old Palmer his devotions sung,
Like pleasing anthems, moduled in time,
For well that aged Syre could tip his tongue
With golden foyle of eloquence, and lime,

And licke his rugged speech with phrases prime.
  Ay me, quoth he, how many yeares have beene,
  Since these old eyes the Sunne of heav'n have seene!
Certes the Sonne of heav'n they now behold I weene.

19

Ah, mote my humble cell so blessed be
As heav'n to welcome in his lowely roofe,
And be the Temple for thy deitie!
Loe how my cottage worships thee aloofe,
That under ground hath hid his head, in proofe
  It doth adore thee with the seeling lowe,
  Here honie, milke, and chesnuts wild doe growe,
The boughs a bed of leaves upon thee shall bestowe.

20

But oh, he said, and therewith sigh't full deepe,   *(Closely tempting*
The heav'ns, alas, too envious are growne,   *him to despaire*
Because our fields thy presence from them keepe;   *of Gods providence,*
For stones doe growe, where corne was lately sowne: *and provide for*
(So stooping downe, he gather'd up a stone)   *himselfe.)*
  But thou with corne canst make this stone to eare,
  What needen we the angrie heav'ns to feare?
Let them envie us still, so we enjoy thee here.

21

Thus on they wandred, but those holy weeds   *But was what he*
A monstrous Serpent, and no man did cover.   *seemed not, Satan*
So under greenest hearbs the Adder feeds: *and would faine*
And round about that stinking corps did hover *have lead him*
The dismall Prince of gloomie night, and over
  His ever-damned head the Shadowes err'd
  Of thousand peccant ghosts, unseene, unheard,
And all the Tyrant feares, and all the Tyrant fear'd.

22

He was the Sonne of blackest Acheron,
Whear many frozen soules doe chattring lie,
And rul'd the burning waves of Phlegethon,
Whear many more in flaming sulphur frie,

At once compel'd to live and forc't to die,
  Whear nothing can be heard for the loud crie
  Of oh, and ah, and out alas that I
Or once againe might live, or once at length might die.

23

Ere long they came neere to a balefull bowre,   *1. To Desperation,*
Much like the mouth of that infernall cave,   *characterd by his*
That gaping stood all Commers to devoure,   *place,*
Darke, dolefull, dreary, like a greedy grave,
That still for carrion carkasses doth crave.
  The ground no hearbs, but venomous did beare,
  Nor ragged trees did leave, but every whear
Dead bones, and skulls wear cast, and bodies hanged wear.

24

Upon the roofe the bird of sorrowe sat
Elonging joyfull day with her sad note,
And through the shady aire, the fluttring bat
Did wave her leather sayles, and blindely flote.
While with her wings the fatall Shreechowle smote
  Th'unblessed house, thear, on a craggy stone,
  Celeno hung, and made his direfull mone,
And all about the murdered ghosts did shreek, and grone.

25

Like clowdie moonshine, in some shadowie grove,   *Countenance,*
Such was the light in which DESPAIRE did dwell,   *Apparell,*
But he himselfe with night for darkenesse strove.   *horrible*
His blacke uncombed locks dishevell'd fell   *apparitions, &c.*
About his face, through which, as brands of hell,
  Sunk in his skull, his staring eyes did glowe,
  That made him deadly looke, their glimpse did showe
Like Cockatrices eyes, that sparks of poyson throwe.

26

His cloaths wear ragged clouts, with thornes pind fast,
And as he musing lay, to stonie fright
A thousand wilde Chimera's would him cast:
As when a fearefull dreame, in mid'st of night,

Skips to the braine, and phansies to the sight
   Some winged furie, strait the hasty foot,
   Eger to flie, cannot plucke up his root,
The voyce dies in the tongue, and mouth gapes without boot.

27

Now he would dreame that he from heaven fell,
And then would snatch the ayre, afraid to fall;
And now he thought he sinking was to hell,
And then would grasp the earth, and now his stall
Him seemed hell, and then he out would crawle,
   And ever, as he crept, would squint aside,
   Lest him, perhaps, some Furie had espide,
And then, alas, he should in chaines for ever bide.

28

Therefore he softly shrunke, and stole away,
Ne ever durst to drawe his breath for feare,
Till to the doore he came, and thear he lay
Panting for breath, as though he dying were,
And still he thought, he felt their craples teare
   Him by the heels backe to his ougly denne,
   Out faine he would have leapt abroad, but then
The heav'n, as hell, he fear'd, that punish guilty men.

29

Within the gloomie hole of this pale wight
The Serpent woo'd him with his charmes to inne,
Thear he might baite the day, and rest the night,
But under that same baite a fearefull grin
Was readie to intangle him in sinne.
   But he upon ambrosia daily fed,
   That grew in Eden, thus he answered,
So both away wear caught, and to the Temple fled.

30

Well knewe our Saviour this the Serpent was,
And the old Serpent knewe our Saviour well,
Never did any this in falshood passe,
Never did any him in truth excell:

With him we fly to heav'n, from heav'n we fell
   With him: but nowe they both together met
   Upon the sacred pinnacles, that threat
With their aspiring tops, Astræas starrie seat.

31

Here did PRESUMPTION her pavillion spread,
Over the Temple, the bright starres among,
(Ah that her foot should trample on the head
Of that most reverend place!) and a lewd throng
Of wanton boyes sung her a pleasant song
   Of love, long life, of mercie, and of grace,
   And every one her deerely did embrace,
And she herselfe enamour'd was of her owne face.

2. To Presumption, characterd by her place,

Attendants, &c.

32

A painted face, belied with vermeyl store,
Which light Eüëlpis every day did trimme,
That in one hand a guilded anchor wore,
Not fixed on the rocke, but on the brimme
Of the wide aire she let it loosely swimme:
   Her other hand a sprinkle carried,
   And ever, when her Ladie wavered,
Court-holy water all upon her sprinkeled.

33

Poore foole, she thought herselfe in wondrous price
With God, as if in Paradise she wear,
But, wear shee not in a fooles paradise,
She might have seene more reason to despere:
But him she, like some ghastly fiend, did feare,
   And therefore as that wretch hew'd out his cell
   Under the bowels, in the heart of hell,
So she above the Moone, amid the starres would dwell.

34

Her Tent with sunny cloudes was seel'd aloft,
And so exceeding shone with a false light,
That heav'n it selfe to her it seemed oft,
Heav'n without cloudes to her deluded sight,

But cloudes withouten heav'n it was aright,
  And as her house was built, so did her braine
  Build castles in the aire, with idle paine,
But heart she never had in all her body vaine.

35

Like as a ship, in which no ballance lies,
Without a Pilot, on the sleeping waves,
Fairely along with winde, and water flies,
And painted masts with silken sayles embraves,
That Neptune selfe the bragging vessell saves,
  To laugh a while at her so proud aray;
  Her waving streamers loosely shee lets play,
And flagging colours shine as bright as smiling day:

36

But all so soone as heav'n his browes doth bend,
Shee veils her banners, and pulls in her beames,
The emptie barke the raging billows send
Up to th'Olympique waves, and Argus seemes
Againe to ride upon our lower streames:
  Right so PRESUMPTION did her selfe behave,
  Tossed about with every stormie wave,
And in white lawne shee went, most like an Angel brave.

37

Gently our Saviour shee began to shrive,   *And by her*
Whither he wear the Sonne of God, or no;   *Temptation.*
For any other shee disdeign'd to wive:
And if he wear, shee bid him fearles throw
Himselfe to ground, and thearwithall did show
  A flight of little Angels, that did wait
  Upon their glittering wings, to latch him strait,
And longed on their backs to feele his glorious weight.

38

But when she saw her speech prevailed nought,
Her selfe she tombled headlong to the flore:
But him the Angels on their feathers caught,
And to an ayrie mountaine nimbly bore,

Whose snowie shoulders, like some chaulkie shore,
  Restles Olympus seem'd to rest upon
  With all his swimming globes: so both are gone,
The Dragon with the Lamb. Ah, unmeet Paragon.

39

All suddenly the hill his snowe devours,
In liew whereof a goodly garden grew,
As if the snow had melted into flow'rs,
Which their sweet breath in subtill vapours threw,
That all about perfumed spirits flew.
  For what so ever might aggrate the sense,
  In all the world, or please the appetence,
Heer it was powred out in lavish affluence.

40

Not lovely Ida might with this compare,
Though many streames his banks besilvered,
Though Xanthus with his golden sands he bare,
Nor Hibla, though his thyme depastured,
As fast againe with honie blossomed.
  Ne Rhodope, ne Tempes flowrie playne,
  Adonis garden was to this but vayne,
Though Plato on his beds a flood of praise did rayne.

41

For in all these, some one thing most did grow,
But in this one, grew all things els beside,
For sweet varietie herselfe did throw
To every banke, here all the ground she dide
In lillie white, there pinks eblazed wide;
  And damask't all the earth, and here shee shed
  Blew violets, and there came roses red,
And every sight the yeelding sense, as captive led.

42

The garden like a Ladie faire was cut,
That lay as if shee slumber'd in delight,
And to the open skies her eyes did shut;
The azure fields of heav'n wear sembled right

K

In a large round, set with the flowr's of light,
　　The flowr's-de-luce, and the round sparks of deaw,
　　That hung upon their azure leaves, did shew
Like twinkling starrs, that sparkle in th'eav'ning blew.

43

Upon a hillie banke her head shee cast,
On which the bowre of Vaine-Delight was built,
White, and red roses for her face wear plac't,
And for her tresses Marigolds wear spilt:
Them broadly shee displaid, like flaming guilt,
　　Till in the ocean the glad day wear drown'd,
　　Then up againe her yellow locks she wound,
And with greene fillets in their prettie calls them bound.

44

What should I here depeint her lillie hand,
Her veines of violets, her ermine brest,
Which thear in orient colours living stand,
Or how her gowne with silken leaves is drest;
Or how her watchmen, arm'd with boughie crest,
　　A wall of prim hid in his bushes bears,
　　Shaking at every winde their leavie spears,
While she supinely sleeps, ne to be waked fears?

45

Over the hedge depends the graping Elme,
Whose greener head, empurpuled in wine,
Seemed to wonder at his bloodie helme;
And halfe suspect the bunches of the vine.
Least they, perhaps, his wit should undermine.
　　For well he knewe such fruit he never bore:
　　But her weake armes embraced him the more,
And with her ruby grapes laught at her paramour.

46

Under the shadowe of these drunken elmes
A Fountaine rose, where Pangloretta uses,
(When her some flood of fancie overwhelms,
And one of all her favourites she chuses)

To bath herselfe, whom she in lust abuses,
　　And from his wanton body sucks his soule,
　　Which drown'd in pleasure, in that shaly bowle,
And swimming in delight, doth amarously rowle.

47

The font of silver was, and so his showrs
In silver fell, onely the guilded bowles
(Like to a fornace, that the min'rall powres)
Seem'd to have moul't it in their shining holes:
And on the water, like to burning coles,
　　On liquid silver, leaves of roses lay:
　　But when PANGLORIE here did list to play,
Rose water then it ranne, and milke it rain'd they say.

48

The roofe thicke cloudes did paint, from which three boyes
Three gaping mermaides with their eawrs did feede,
Whose brests let fall the streame, with sleepie noise,
To Lions mouths, from whence it leapt with speede,
And in the rosie laver seem'd to bleed.
　　The naked boyes unto the waters fall,
　　Their stonie nightingales had taught to call,
When Zephyr breath'd into their watry interall.

49

And all about, embayed in soft sleepe,
A heard of charmed beasts aground wear spread,
Which the faire Witch in goulden chaines did keepe,
And them in willing bondage fettered,
Once men they liv'd, but now the men were dead,
　　And turn'd to beasts, so fabled Homer old,
　　That Circe, with her potion, charm'd in gold,
Us'd manly soules in beastly bodies to immould.

50

Through this false Eden, to his Lemans bowre,
(Whome thousand soules devoutly idolize)
Our first destroyer led our Saviour.
Thear in the lower roome, in solemne wise,

From her Court, and Courtiers.
1. Pleasure in drinking.

They daunc't a round, and powr'd their sacrifice
  To plumpe Lyæus, and among the rest,
  The jolly Priest, in yvie garlands drest,
Chaunted wild Orgialls, in honour of the feast.

51

Others within their arbours swilling sat,
(For all the roome about was arboured)
With laughing Bacchus, that was growne so fat,
That stand he could not, but was carried,
And every evening freshly watered,
  To quench his fierie cheeks, and all about
  Small cocks broke through the wall, and sallied out
Flaggons of wine, to set on fire that spueing rout.

52

This their inhumed soules esteem'd their wealths,
To crowne the bouzing kan from day to night,
And sicke to drinke themselves with drinking healths,
Some vomiting, all drunken with delight.
Hence to a loft, carv'd all in yvorie white,   *in Luxurie.*
  They came, whear whiter Ladies naked went,
  Melted in pleasure, and soft languishment,
And sunke in beds of roses, amourous glaunces sent.

53

Flie, flie thou holy child that wanton roome,
And thou my chaster Muse those harlots shun,
And with him to a higher storie come,   *2. Avarice.*
Whear mounts of gold, and flouds of silver run,
The while the owners, with their wealth undone,
  Starve in their store, and in their plentie pine,
  Tumbling themselves upon their heaps of mine.
Glutting their famish't soules with the deceitfull shine.

54

Ah, who was he such pretious perills found?
How strongly Nature did her treasures hide;
And threw upon them mountains of thicke ground,
To darke their orie lustre; but queint Pride

Hath taught her Sonnes to wound their mothers side,
    And gage the depth, to search for flaring shells,
    In whose bright bosome spumie Bacchus swells,
That neither heav'n, nor earth henceforth in safetie dwells.

55

O sacred hunger of the greedie eye,
Whose neede hath end, but no end covetise,
Emptie in fulnes, rich in povertie,
That having all things, nothing can suffice,
How thou befanciest the men most wise?
    The poore man would be rich, the rich man great,
    The great man King, the King, in Gods owne seat
Enthron'd, with mortal arme dares flames, and thunder threat.

56

Therefore above the rest Ambition sat: *3. Ambitious*
His Court with glitterant pearle was all enwall'd,   *honour.*
And round about the wall in chaires of State,
And most majestique splendor, wear enstall'd
A hundred Kings, whose temples wear impal'd
    In goulden diadems, set here, and thear
    With diamounds, and gemmed every whear,
And of their golden virges none disceptred wear.

57

High over all, *Panglories* blazing throne,   *From her throne.*
In her bright turret, all of christall wrought,
Like Phœbus lampe in midst of heaven, shone:
Whose starry top, with pride infernall fraught,
Selfe-arching columns to uphold wear taught:
    In which, her Image still reflected was
    By the smooth christall, that most like her glasse,
In beauty, and in frailtie, did all others passe.

58

A Silver wande the sorceresse did sway,
And, for a crowne of gold, her haire she wore,
Onely a garland of rosebuds did play
About her locks, and in her hand, she bore

A hollowe globe of glasse, that long before,
   She full of emptinesse had bladdered,
   And all the world therein depictured,
Whose colours, like the rainebowe, ever vanished.

59

Such watry orbicles young boyes doe blowe
Out from their sopy shells, and much admire
The swimming world, which tenderly they rowe
With easie breath, till it be waved higher,
But if they chaunce but roughly once aspire,
   The painted bubble instantly doth fall.
   Here when she came, she gan for musique call,
And sung this wooing song, to welcome him withall.

Love is the blossome whear thear blowes   *From her*
Every thing, that lives, or growes,   *temptation.*
Love doth make the heav'ns to move,
And the Sun doth burne in love;
Love the strong, and weake doth yoke,
And makes the yvie climbe the oke,
Under whose shadowes Lions wilde,
Soft'ned by Love, growe tame, and mild;
Love no med'cine can appease,
He burnes the fishes in the seas,
Not all the skill his wounds can stench,
Not all the sea his fire can quench;
Love did make the bloody spear
Once a levie coat to wear,
While in his leaves thear shrouded lay
Sweete birds, for love, that sing, and play;
And of all loves joyfull flame,
I the bud, and blossome am.
   Onely bend thy knee to me,
   Thy wooing, shall thy winning be.

See, see the flowers that belowe,
Now as fresh as morning blowe,
And of all, the virgin rose,
That as bright Aurora showes,

How they all unleaved die,
Loosing their virginitie:
Like unto a summer-shade,
But now borne, and now they fade.
Every thing doth passe away,
Thear is danger in delay,
Come, come gather then the rose,
Gather it, or it you lose.
All the sande of Tagus shore
Into my bosome casts his ore;
All the valleys swimming corne
To my house is yeerely borne;
Every grape, of every vine
Is gladly bruis'd to make me wine,
While ten thousand kings, as proud,
To carry up my traine, have bow'd,
And a world of Ladies send me
In my chambers to attend me:
All the starres in heav'n that shine,
And ten thousand more, are mine:
    Onely bend thy knee to mee,
    Thy wooing shall thy winning bee.

60

Thus sought the dire Enchauntress in his minde
Her guilefull bayt to have embosomed,
But he her charmes dispersed into winde,
And her of insolence admonished,
And all her optique glasses shattered.   *The effect of this*
    So with her Syre to hell shee tooke her flight,   *victorie in Satan.*
    (The starting ayre flew from the damned spright,)
Whear deeply both aggriev'd, plunged themselves in night.

61

But to their Lord, now musing in his thought,   *The Angels.*
A heavenly volie of light Angels flew,
And from his Father him a banquet brought,
Through the fine element, for well they knew,
After his lenten fast, he hungrie grew,
    And, as he fed, the holy quires combine

To sing a hymne of the celestiall Trine;
All thought to passe, and each was past all thought divine.

62

The birds sweet notes, to sonnet out their joyes,   *The Creatures.*
Attemper'd to the layes Angelicall,
And to the birds, the winds attune their noyse,
And to the winds, the waters hoarcely call,
And Eccho back againe revoyced all,
    That the whole valley rung with victorie.
    But now our Lord to rest doth homewards flie:
See how the Night comes stealing from the mountains high.

Christs Triumph over Death

1

So downe the silver streames of Eridan,   *Christs Tryumph*
On either side bank't with a lilly wall,   *over death, on the*
Whiter then both, rides the truimphant Swan,   *crosse, exprest. 1.*
And sings his dirge, and prophesies his fall,   *in generall by his*
Diving into his watrie funerall: *joy to undergoe it:*
                                                          singing before he
    But Eridan to Cedron must submit   *went to the garden,*
    His flowry shore, nor can he envie it,   *Mat. 26. 30.*
If when Apollo sings, his swans doe silent sit.

2

That heav'nly voice I more delight to heare,
Then gentle ayres to breath, or swelling waves
Against the sounding rocks their bosomes teare,
Or whistling reeds, that rutty Jordan laves,
And with their verdure his white head embraves,
    To chide the windes, or hiving bees, that flie
    About the laughing blooms of sallowie,
Rocking asleepe the idle groomes that lazie lie.

3

And yet, how can I heare thee singing goe,
When men incens'd with hate, thy death foreset?
Or els, why doe I heare thee sighing so,
When thou, inflam'd with love, their life doest get?

That Love, and hate, and sighs, and songs are met;
  But thus, and onely thus thy love did crave,
  To sende thee singing for us to thy grave,
While we sought thee to kill, and thou sought'st us to save.

4

When I remember Christ our burden beares,   *By his griefe*
I looke for glorie, but finde miserie;   *in the under-*
I looke for joy, but finde a sea of teares;   *going it.*
I looke that we should live, and finde him die;
I looke for Angels songs, and heare him crie:
  Thus what I looke, I cannot finde so well,
  Or rather, what I finde, I cannot tell,
These bankes so narrowe are, those streames so highly swell.

5

Christ suffers, and in this, his teares begin,
Suffers for us, and our joy springs in this,
Suffers to death, here is his Manhood seen,
Suffers to rise, and here his Godhead is.
For Man, that could not by himselfe have ris,
  Out of the grave doth by the Godhead rise,
  And God, that could not die, in Manhood dies,
That we in both might live, by that sweete sacrifice.

6

Goe giddy braines, whose witts are thought so fresh,
Plucke all the flowr's that Nature forth doth throwe,
Goe sticke them on the cheekes of wanton flesh;
Poore idol, (forc't at once to fall and growe)
Of fading roses, and of melting snowe:
  Your songs exceede your matter, this of mine,
  The matter, which it sings, shall make divine,
As starres dull puddles guild, in which their beauties shine.

7

Who doth not see drown'd in Deucalions name,   *By the obscure*
(When earth his men, and sea had lost his shore)   *fables of the*
Old Noah; and in Nisus lock, the fame   *Gentiles, typing it.*
Of Sampson yet alive; and long before

In Phaethons, mine owne fall I deplore:
  But he that conquer'd hell, to fetch againe
  His virgin widowe, by a serpent slaine,
Another Orpheus was then dreaming poets feigne.

8

That taught the stones to melt for passion,
And dormant sea, to heare him, silent lie,
And at his voice, the watrie nation
To flocke, as if they deem'd it cheape, to buy
With their owne deaths his sacred harmonie:
  The while the waves stood still to heare his song,
  And steadie shore wav'd with the reeling throng
Of thirstie soules, that hung upon his fluent tongue.

9

What better friendship, then to cover shame?
What greater love, then for a friend to die?
Yet this is better to asself the blame,
And this is greater, for an enemie:
But more then this, to die, not suddenly,
  Not with some common death, or easie paine,
  But slowely, and with torments to be slaine,
O depth, without a depth, farre better seene, then saine!

By the cause of it in him, his Love.

10

And yet the Sonne is humbled for the Slave,
And yet the Slave is proude before the Sonne:
Yet the Creator for his creature gave
Himselfe, and yet the creature hasts to runne
From his Creator, and self-good doth shunne:
  And yet the Prince, and God himselfe doth crie
  To Man, his Traitour, pardon not to flie,
Yet Man his God, and Traytour doth his Prince defie.

By the effect it should have in us.

11

Who is it sees not that he nothing is,
But he that nothing sees; what weaker brest,
Since Adams Armour fail'd, dares warrant his?
That made by God of all his creatures best,

Strait made himselfe the woorst of all the rest:
  'If any strength we have, it is to ill,
  'But all the good is Gods, both pow'r, and will:'
The dead man cannot rise, though he himselfe may kill.

12

But let the thorny schools these punctualls
Of wills, all good, or bad, or neuter diss;
Such joy we gained by our parentalls,
That good, or bad, whither I cannot wiss,
To call it a mishap, or happy miss
    That fell from Eden, and to heav'n did rise:
    Albee the mitred Card'nall more did prize
His part in Paris, then his part in Paradise.

13

A Tree was first the instrument of strife,
Whear Eve to sinne her soule did prostitute,
A Tree is now the instrument of life,
Though ill that trunke, and this faire body suit:
Ah, cursed tree, and yet O blessed fruit!
    That death to him, this life to us doth give:
    Strange is the cure, when things past cure revive,
And the Physitian dies, to make his patient live.

By the instrument, the cursed Tree,

14

Sweete Eden was the arbour of delight,
Yet in his hony flowr's our poyson blew;
Sad Gethseman the bowre of balefull night,
Whear Christ a health of poison for us drewe,
Yet all our hony in that poyson grewe:
    So we from sweetest flowr's, could sucke our bane,
    And Christ from bitter venome, could againe
Extract life out of death, and pleasure out of paine.

2. exprest in particular,
1. by his fore-passion in the Garden.

15

A Man was first the author of our fall,
A Man is now the author of our rise,
A Garden was the place we perisht all,
A Garden is the place he payes our price,

And the old Serpent with a newe devise,
  Hath found a way himselfe for to beguile,
  So he, that all men tangled in his wile,
Is now by one man caught, beguil'd with his owne guile.

16

The dewie night had with her frostie shade
Immant'led all the world, and the stiffe ground
Sparkled in yce, onely the Lord, that made
All for himselfe, himselfe dissolved found,
Sweat without heat, and bled without a wound:
  Of heav'n and earth, and God, and Man forlore,
  Thrice begging helpe of those, whose sinnes he bore,
And thrice denied of those, not to denie had swore.

17

Yet had he beene alone of God forsaken,
Or had his bodie beene imbroyl'd alone
In fierce assault, he might, perhaps, have taken
Some joy in soule, when all joy els was gone,
But that with God, and God to heav'n is flow'n;
  And Hell it selfe out from her grave doth rise,
  Black as the starles night, and with them flies,
Yet blacker then they both, the Sonne of blasphemies.

18

As when the Planets, with unkind aspect,
Call from her caves the meager pestilence,
The sacred vapour, eager to infect,
Obeyes the voyce of the sad influence,
And vomits up a thousand noysome sents,
  The well of life, flaming his golden flood
  With the sicke ayre, fevers the boyling blood,
And poisons all the bodie with contagious food.

19

The bold Physitian, too incautelous,
By those he cures, himselfe is murdered,
Kindnes infects, pitie is dangerous,
And the poore infant, yet not fully bred,

Thear where he should be borne, lies buried:
  So the darke Prince, from his infernall cell,
  Casts up his griesly Torturers of hell,
And whets them to revenge, with this insulting spell.

20

See how the world smiles in eternall peace;
While we, the harmles brats, and rustie throng
Of Night, our snakes in curles doe pranke, and dresse:
Why sleepe our drouzie scorpions so long?
Whear is our wonted vertue to doe wrong?
  Are we our selves; or are we Graces growen?
  The Sonnes of hell, or heav'n? was never knowne
Our whips so over-moss't, and brands so deadly blowne.

21

O long desired, never hop't for howre,
When our Tormentour shall our torments feele!
Arme, arme your selves, sad Dires of my pow'r,
And make our Judge for pardon to us kneele,
Slise, launch, dig, teare him with your whips of steele:
  My selfe in honour of so noble prize,
  Will powre you reaking blood, shed with the cries
Of hastie heyres, who their owne fathers sacrifice.

22

With that a flood of poyson, blacke as hell,
Out from his filthy gorge, the beast did spue,
That all about his blessed bodie fell,
And thousand flaming serpents hissing flew
About his soule, from hellish sulphur threw,
  And every one brandisht his fierie tongue,
  And woorming all about his soule they clung,
But he their stings tore out, and to the ground them flung.

23

So have I seene a rocks heroique brest,
Against proud Neptune, that his ruin threats,
When all his waves he hath to battle prest,
And with a thousand swelling billows beats

The stubborne stone, and foams, and chafes, and frets
  To heave him from his root, unmooved stand;
  And more in heapes the barking surges band,
The more in pieces beat, flie weeping to the strand.

24

So may wee oft a vent'rous father see,
To please his wanton sonne, his onely joy,
Coast all about, to catch the roving bee,
And stung himselfe, his busie hands employ
To save the honie, for the gamesome boy:
  Or from the snake her rank'rous teeth erace,
  Making his child the toothles Serpent chace,
Or, with his little hands, her tum'rous gorge embrace.

25

Thus Christ himselfe to watch, and sorrow gives,
While, deaw'd in easie sleepe, dead Peter lies:
Thus Man in his owne grave securely lives,
While Christ alive, with thousand horrours dies,
Yet more for theirs, then his owne pardon cries:
  No sinnes he had, yet all our sinnes he bare,
  So much doth God for others evills care,
And yet so careles men for their owne evills are.

26

See drouzie Peter, see whear Judas wakes,
Whear Judas kisses him whom Peter flies:
O kisse more deadly then the sting of snakes!
False love more hurtfull then true injuries!
Aye me! how deerly God his Servant buies?
  For God his man, at his owne blood doth hold,
  And Man his God, for thirtie pence hath sold.
So tinne for silver goes, and dunghill drosse for gold.

*By his passion
it selfe,
amplified, 1.
from the genera
causes.*

27

Yet was it not enough for Sinne to chuse
A Servant, to betray his Lord to them;
But that a Subject must his King accuse,
But that a Pagan must his God condemne,

But that a Father must his Sonne contemne,
   But that the Sonne must his owne death desire,
   That Prince, and People, Servant, and the Sire,
Gentil, and Jewe, and he against himselfe conspire?

28

Was this the oyle, to make thy Saints adore thee,   *Parts, and*
The froathy spittle of the rascall throng?
Ar these the virges, that ar borne before thee,
Base whipps of corde, and knotted all along?
Is this thy golden scepter, against wrong,
   A reedie cane? is that the crowne adornes
   Thy shining locks, a crowne of spiny thornes?
Ar theas the Angels himns, the Priests blasphemous scornes?

29

Who ever sawe Honour before asham'd;   *Effects of it.*
Afflicted Majestie, debased height;
Innocence guiltie, Honestie defam'd;
Libertie bound, Health sick, the Sunne in night?
But since such wrong was offred unto right,
   Our night is day, our sicknes health is growne,
   Our shame is veild, this now remaines alone
For us, since he was ours, that wee bee not our owne.

30

Night was ordeyn'd for rest, and not for paine,   *2. From the*
But they, to paine their Lord, their rest contemne,   *particular causes.*
Good lawes to save, what bad men would have slaine,
And not bad Judges, with one breath, by them
The innocent to pardon, and condemne:
   Death for revenge of murderers, not decaie
   Of guiltles blood, but now, all headlong sway
Mans Murderer to save, mans Saviour to slaie.

31

Fraile Multitude, whose giddy lawe is list,
And best applause is windy flattering,
Most like the breath of which it doth consist,
No sooner blowne, but as soone vanishing,

As much desir'd, as little profiting,
   That makes the men that have it oft as light,
   As those that give it, which the proud invite,
And feare: the bad mans friend, the good mans hypocrite.

32

It was but now their sounding clamours sung,   *Parts, and*
Blessed is he, that comes from the most high,
And all the mountaines with Hosanna rung,
And nowe, away with him, away they crie,
And nothing can be heard but crucifie:
   It was but now, the Crowne it selfe they save,
   And golden name of King unto him gave,
And nowe, no King, but onely Cæsar, they will have:

33

It was but now they gathered blooming May,
And of his armes disrob'd the branching tree,
To strowe with boughs, and blossomes all thy way,
And now, the branchlesse truncke a crosse for thee,
And May, dismai'd, thy coronet must be:
   It was but now they wear so kind, to throwe
   Their owne best garments, whear thy feet should goe,
And now, thy selfe they strip, and bleeding wounds they show.

34

See whear the author of all life is dying:
O fearefull day! he dead, what hope of living?
See whear the hopes of all our lives are buying:
O chearfull day! they bought, what feare of grieving?
Love love for hate, and death for life is giving:
   Loe how his armes are stretch't abroad to grace thee,
   And, as they open stand, call to embrace thee,
Why stai'st thou then my soule; ô flie, flie thither hast thee.

35

His radious head, with shamefull thornes they teare,
His tender backe, with bloody whipps they rent,
His side, and heart they furrowe with a spear,
His hands, and feete, with riving nayles they tent,

And, as to disentrayle his soule they meant,
  They jolly at his griefe, and make their game,
  His naked body to expose to shame,
That all might come to see, and all might see, that came.

36

Whereat the heav'n put out his guiltie eye,   *Effects of it in*
That durst behold so execrable sight,   *heaven.*
And sabled all in blacke the shadie skie,
And the pale starres, strucke with unwonted fright,
Quenched their everlasting lamps in night:
  And at his birth as all the starres heav'n had,
  Wear not enough, but a newe star was made,
So now both newe, and old, and all away did fade.

37

The mazed Angels shooke their fierie wings,   *in the heavenly*
Readie to lighten vengeance from Gods throne,   *Spirits.*
One downe his eyes upon the Manhood flings,
Another gazes on the Godhead, none
But surely thought his wits wear not his owne:
  Some flew, to looke if it wear very hee,
  But, when Gods arme unarmed they did see,
Albee they sawe it was, they vow'd it could not bee.

38

The sadded aire hung all in cheerelesse blacke, *in the Creatures*
Through which, the gentle windes soft sighing flewe, *subcœlestiall.*
And Jordan into such huge sorrowe brake,
(As if his holy streame no measure knewe,)
That all his narrowe bankes he overthrewe,
  The trembling earth with horrour inly shooke,
  And stubborne stones, such griefe unus'd to brooke,
Did burst, and ghosts awaking from their graves gan looke.

39

The wise Philosopher cried, all agast,
The God of nature surely lanquished,
The sad Centurion cried out as fast,
The Sonne of God, the Sonne of God was dead,

The headlong Jew hung downe his pensive head,   *In the wicked*
  And homewards far'd, and ever, as he went,   *Jewes.*
  He smote his brest, halfe desperately bent,
The verie woods, and beasts did seeme his death lament.

40

The gracelesse Traytour round about did looke,   *In Judas.*
(He lok't not long, the Devill quickely met him)
To finde a halter, which he found, and tooke,
Onely a gibbet nowe he needes must get him,
So on a wither'd tree he fairly set him,
  And helpt him fit the rope, and in his thought
  A thousand furies, with their whippes, he brought,
So thear he stands, readie to hell to make his vault.

41

For him a waking bloodhound, yelling loude,
That in his bosome long had sleeping layde,
A guiltie Conscience, barking after blood,
Pursued eagerly, ne ever stai'd,
Till the betrayers selfe it had betray'd.
  Oft chang'd he place, in hope away to winde,
  But change of place could never change his minde,
Himselfe he flies to loose, and followes for to finde.

42

Thear is but two wayes for this soule to have,
When parting from the body, forth it purges,
To flie to heav'n, or fall into the grave,
Where whippes of scorpions, with the stinging scourges,
Feed on the howling ghosts, and firie Surges
  Of brimstone rowle about the cave of night,
  Where flames doe burne, and yet no sparke of light,
And fire both fries, and freezes the blaspheming spright.

43

Thear lies the captive soule, aye-sighing sore,
Reck'ning a thousand yeares since her first bands,
Yet staies not thear, but addes a thousand more,
And at another thousand never stands,

But tells to them the starres, and heapes the sands,
    And now the starres are told, and sands are runne,
    And all those thousand thousand myriads done,
And yet but now, alas! but now all is begunne.

44

With that a flaming brand a Furie catch't,
And shooke, and tost it round in his wilde thought,
So from his heart all joy, all comfort snatch't,
With every starre of hope, and as he sought,
(With present feare, and future griefe distraught)
    To flie from his owne heart, and aide implore
    Of him, the more he gives, that hath the more,
Whose storehouse is the heavens, too little for his store.

45

Stay wretch on earth, cried Satan, restles rest,
Know'st thou not Justice lives in heav'n; or can
The worst of creatures live among the best;
Among the blessed Angels cursed man?
Will Judas now become a Christian?
    Whither will hopes long wings transport thy minde;
    Or canst thou not thy selfe a sinner finde;
Or cruell to thy selfe, wouldst thou have Mercie kinde?

46

He gave thee life: why shouldst thou seeke to slay him?
He lent thee wealth: to feed thy avarice?
He cal'd thee friend: what, that thou shouldst betray him?
He kist thee, though he knew his life the price:
He washt thy feet: should'st thou his sacrifice?
    He gave thee bread, and wine, his bodie, blood,
    And at thy heart to enter in he stood,
But then I entred in, and all my snakie brood.

47

As when wild Pentheus, growne madde with fear,
Whole troups of hellish haggs about him spies,
Two bloodie Sunnes stalking the duskie sphear,
And twofold Thebes runs rowling in his eyes:

Or through the scene staring Orestes flies,
 With eyes flung back upon his Mothers ghost,
 That, with infernall serpents all embost,
And torches quencht in blood, doth her stern sonne accost.

48

Such horrid gorgons, and misformed formes
Of damned fiends, flew dauncing in his heart,
That now, unable to endure their stormes,
Flie, flie, he cries, thy selfe, what ere thou art,
Hell, hell alreadie burnes in every part.
 So downe into his Torturers armes he fell,
 That readie stood his funeralls to yell,
And in a clowd of night to waft him quick to hell.

49

Yet oft he snacht, and started as he hung:
So when the senses halfe enslumb'red lie,
The headlong bodie, readie to be flung,
By the deluding phansie, from some high,
And craggie rock, recovers greedily,
 And clasps the yeelding pillow, halfe asleepe,
 And, as from heav'n it tombled to the deepe,
Feeles a cold sweat through every trembling member creepe.

50

Thear let him hang, embowelled in blood,
Whear never any gentle Sheapheard feed
His blessed flocks, nor ever heav'nly flood
Fall on the cursed ground, nor holesome seed,
That may the least delight, or pleasure breed:
 Let never Spring visit his habitation,
 But nettles, kixe, and all the weedie nation,
With emptie elders grow, sad signes of desolation.

51

Thear let the Dragon keepe his habitance,
And stinking karcases be throwne avaunt,
Faunes, Sylvans, and deformed Satyrs daunce,
Wild-cats, wolves, toads, and shreechowles direly chaunt,

Thear ever let some restles spirit haunt,
  With hollow sound, and clashing cheynes, to scarr
  The passenger, and eyes like to the starr,
That sparkles in the crest of angrie Mars afarr.

52

But let the blessed deawes for ever showr
Upon that ground, in whose faire fields I spie
The bloodie ensigne of our Saviour:
Strange conquest, whear the Conquerour must die,
And he is slaine, that winns the victorie:
  But he, that living, had no house to owe it,   *In the blessed*
  Now had no grave, but Joseph must bestowe it,   *Saints,*
  Joseph, &c.
O runne ye Saints apace, and with sweete flowr's bestrowe it.

53

And ye glad Spirits, that now sainted sit
On your cœlestiall thrones, in beawtie drest,
Though I your teares recoumpt, O let not it
With after-sorrowe wound your tender brest,
Or with new griefe unquiet your soft rest:
  Inough is me your plaints to sound againe,
  That never could inough my selfe complaine,
Sing then, O sing aloude thou Arimathean Swaine.

54

But long he stood, in his faint armes upholding
The fairest spoile heav'n ever forfeited,
With such a silent passion griefe unfoulding,
That, had the sheete but on himselfe beene spread,
He for the corse might have beene buried:
  And with him stood the happie theefe, that stole
  By night his owne salvation, and a shole
Of Maries drowned, round about him, sat in dole.

55

At length (kissing his lipps before he spake,
As if from thence he fetcht againe his ghost)
To Mary thus, with teares, his silence brake.
Ah woefull soule! what joy in all our cost,

When him we hould, we have alreadie lost?
   Once did'st thou loose thy Sonne, but found'st againe,
   Now find'st thy Sonne, but find'st him lost, and slaine.
Ay mee! though he could death, how canst thou life sustaine?

56

Whear ere, deere Lord, thy Shadowe hovereth,
Blessing the place, wherein it deigns abide,
Looke how the earth darke horrour covereth,
Cloathing in mournfull black her naked side,
Willing her shadowe up to heav'n to glide,
   To see and if it meet thee wandring thear,
   That so, and if her selfe must misse thee hear,
At least her shadow may her dutie to thee bear.

57

See how the Sunne in daytime cloudes his face,
And lagging Vesper, loosing his late teame,
Forgets in heav'n to runne his nightly race,
But, sleeping on bright Oetas top, doeth dreame
The world a Chaos is, no joyfull beame
   Looks from his starrie bowre, the heav'ns doe mone,
   And Trees drop teares, least we should greeve alone,
The windes have learnt to sigh, and waters hoarcely grone.

58

And you sweete flow'rs, that in this garden growe,
Whose happie states a thousand soules envie,
Did you your owne felicities but knowe,
Your selves unpluckt would to his funerals hie,
You never could in better season die:
   O that I might into your places slide,
   The gate of heav'n stands gaping in his side,
Thear in my soule should steale, and all her faults should hide.

59

Are theas the eyes, that made all others blind;
Ah why ar they themselves now blemished?
Is this the face, in which all beawtie shin'd;
What blast hath thus his flowers debellished?

Ar these the feete, that on the watry head
  Of the unfaithfull Ocean passage found;
  Why goe they now so lowely under ground,
Wash't with our woorthles teares, and their owne precious wound?

60

One hem but of the garments that he wore,
Could medicine whole countries of their paine,
One touch of this pale hand could life restore,
One word of these cold lips revive the slaine:
Well the blinde man thy Godhead might maintaine,
  What though the sullen Pharises repin'd?
  He that should both compare, at length would finde
The blinde man onely sawe, the Seers all wear blinde.

61

Why should they thinke thee worthy to be slaine?
Was it because thou gav'st their blinde men eyes;
Or that thou mad'st their lame to walke againe;
Or for thou heal'dst their sick mens maladies;
Or mad'st their dumbe to speake; and dead to rise?
  O could all these but any grace have woon,
  What would they not to save thy life have done?
The dumb man would have spoke, and lame man would have runne.

62

Let mee, O let me neere some fountaine lie,
That through the rocke heaves up his sandie head,
Or let me dwell upon some mountaine high,
Whose hollowe root, and baser parts ar spread
On fleeting waters, in his bowells bred,
  That I their streames, and they my teares may feed,
  Or, cloathed in some Hermits ragged weed,
Spend all my daies, in weeping for this cursed deed.

63

The life, the which I once did love, I leave,
The love, in which I once did live, I loath,
I hate the light, that did my light bereave,
Both love, and life, I doe despise you both,

O that one grave might both our ashes cloath!
　A Love, a Life, a Light I now obteine,
　Able to make my Age growe young againe,
Able to save the sick, and to revive the slaine.

64

Thus spend we teares, that never can be spent,
On him, that sorrow now no more shall see:
Thus send we sighs, that never can be sent,
To him, that died to live, and would not be,
To be thear whear he would; here burie we
　This heav'nly earth, here let it softly sleepe,
　The fairest Sheapheard of the fairest sheepe.
So all the bodie kist, and homewards went to weepe.

65

So home their bodies went, to seeke repose,
But at the grave they left their soules behinde;
O who the force of love cœlestiall knowes!
That can the cheynes of natures selfe unbinde,
Sending the Bodie home, without the minde.
　Ah blessed Virgin, what high Angels art
　Can ever coumpt thy teares, or sing thy smart,
When every naile, that pierst his hand, did pierce thy heart?

66

So Philomel, perch't on an aspin sprig,
Weeps all the night her lost virginitie,
And sings her sad tale to the merrie twig,
That daunces at such joyfull miserie,
Ne ever lets sweet rest invade her eye:
　But leaning on a thorne her daintie chest,
　For feare soft sleepe should steale into her brest,
Expresses in her song greefe not to be exprest.

67

So when the Larke, poore birde, afarre espi'th
Her yet unfeather'd children (whom to save
She strives in vaine) slaine by the fatall sithe,

Which from the medowe her greene locks doeth shave,
That their warme nest is now become their grave;
    The woefull mother up to heaven springs,
    And all about her plaintive notes she flings,
And their untimely fate most pittifully sings.

Christ's Triumph after Death

I

But now the second Morning, from her bowre,   *Christs Triumph*
Began to glister in her beames, and nowe   *after death. 1. in*
                                     his Resurrection,
The roses of the day began to flowre   *manifested by the*
In th'easterne garden; for heav'ns smiling browe *effects of it in*
Halfe insolent for joy begunne to showe: *the Creatures.*
    The early Sunne came lively dauncing out,
    And the bragge lambes ranne wantoning about,
That heav'n, and earth might seeme in tryumph both to shout.

2

Th'engladded Spring, forgetfull now to weepe,
Began t'eblazon from her leavie bed,
The waking swallowe broke her halfe-yeares sleepe,
And everie bush lay deepely purpured
With violets, the woods late-wintry head
    Wide flaming primroses set all on fire,
    And his bald trees put on their greene attire,
Among whose infant leaves the joyeous birds conspire.

3

And now the taller Sonnes (whom Titan warmes)
Of unshorne mountaines, blowne with easie windes,
Dandled the mornings childhood in their armes,
And, if they chaunc't to slip the prouder pines,
The under Corylets did catch the shines,
    To guild their leaves, sawe never happie yeare
    Such joyfull triumph, and triumphant cheare,
As though the aged world anew created wear.

4

Say Earth, why hast thou got thee new attire,
And stick'st thy habit full of dazies red?
Seems that thou doest to some high thought aspire,
And some newe-found-out Bridegroome mean'st to wed:
Tell me ye Trees, so fresh apparelled,
    So never let the spitefull Canker wast you,
    So never let the heav'ns with lightening blast you,
Why goe you now so trimly drest, or whither hast you?

5

Answer me Jordan, why thy crooked tide
So often wanders from his neerest way,
As though some other way thy streame would slide,
And faine salute the place where something lay?
And you sweete birds, that shaded from the ray,
    Sit carolling, and piping griefe away,
    The while the lambs to heare you daunce, and play,
Tell me sweete birds, what is it you so faine would say?

6

And, thou faire Spouse of Earth, that everie yeare,
Gett'st such a numerous issue of thy bride,
How chance thou hotter shin'st, and draw'st more neere?
Sure thou somewhear some worthie sight hast spide,
That in one place for joy thou canst not bide:
    And you dead Swallowes, that so lively now
    Through the flit aire your winged passage rowe,
How could new life into your frozen ashes flowe?

7

Ye Primroses, and purple violets,
Tell me, why blaze ye from your leavie bed,
And wooe mens hands to rent you from your sets,
As though you would somewhear be carried,
With fresh perfumes, and velvets garnished?
    But ah, I neede not aske, t'is surely so,
    You all would to your Saviours triumphs goe,
Thear would ye all awaite, and humble homage doe.

8

Thear should the Earth herselfe with garlands newe   *In himselfe.*
And lovely flowr's embellished adore,
Such roses never in her garland grewe,
Such lillies never in her brest she wore,
Like beautie never yet did shine before:
 Thear should the Sunne another Sunne behold,
 From whence himselfe borrowes his locks of gold,
That kindle heav'n, and earth with beauties manifold.

9

Thear might the violet, and primrose sweet
Beames of more lively, and more lovely grace,
Arising from their beds of incense meet;
Thear should the Swallowe see newe life embrace
Dead ashes, and the grave unheale his face,
 To let the living from his bowels creepe,
 Unable longer his owne dead to keepe:
Thear heav'n, and earth should see their Lord awake from sleepe.

10

Their Lord, before by other judg'd to die,
Nowe Judge of all himselfe, before forsaken
Of all the world, that from his aide did flie,
Now by the Saints into their armies taken,
Before for an unworthie man mistaken,
 Nowe worthy to be God confest, before
 With blasphemies by all the basest tore,
Now worshipped by Angels, that him lowe adore.

11

Whose garment was before indipt in blood,
But now, imbright'ned into heav'nly flame,
The Sun it selfe outglitters, though he should
Climbe to the toppe of the celestiall frame,
And force the starres go hide themselves for shame:
 Before that under earth was buried,
 But nowe about the heav'ns is carried,
And thear for ever by the Angels heried.

12

So fairest Phosphor the bright Morning starre,
But neewely washt in the greene element,
Before the drouzie Night is halfe aware,
Shooting his flaming locks with deaw besprent,
Springs lively up into the orient,
    And the bright drove, fleec't all in gold, he chaces
    To drinke, that on the Olympique mountaine grazes,
The while the minor Planets forfeit all their faces.

13

So long he wandred in our lower spheare,
That heav'n began his cloudy starres despise,
Halfe envious, to see on earth appeare
A greater light, then flam'd in his owne skies:
At length it burst for spight, and out thear flies
    A globe of winged Angels, swift as thought,
    That, on their spotted feathers, lively caught
The sparkling Earth, and to their azure fields it brought.

2. In his Ascension to heaven, whose joyes are described,

14

The rest, that yet amazed stood belowe,
With eyes cast up, as greedie to be fed,
And hands upheld, themselves to ground did throwe,
So when the Trojan boy was ravished,
As through th'Idalian woods they saie he fled,
    His aged Gardians stood all dismai'd,
    Some least he should have fallen back afraid,
And some their hasty vowes, and timely prayers said.

15

Tosse up your heads ye everlasting gates,
And let the Prince of glorie enter in:
At whose brave voly of sideriall States,
The Sunne to blush, and starres growe pale wear seene,
When, leaping first from earth, he did begin
    To climbe his Angells wings; then open hang
    Your christall doores, so all the chorus sang
Of heav'nly birds, as to the starres they nimbly sprang.

16

Hearke how the floods clap their applauding hands,
The pleasant valleyes singing for delight,
And wanton Mountaines daunce about the Lands,
The while the fieldes, struck with the heav'nly light,
Set all their flowr's a smiling at the sight,
　　The trees laugh with their blossoms, and the sound
　　Of the triumphant shout of praise, that crown'd
The flaming Lambe, breaking through heav'n, hath passage found.

17

Out leap the antique Patriarchs, all in hast,
To see the powr's of Hell in triumph lead,
And with small starres a garland intercha'st
Of olive leaves they bore, to crowne his head,
That was before with thornes degloried,
　　After them flewe the Prophets, brightly stol'd
　　In shining lawne, and wimpled manifold,
Striking their yvorie harpes, strung all in chords of gold.

1. By the accesse of all good, the blessed Societie of the Saints,

18

To which the Saints victorious carolls sung,
Ten thousand Saints at once, that with the sound,
The hollow vaults of heav'n for triumph rung:
The Cherubins their clamours did confound
With all the rest, and clapt their wings around:
　　Downe from their thrones the Dominations flowe,
　　And at his feet their crownes, and scepters throwe,
And all the princely Soules fell on their faces lowe.

Angels, &c.

19

Nor can the Martyrs wounds them stay behind,
But out they rush among the heav'nly crowd,
Seeking their heav'n out of their heav'n to find,
Sounding their silver trumpets out so loude,
That the shrill noise broke through the starrie cloude,
　　And all the virgin Soules, in pure araie,
　　Came dauncing forth, and making joyeous plaie;
So him they lead along into the courts of day.

20

So him they lead into the courts of day,
Whear never warre, nor wounds abide him more,
But in that house, eternall peace doth plaie,
Acquieting the soules, that newe before
Their way to heav'n through their owne blood did skore,
   But now, estranged from all miserie,
   As farre as heav'n, and earth discoasted lie,
Swelter in quiet waves of immortalitie.

*The sweete
quiet and peace,
injoyed under God.*

21

And if great things by smaller may be ghuest,
So, in the mid'st of Neptunes angrie tide,
Our Britan Island, like the weedie nest
Of true Halcyon, on the waves doth ride,
And softly sayling, skornes the waters pride:
   While all the rest, drown'd on the continent,
   And tost in bloodie waves, their wounds lament,
And stand, to see our peace, as struck with woonderment.

*Shadowed by the
peace we enjoy
under our
Soveraigne.*

22

The Ship of France religious waves doe tosse,
And Greec it selfe is now growne barbarous,
Spains Children hardly dare the Ocean crosse,
And Belges field lies wast, and ruinous,
That unto those, the heav'ns ar invious,
   And unto them, themselves ar strangers growne,
   And unto these, the Seas ar faithles knowne,
And unto her, alas, her owne is not her owne.

23

Here onely shut we Janus yron gates,
And call the welcome Muses to our springs,
And ar but Pilgrims from our heav'nly states,
The while the trusty Earth sure plentie brings,
And Ships through Neptune safely spread their wings.
   Goe blessed Island, wander whear thou please,
   Unto thy God, or men, heav'n, lands, or seas,
Thou canst not loose thy way, thy King with all hath peace.

24

Deere Prince, thy Subjects joy, hope of their heirs,
Picture of peace, or breathing Image rather,
The certaine argument of all our pray'rs,
Thy Harries, and thy Countries lovely Father,
Let Peace, in endles joyes, for ever bath her
   Within thy sacred brest, that at thy birth
   Brought'st her with thee from heav'n, to dwell on earth,
Making our earth a heav'n, and paradise of mirth.

25

Let not my Liege misdeem these humble laies,
As lick't with soft, and supple blandishment,
Or spoken to disparagon his praise;
For though pale Cynthia, neere her brothers tent,
Soone disappeares in the white firmament,
   And gives him back the beames, before wear his,
   Yet when he verges, or is hardly ris,
She the vive image of her absent brother is.

26

Nor let the Prince of peace his beadsman blame,
That with his Stewart dares his Lord compare,
And heav'nly peace with earthly quiet shame:
So Pines to lowely plants compared ar,
And lightning Phœbus to a little starre:
   And well I wot, my rime, albee unsmooth,
   Ne, saies but what it meanes, ne meanes but sooth,
Ne harmes the good, ne good to harmefull person doth.

27

Gaze but upon the house, whear Man embowr's: *The beauty of*
With flowr's, and rushes paved is his way, *the place.*
Whear all the Creatures ar his Servitours,
The windes doe sweepe his chambers every day,
And cloudes doe wash his rooms, the seeling gay,
   Starred aloft the guilded knobs embrave:
   If such a house God to another gave,
How shine those glittering courts, he for himselfe will have?

28

And if a sullen cloud, as sad as night,
In which the Sunne may seeme embodied,
Depur'd of all his drosse, we see so white,
Burning in melted gold his watrie head,
Or round with yvorie edges silvered,
 What lustre superexcellent will he
 Lighten on those, that shall his sunneshine see,
In that all-glorious court, in which all glories be?

The Claritie (as the schoole cals it) of the Saints bodies.

29

If but one Sunne, with his diffusive fires,
Can paint the starres, and the whole world with light,
And joy, and life into each heart inspires,
And every Saint shall shine in heav'n, as bright
As doth the Sunne in his transcendent might,
 (As faith may well beleeve, what Truth once sayes)
 What shall so many Sunnes united rayes
But dazle all the eyes, that nowe in heav'n we praise?

30

Here let my Lord hang up his conquering launce,
And bloody armour with late slaughter warme,
And looking downe on his weake Militants,
Behold his Saints, mid'st of their hot alarme,
Hang all their golden hopes upon his arme.
 And in this lower field dispacing wide,
 Through windie thoughts, that would their sayles misguide,
Anchor their fleshly ships fast in his wounded side.

31

Here may the Band, that now in Tryumph shines,
And that (before they wear invested thus)
In earthly bodies carried heavenly mindes,
Pitcht round about in order glorious,
Their sunny Tents, and houses luminous,
 All their eternall day in songs employing,
 Joying their ende, without ende of their joying,
While their almightie Prince Destruction is destroying.

32

Full, yet without satietie, of that   *The impletion of*
Which whetts, and quiets greedy Appetite,   *the Appetite.*
Whear never Sunne did rise, nor ever sat,
But one eternall day, and endles light
Gives time to those, whose time is infinite,
   Speaking with thought, obtaining without fee,
   Beholding him, whom never eye could see,
And magnifying him, that cannot greater be.

33

How can such joy as this want words to speake?
And yet what words can speake such joy as this?
Far from the world, that might their quiet breake,
Here the glad Soules the face of beauty kisse,
Powr'd out in pleasure, on their beds of blisse,
   And drunke with nectar torrents, ever hold
   Their eyes on him, whose graces manifold,
The more they doe behold, the more they would behold.

34

Their sight drinkes lovely fires in at their eyes,   *The joy of the*
Their braine sweete incense with fine breath accloyes, *senses, &c.*
That on Gods sweating altar burning lies,
Their hungrie eares feede on their heav'nly noyse,
That Angels sing, to tell their untould joyes;
   Their understanding naked Truth, their wills
   The all, and selfe-sufficient Goodnesse fills,
That nothing here is wanting, but the want of ills.

35

No Sorrowe nowe hangs clowding on their browe,   *2. By the*
No bloodles Maladie empales their face,   *amotion of all*
No Age drops on their hayrs his silver snowe,   *evill.*
No Nakednesse their bodies doeth embase,
No Povertie themselves, and theirs disgrace,
   No feare of death the joy of life devours,
   No unchast sleepe their precious time deflowrs,
No losse, no griefe, no change waite on their winged hour's.

L

36

But now their naked bodies skorne the cold,
And from their eyes joy lookes, and laughs at paine,
The Infant wonders how he came so old,
And old man how he came so young againe;
Still resting, though from sleepe they still refraine,
 Whear all are rich, and yet no gold they owe,
 And all are Kings, and yet no Subjects knowe,
All full, and yet no time on foode they doe bestowe.

37

For things that passe are past, and in this field,
The indeficient Spring no Winter feares,
The Trees together fruit, and blossome yeild,
Th'unfading Lilly leaves of silver beares,
And crimson rose a skarlet garment weares:
 And all of these on the Saints bodies growe,
 Not, as they woont, on baser earth belowe;   *By the accesse*
Three rivers heer of milke, and wine, and honie flowe. *of all good againe.*

38

About the holy Cittie rowles a flood   *in the glorie of*
Of moulten chrystall, like a sea of glasse,   *the Holy Cittie.*
On which weake streame a strong foundation stood,
Of living Diamounds the building was,
That all things else, besides it selfe, did passe.
 Her streetes, in stead of stones, the starres did pave,
 And little pearles, for dust, it seem'd to have,
On which soft-streaming Manna, like pure snowe, did wave.

39

In mid'st of this Citie cœlestiall,   *in the beatificall*
Whear the eternall Temple should have rose,   *vision of God.*
Light'ned th'Idea Beatificall:
End, and beginning of each thing that growes,
Whose selfe no end, nor yet beginning knowes,
 That hath no eyes to see, nor ears to heare,
 Yet sees, and heares, and is all-eye, all-eare,
That no whear is contain'd, and yet is every whear.

40

Changer of all things, yet immutable,
Before, and after all, the first, and last,
That mooving all, is yet immoveable,
Great without quantitie, in whose forecast,
Things past are present, things to come are past,
    Swift without motion, to whose open eye
    The hearts of wicked men unbrested lie,
At once absent, and present to them, farre, and nigh.

41

It is no flaming lustre, made of light,
No sweet concent, or well-tim'd harmonie,
Ambrosia, for to feast the Appetite,
Or flowrie odour, mixt with spicerie.
No soft embrace, or pleasure bodily,
    And yet it is a kinde of inward feast,
    A harmony, that sounds within the brest,
An odour, light, embrace, in which the soule doth rest.

42

A heav'nly feast, no hunger can consume,
A light unseene, yet shines in every place,
A sound, no time can steale, a sweet perfume,
No windes can scatter, an intire embrace,
That no satietie can ere unlace,
    Ingrac't into so high a favour, thear
    The Saints, with their Beaw-peers, whole worlds outwear,
And things unseene doe see, and things unheard doe hear.

43

Ye blessed soules, growne richer by your spoile,   *And of Christ.*
Whose losse, though great, is cause of greater gaines,
Here may your weary Spirits rest from toyle,
Spending your endlesse eav'ning, that remaines,
Among those white flocks, and celestiall traines,
    That feed upon their Sheapheards eyes, and frame
    That heav'nly musique of so woondrous fame,
Psalming aloude the holy honours of his name.

44

Had I a voice of steel to tune my song,
Wear every verse as smoothly fil'd as glasse,
And every member turned to a tongue,
And every tongue wear made of sounding brasse,
Yet all that skill, and all this strength, alas,
　　Should it presume to guild, wear misadvis'd,
　　The place, whear David hath new songs devis'd,
As in his burning throne he sits emparadis'd.

45

Most happie Prince, whose eyes those starres behould,
Treading ours under feet, now maist thou powre
That overflowing skill, whearwith of ould
Thou woont'st to combe rough speech, now maist thou showr
Fresh streames of praise upon that holy bowre,
　　Which well we heaven call, not that it rowles,
　　But that it is the haven of our soules.
Most happie Prince, whose sight so heav'nly sight behoulds.

46

Ah foolish Sheapheards, that wear woont esteem,
Your God all rough, and shaggy-hair'd to bee;
And yet farre wiser Sheapheards then ye deeme,
For who so poore (though who so rich) as hee,
When, with us hermiting in lowe degree,
　　He wash't his flocks in Jordans spotles tide,
　　And, that his deere remembrance aie might bide,
Did to us come, and with us liv'd, and for us di'd?

47

But now so lively colours did embeame
His sparkling forehead, and so shiny rayes
Kindled his flaming locks; that downe did streame
In curles, along his necke, whear sweetly playes
(Singing his wounds of love in sacred layes)
　　His deerest Spouse, Spouse of the deerest Lover,
　　Knitting a thousand knots over, and over,
And dying still for love, but they her still recover.

48

Faire Egliset, that at his eyes doth dresse
Her glorious face, those eyes, from whence ar shed
Infinite belamours, whear to expresse
His love, high God all heav'n as captive leads,
And all the banners of his grace dispreads,
  And in those windowes, doth his armes englaze,
  And on those eyes, the Angels all doe gaze,
And from those eies, the lights of heav'n do gleane their blaze.

49

But let the Kentish lad, that lately taught
His oaten reed the trumpets silver sound,
Young Thyrsilis, and for his musique brought
The willing sphears from heav'n, to lead a round
Of daxncing Nymphs, and Heards, that sung, and crown'd
  Eclectas hymen with ten thousand flowrs
  Of choycest prayse, and hung her heav'nly bow'rs
With saffron garlands, drest for Nuptiall Paramours,

50

Let his shrill trumpet, with her silver blast,
Of faire Eclecta, and her Spousall bed,
Be the sweet pipe, and smooth Encomiast:
But my greene Muse, hiding her younger head
Under old Chamus flaggy banks, that spread
  Their willough locks abroad, and all the day
  With their owne watry shadowes wanton play,
Dares not those high amours, and love-sick songs assay.

51

Impotent words, weake sides, that strive in vaine,
In vaine, alas, to tell so heav'nly sight,
So heav'nly sight, as none can greater feigne,
Feigne what he can, that seemes of greatest might,
  Might any yet compare with Infinite?
  Infinite sure those joyes, my words but light,
Light is the pallace whear she dwells. O blessed wight!

Notes

An asterisk before a note indicates that it appears in the original edition.

The fable of Ovid treting of Narcissus

This translation of Ovid *Metamorphoses* III. line 341 ff. was first published in 1560 but may have been composed some years before publication. In the original the translation is followed by a lengthy moralization. The author is unknown but the words, 'FINIS. QUOD. T.H.' at the end of the moralization caused some scholars to ascribe it to Thomas Howell, author of the *Arbor of Amitie* (1568). This is unlikely since it does not resemble Howell's style and the initials are probably those of the printer, Thomas Hacket. (Cf. O. L. Jiriczek, *Specimens of Tudor Translations from the Classics*, Heidelberg 1923, p. 74, and D. Bush, *Mythology and the Renaissance Tradition in English Poetry*, Minneapolis 1932, p. 48.)

The black-letter quarto of 1560 is the only known edition. I have used the Bodleian copy as copy text.

   1 Lireope: one of the daughters of Oceanus.
      Ciphicious: the river Cephisus in Greece.
  20 dobbeler: doubler, repeater.
  46 here: her 1560. 'dixerat "hic quis adest?" et "adest" responderat Echo. Ovid.
  48 yeke: also.
  50 flyst: why/tlyst 1560. 'quid,' inquit, 'me fugis?' Ovid. Cf. Jiriczek.
  65 eare: air. in aera, Ovid.
  70 nowe: none 1560. em. Jiriczek.
  73 some: soone 1560. 'aliquis', Ovid. em. Jiriczek.
  75 Ramusya: Nemesis. 'Rhamnusia', Ovid. ʽΡαμνοῦς was a deme of Attica, so called on account of the prickly shrubs (ῥάμνοι) growing there. It was famous for its temple and later for its statue of Nemesis by Phidias.
  91 cheare: cheer, frame of mind, face.
 112 thence: thus 1560. 'inde', Ovid. em. Jiriczek.
      astarte: draw or drag away. 'abstrahere', Ovid.
 116 raught: raised up.
 123 say: sea.
 124 waleys: valeys 1560. 'moenia', Ovid. 'walles', Jiriczek.

129 be done:⎫
130 shone: ⎬ be dime, shine, 1560. 'posse putes tangi', Ovid. em. Jiriczek.

132 the: thee.
138 steares: stirs, moves.
142 gloue: glow. 'flammas moveoque feroque.' Ovid.
146 In hym that loves this: In hym loves this that, 1560. em. Jiriczek.
strang: strange.
149 sure: sour.
151 two to one: to one, 1560. 'duo concordes', Ovid. A stressed syllable is omitted. Jiriczek 'we to one'.
153 starte: stirred up. 'turbavit', Ovid.
161 Wyth: Jiriczek emends to 'Whych'.
163 strepe: stripe—to assume various colours, here: to turn purple.
171 hewe: heare, 1560. 'color', Ovid. em. Jiriczek.
185 hellye: hellish, infernal. hyllye, 1560. 'inferna', Ovid. em. Jiriczek.
186 Styxe: stype, 1560. 'Stygia', Ovid. em. Jiriczek.

Scillaes Metamorphosis

Thomas Lodge (? 1558–1625) is recorded as having been in the household of the Earl of Derby. Admitted to Merchant Taylors School on March 23rd 1571, he proceeded in 1573 as a scholar to Trinity College, Oxford, and took his degree on July 8th 1577. He entered Lincoln's Inn on April 26th 1578 but apparently preferred the practice of literature to the study of law. Between 1584 and 1589 he was on a voyage with Captain Clark to the Canaries and Azores. In 1591, on Cavendish's voyage, he endured the severe winter at the Straits of Magellan. After *Scillaes Metamorphosis* his principal literary works are the prose romance *Rosalynde* (1590), the sonnet sequence *Phillis* with the *Tragicall Complaynt of Elstred* (1593), the drama *A Looking glasse for London and England* (1594) in collaboration with Robert Greene, the verse satire *A Fig for Momus* (1595), and the romance *A Margarite of America* (1596). Forced, either by debt or religious difficulties, to leave England in 1596/7, he studied medicine at Avignon and graduated in 1598. He practised medicine on his return to England but still found time to translate the works of Flavius Josephus (1602) and the prose works of Seneca (1614).

(Cf. N. B. Paradise, *Thomas Lodge*, New Haven 1931; C. J. Sisson, *Thomas Lodge and other Elizabethans*, Harvard 1933; A. Walker *R.E.S.* vols IX, X. 1933/4.)

Scillaes Metamorphosis, first published in 1589 (in some copies the date is changed to 1590 and the title-page altered; see F. Bowers, *Bibliography and Textual Criticism*, Oxford 1964, p. 132), proved popular enough to be reissued in 1610 under the title of *A most pleasant historie of Glaucus and Scilla*. The story of Scilla is told by Ovid in *Metamorphoses* XIII. 898–968, and XIV. Lodge uses Ovid only for the framework of his story. L. E. Kastner has demonstrated Lodge's debt in other poems to Italian and French sources and Bush suggests that Lodge may have known Ronsard's *Complainte de Glauce a Scylle Nimphe* and *Le Ravissement de Cephale* (see Bush, p. 83). John Forrest in his thesis *The Elizabethan Ovid*, Edinburgh 1945, suggests also that Lodge may have consulted Peele's *The Araygnement of Paris* (1584).

Texts A: 1589. B: 1610. B is a reprint of A. This edition takes the British Museum copy of 1589 as copy text.

4 wood: mad.

52 sallowes: plant of genus *Salix*, a willow.

56 Themis: the daughter of Uranus and Gaea, the mother of Prometheus and later a personification of Justice. Lodge may be thinking of her in this sense or he may have confused her with Tethys, the wife of Oceanus, who would be more appropriate in this context.

64 Ariadnes crowne: the constellation Corona which is identified as the garland given by Dionysus to Ariadne when he married her on the island of Naxos.

97 the Thebans ivorie brow: Hercules was frequently represented crowned with poplar leaves.

99 bowe: E. S. Donno, *Elizabethan Minor Epics*, Routledge 1963, reads vowe.

133 dawe: waken.

139 Angelica: the daughter of Galafron, King of Cathay, in Ariosto, *Orlando Furioso*.

170 betimed: bedtime 1589. Donno, betime.

200 Moly: the herb given by Hermes to Odysseus on Circe's island. *Od.* X. 302–6. The name is magical and not identifiable but the name was later applied to garlic and relatives of chives. See Gerarde, *The herball or generall historie of Plants*, 1597.

203 Amaranthus: an introduced semi-tropical plant, perhaps love-lies-bleeding. Since it does not fade (ἀμάραντος, unwithering) it was a symbol of immortality and was supposed to have special healing properties.

204 Ajax blossom: the iris. Ovid *Met.* XIII. 394 ff. The flower which sprang from the blood of Ajax and is therefore marked A.I. for Aias. Like the other plants mentioned in this stanza it was regarded as medicinal.

227 with: which 1589. em. Donno.

308 saples: saplings.

380 flouds: waves.

394 flouds repaire: the retreat or home of the waves.

484 Shepeheards: Seepeheards 1589. em. Donno.

487 th'Arcadian: Th'arcadian 1589. em. Donno.

506 Amyntas: a shepherd in Virgil's *Eclogues* and the hero of Tasso's pastoral play *Aminta* (1573). cf. Thomas Watson, *Amyntas* (1585).

532 with: which 1589. em. Donno.

657 was so full: Donno omits 'so'.

672 Cayster: a river of Asia near Ephesus, famous for its swans.

Hero and Leander by Christopher Marlowe

Christopher Marlowe (1564–1593) was born the son of a Canterbury cobbler. After a year at the King's School he went as a scholar to Corpus Christi College, Cambridge. He took his M.A. in 1587 but only after the Privy Council had intervened to clear him of the charge of remaining at Rheims—presumably the suspicion was that he might enter the English Catholic seminary there. Since the same document says that he 'had done her Majestie good service, and deserved to be rewarded for his faithfull dealinge' it has been supposed that he was a government agent. In the same year *Tamburlaine* was produced in London and Marlowe's brief but effective dramatic career had begun. The exact dates and the order of composition of *The Tragedy of Dido*, *Dr Faustus*, *The Jew of Malta*, *Edward II*, and *The Massacre at Paris* are uncertain. On at least two occasions Marlowe is recorded as being involved in breaches of the peace before the final affray after supper at Deptford in 1593 when he was killed by Ingram Frizer.

In the preface to his continuation of *Hero and Leander* Henry Petowe says that the poem was interrupted by Marlowe's death. Some scholars, however, prefer to give an early date for its composition because of similarities between it and Marlowe's translation of Ovid's *Elegies*. Early or late it is the kind of subject that occupied Marlowe all his working life. The story is referred to by Ovid in *Amores* II. xvi and given in *Heroides* XVIII and XIX. Marlowe also used the Greek poem ascribed to Musaeus, an Alexandrian of the fifth century A.D. The Elizabethans confused this poet with the mythical Musaeus described by Virgil in *Aeneid* VI. 667 as a head taller than his fellow poets in the Elisian fields, and consequently regarded this version of *Hero and Leander* as one of the earliest examples of poetry. It seems possible that Marlowe had consulted it in Greek—see T. W. Baldwin, 'Marlowe's Musaeus', *J.E.G.P.* liv. no. 4, Oct. 1955.

Hero and Leander was entered to J. Wolfe in the Stationers' Register in 1593 but, so far as we know, no edition was printed until 1598. In that year Edward Blount published an edition of Marlowe's poem only. Later that same year he transferred his rights to Paul Linley who published an edition containing Chapman's continuation as well. Both appear to be good texts but the relation between them and the nature of the copy used has never been definitely established.

This edition takes 1598 A, Blount's edition, as copy text.

The reader should consult C. F. Tucker Brooke, *The Works of Christopher Marlowe*, Oxford 1910, and L. C. Martin, *Marlowe's Poems*, Methuen 1931, for a discussion of the text and fuller annotation than can be given here. Gertrud Lazarus, *Technik und Stil von Hero and Leander*, Bonn 1915, is useful for Marlowe's debt to Ovid. M. C. Bradbrook, 'Hero and Leander', *Scrutiny* II. i. 1933, and C. S. Lewis, *Hero and Leander* (British Academy Lecture, 1952), give interesting and different accounts of the poem. J. B. Steane, *Marlowe, a critical study*, Cambridge 1964, has a good chapter on *Hero and Leander* and a critical bibliography.

The division into Sestyads and the head-links only occur in 1598 B, and are probably due to Chapman. Sestyad is formed from the name of the town Sestos as Iliad comes from Ilium.

1 L. C. Martin quotes a Latin translation of Musaeus for the form of the opening lines, but see T. W. Baldwin, op. cit., for Marlowe's use of the Greek text.

3 Seaborderers: Seaborders 1598 A and B. But Thomas Nashe in *Nashe's Lenten Stuffe* uses 'Seaborderers'. See R. B. McKerrow, *The Works of Thomas Nashe*, III. 199 or S. Wells, *Thomas Nashe*, Stratford Library I. 320.

45 Venus Nun: Baldwin points out that this was the normal translation of 'priestess'.

59 spheare: circuit of motion, range, orbit.

65 Pelops shoulder: in order to test the divinity of the gods Tantalus served them his son, Pelops, at a banquet. Demeter ate his shoulder and Zeus, when he restored him to life, replaced it with one of ivory.

73 orient: glowing, fresh—from eastern, either as 'an eastern gem' L. C. Martin, or associated with the colour of the dawn.

86 banquet: the banquet of love made from the person of the beloved is a vital part of Shakespeare's *Venus and Adonis* and Chapman's *Ovids Banquet of Sence*.

108 thirling: twirl or roll, of the wheels of the car.

114 Ixion: attempted to seduce Hera but was frustrated by Zeus who substituted a cloud. The result of this union was the race of Centaurs. Ixion was later bound on a perpetual wheel in hell.

137 carved: carv'd 1598 B.
o'rehead: overhead 1598 B.

146 Danae: daughter of Acrisius, king of Argos. She was confined in a brazen tower by her father because of an oracle that he should be killed by her son. Zeus fell in love with her, assumed the shape of a shower of gold, and gave her a son, Perseus.

154 Sylvanus: a god of the woods, in love with Cyparissus who was metamorphosed into a cypress tree.

159 Vaild: Taild 1598 B. vail: to bow.

161 Loves arrow: Cupid had two arrows, golden for inflicting love and leaden for removing it.

184 hardly: with difficulty.

185 parled: spoke.

190 a periphrasis of night (marginal note, 1598).

203 stuffe: material for creation, hence, persons.

214 flaring: glittering, gaudy.

231 The argument is from Ovid *Amores* I. viii.

233 mold: earth.

242 Lone: Love 1598 B.

243 sinnes: since 1598 B.

255 One is traditionally not regarded as a number. L. C. Martin quotes Aristotle *Metaphysics* XIV. i.

270 essence: something in existence.

298 trace: to follow.

420 pleasure: pleasures 1598 B.

458 Emperie 1598 B: Emprie 1598 A. em. Donno.

Second Sestyad

26 affied: affianced, engaged.

51 Aesops cocke: preferred a barleycorn to a precious stone. L. C. Martin quotes various possible sources and points out that there is no such fable by Aesop himself.

61 rude: inexperienced.

75 Tantalus: in hell he could neither drink water from the river he was standing in nor reach the fruit on the tree above him.

123 Dyameter: in a straight line, directly.

179 Helles bracelet: Helle attempted to escape from the jealousy of her stepmother by flying on a golden ram to Colchis, but fell into the sea which was later called the Hellespont.

187 threw: L. C. Martin emends to 'throw'.

200 up-staring: L. C. Martin upstarting. Donno quotes T. Edwards, *Cephalus and Procris* (1595), 508: up looke,/Like rurall Faunes.

246 Through: Though 1598 B.

255 fet: fetched.

lines 291–300 follow 278 in editions of 1598. The order was first changed in an edition of *Select English Poets* (1821) whose general editor was S. W. Singer.

305 Ericine: Venus.

316 One: And 1598 B.

320 glymse: shine or gleam. Cf. *Salmacis and Hermaphroditus*, 596.

334 Dang'd: Hurld 1598 B.

1598 A reads 'Desunt nonulla' at the end of the Second Sestyad.

Hero and Leander by George Chapman

George Chapman (? 1559–1634) was born near Hitchin in Hertfordshire and Anthony Wood records him as having gone to Oxford University, but

there is no record of his taking a degree. In 1583 he was in the service of Sir
Ralph Sadler and it is possible that he served as a soldier in the Netherlands.
In 1594 he began his public career as a poet with *The Shadow of Night*, a
poem which is based on Natalis Comes and connects Chapman with Mathew
Roydon and the Raleigh circle. The volume of poetry containing *Ovids
Banquet of Sence* is also dedicated to Roydon. By 1598 Chapman had begun
his work as a dramatist with *The Blind Beggar of Alexandria*, had published
the first two instalments of his translation of *The Iliad*, and had completed
Hero and Leander. Between then and his death he wrote or collaborated in a
number of plays. *Bussy d'Ambois*, *The Conspiracy of Byron*, *The Revenge of
Bussy d'Ambois* and *Caesar and Pompey* are the most popular. Prince Henry
became his patron in 1604 and commanded him to finish his translation of the
Iliad. His death in 1612 was a severe blow to Chapman but the translation
was finally completed and a complete version of the *Iliad* and the *Odyssey*
published in 1616.

Chapman published a translation of Musaeus in 1616 but is perhaps more
indebted to Latin versions than Marlowe was. The story of Hymen comes
from Servius on *Aeneid* I 651. F. L. Schoell has pointed out that Chapman
makes fairly extensive use of the Latin translation of Plutarch's *Moralia*
made by Gulielmus Xylander (Wilhelm Holtzman) which is used in the
1572 Greek–Latin edition of Plutarch by Estienne.

The text is from the 1598 edition of *Hero and Leander* published by Paul
Linley. Later reprints have no independent authority.

Chapman's continuation of *Hero and Leander* has been edited by Tucker
Brooke and L. C. Martin in their editions of Marlowe, by P. B. Bartlett, *The
Poems of George Chapman*, Oxford 1941 and by E. S. Donno. See also
D. J. Gordon, 'Chapman's "Hero and Leander" ', *English Miscellany*, ed.
Mario Praz, No. 5, Rome 1954, pp. 41–92.

Argument   4 Thesme: Θεσμός, law or rite.

24 (* Chapman's note in 1598 B) He cals Phœbus the God of Gold, since
   the vertue of his beams creates it.
60 Pythagoras was supposed to have a golden thigh and his philosophy is
   concerned with number and harmony as the principles of the universe.
   For the influence of Pythagorean doctrine on literature see L. Spitzer,
   Classical and Christian Ideas of World Harmony, Johns Hopkins 1963.
90 meere: unmixed, pure; hence, completely 'insensuall'.
102 Carquenet: a collar for the neck or a crown for the hair.
123 disparent: diversely coloured.
   Pentackle: a figure used in magic, a pentagon with the sides produced to
   form a five-pointed star.
167 his: her 1598 B. em. L. C. Martin.
173 on: of 1598 B, changed to 'on' in 1629. L. C. Martin and P. Bartlett read

'on', E. S. Donno reads 'of'. Probably 'faults he' in 174 should also be emended to 'fault she'.

183 thou: how 1598 B. em. Brooke.
204 The assault by Essex on Cadiz in 1596.
241 rorid: dewy.
261 Lapwing: deceitful.
265 Apoplexie: an effusion of blood to the brain.
266 beddred: worn out, decrepit.
302 Embrion: embryo.
    never: ne'er Donno.
383 she: he 1598 B. em. Donno.
392 imperance: commanding power.
409 Oribiculer: round like a globe, circular. L. C. Martin punctuates with a comma after 'Heaven's'.

The Fourth Sestyad

The Argument.   9 Ecte
             11 Leucote
             14 Eronusis

Chapman introduces many allegorical or mythological figures of his own creation, often transliterated from Greek: οἶκτος, pity; λευκότης, whiteness. Chapman's own note to 14 reads '*Eronusis*, Dissimulation' and this has been taken as coming from ἔρως, love, and νόσος, disease.

20 Peristera: περιστερά, dove.
31 adumbrate: shadow, shadow forth, represent.
117 eyas: 1598 B. yas. eyas, youthful. Donno.
130 ostents: signs, shows, prodigies.
198 Excellence: Excellencie 1598 B. em. Donno.
227 pheres: fere, a companion.
231 Ædone: ἡδονή, pleasure.
232 ruffoot: rufous, a brownish-red colour.
    Chreste: χρηστός, good.
235 proyne: preen, dress.
236 Leucote: λευκότης, whiteness.
237 Dapsilis: δαψιλής, abundant, bounteous.
264 savor: T. Brooke emends to 'favor'. P. Bartlett compares *Ovids Banquet of Sence* 282, the sensor of his savor = nose.
267 Epicedians: singers of a dirge at a funeral. ἐπικηδεία, funeral.
269 Ecte: οἶκτος, pity.
290 (*) *Description and creation of Dissimulation.*
300 Cares: Caria, a division of Asia Minor.
302 Arachne: turned into a spider for competing against Athena in weaving.
336 Anademe: ἀνάδημα, wreath, garland for the head.

346 Persian shield: L. C. Martin reads 'Persean shield'. Perseus used a mirror to kill the Gorgon Medusa without looking at her face. Her head was then fixed in his shield.

The Fift Sestyad

The Argument. 12 Teras: τέρας, a sign or portent.

62 ebon: L. C. Martin quotes *N.E.D.* ebon: Art.B4 as showing that this is a mistake for ivory.
119 Eucharis: εὔχαρις, pleasing, gracious.
124 interminate: without end or limit.
142 prayers: prayes 1598 B. em. Dyce.
207 Inggl'd: cajole, coax. ingle: a catamite.
225 superficies: surface, outward show.
265 plat: plot.
287 Adolesches: ἀδολέσχης, a talker, chatterer.
289 neither: nether.
375 Agneia: ἀγνεία, purity, chastity.
381 Phemonoe: a priestess of Apollo and the inventor of heroic verse.
408 Tellus: the Earth.

The Sixt Sestyad

The Argument. 14 Acanthides: ἀκανθίς, goldfinch; ἄκανθα, thorn or thistle.

21 devotes: acts of devotion.
22 pricks: to write down music.
120 Rhene: Rhine.
144 cockhorse: 'The phrase *cockhorse Pessantrie* means people in exalted positions who are really no better than peasants.' P. Bartlett.
188 Statists: politicians.
191 Atthæa: Orithyia, a daughter of Erechtheus, king of Athens, who was carried off by Boreas. Cf. line 47. This form is from ᾿Ατθίς, Attic.
216 bating: growing smaller.
226 Lachesis: λαχεῖν, to measure out by lot. One of the Parcae, she measured out the wool which represented each person's span of life.

Hero and Leander by Henry Petowe

Henry Petowe (circa 1612) is almost too obscure to be recorded as a poet. As well as his continuation of *Hero and Leander* he published a romance, *Philochasander and Elanira*, in 1599, and poems upon the funeral of Elizabeth and the coronation of King James. He was master of the Artillery Garden in 1622 and later published verses on it in Munday's edition of Stowe's *Survey of London* 1633.

The text exists only in the quarto of 1598. The copy text is the Bodleian copy.

The poem has been reprinted by L. Chabalier, *Héro et Léandre* (1911), and there is an article by A. T. Crathern, 'A Romanticized Version of Hero and Leander', *M.L.N.* xlvi, 1931, pp. 382–5.

3 Tellus: Earth.
19 Tysiphone: one of the Furies who executed divine vengeance on mankind.
91 Compare Shakespeare, *Love's Labour's Lost* V. ii. 911: 'The Words of Mercurie/Are harsh after the songs of Apollo.' Lyly has the same comparison in *Mydas* V. 2.
149 phere: fere, companion.
216 rinde: bark.
258 horce: hoarse.
290 Grown'd of the graft: grown from a shoot inserted in another stock.
329 wood: mad, furious.
354 sound: faint.
412 impleat: to fill full.
440 spoyle: decay.
447 soile: a marshy area where hunted animals find refuge.
487 Spectatum veniunt, veniunt spectentur ut ipsae: They come to watch and to be watched themselves. Ovid *Ars Amatoria* I. 99.
    spectentur: spectantur 1598.
548 sad extacie: unconsciousness.

Ovids Banquet of Sence

Ovids Banquet of Sence is clearly influenced by Natalis Comes (see Schoell) and the doctrines of Renaissance Platonism. Douglas Bush has pointed out that the most likely source for the scheme of the poem is Marsilio Ficino's Latin commentary on Plato's *Symposium*. The *Commentarii in Convivium* (*Omnia Divini Platonis Opera*, Lyons 1548) contains a discussion of Ratio, Visus, Auditus, Olfactus, Gustus and Tactus (see Bush, *Mythology*, p. 204). See also J. F. Kermode, 'The Banquet of Sence', *Bulletin of the John Rylands Library*, xliv. Sept. 1961, pp. 68–99. Chapman had also consulted Aristotle's similar discussion of the senses in *De Anima*.

The poem was first printed in 1595 and another edition was issued in 1639. The copy text for this edition is the British Museum copy of 1595.

10 (* Chapman's note) *Cyrrhus* is a surname of the Sun, from a towne called *Cyrrha*, where he was honored.
15 (*) By *Prosopopœia*, he makes the fountaine the eye of the round Arbor, as a Diamant seemes to be the eye of a Ring: and therefore sayes, the Arbor sees with the Fountaine.

74 Chloris: Flora, goddess of flowers.

75 Melanthy: μελάνθιον, a kind of mint, sometimes called Gith, which is a name for plants of the genus *Nigella*. Gerarde, *Herball*, p. 553, writing of mint says, 'they laie it to the stinging of waspes and bees with good success'.

76 Amareus: Donno suggests this refers to 'amaracus', sweet marjoram, which Gerarde says produces 'an excellent oyle'.

77 Enameld Pansies: This is probably Heartsease, a wild flower, very different from modern cultivated varieties of pansy.

78 Dianas arrow: artemisia, a wild poisonous flower.
   Cupids crimson shielde: love-in-idleness, a violet.

79 Ope-morn: bindweed, a related species to nightshade.
   night-shade: a plant whose berry is a deadly poison.
   Venus navill: since 'Venus navill' is the same as 'Ladies navill' it is pennywort, a plant poisonous to sheep.

81 Calaminth: catmint. Gerarde, 'the whole plant is of a very good smell'.

82 Nepenthe: another aromatic mint.

83 Rumex: the dock, used on bee stings.

84 Sya: Donno suggests 'syve', chive or garlic, also regarded as having medicinal properties.

85 Jessamines: Jasmine is a flowering shrub, usually white or yellow, from which a sweet-smelling oil is made.
   Merry: black cherry.
   Melliphill: honey leaf or balm.

86 Crowne-imperiall: fritillary or snakes-head lily.

87 Amaranth: a plant genus containing several well-known semi-tropical garden plants such as love-lies-bleeding. Since they were unwithering (ἀμάραντος) the Greeks regarded them as symbols of immortality with special healing powers. Gerarde refers to Pliny.

87 Aphrodill: possibly asphodel, a plant which the Greeks believed grew in the underworld—hence its association with Amaranth. William Turner, *A new herball*, 1551, calls it 'ryght affodil' and 'whyte affodil'.

88 Twillpants: Shakespeare, *Tempest* IV. i. 64; 'Pioned and twilled brims' may be a parallel but is itself a crux. W. A. Wright regarded 'twillpants' as a variant of 'tulipant', a tulip. Twilled has often been given the sense 'woven', in which case it might be applied to a plant which makes weaving possible, *Linum* or flax. After her bath Corynna will be covered by the linen of 63 but is now covered by the plant itself. Linseed oil from flax is used on burns while a related species is a purgative. Purgatives occur at 82 and it seems hardly accidental that Chapman should link a plant capable of covering and purging Corynna with the bees whose actions parallel Ovid's intentions.

158 species: an element or image presented to the senses. Cf. Chapman's note on 210.

198 grissells: pieces of gristle. P. Bartlett refers to Vicary's *Anatomie* Ch. 5, for evidence that the ear was thought to be formed of gristle.

210 first conceived: (*) In this allusion to the birth of *Pallas*; he shewes the conceit of her Sonnet; both for matter and note, and by Metaphor hee expresseth how shee delivered her words, and tunes, which was by commision of the order, Philosophers set downe in apprehension of our knowledge, and effection of our sences, for first they affirme, the species of every object propagates it selfe by our spirites to our common sence, that, delivers it to the imaginative part, that to the Cogitative: the Cogitative to the Passive Intelect. the Passive Intelect, to that which is called *Dianoia*, or *Discursus*; and that delivers it up to the minde, which order hee observes in her utterance.

P. Bartlett suggests that this is derived from Aristotle *De Anima* III.

221 Intellects: (*) The Philosopher saith, *Intellectus in ipsa intellegibilia transit*, upon which is grounded thys invention, that in the same manner his life might passe into hys Mistres conceite, intending his intellectuall life, or soule: which by this Analogie, should bee *Intellectus*, and her conceit, *Intellegibilis*.

Aristotle *De Anima* III 429a 15–18 says that $νοῦς$, reason, must be like its objects, $τά νοητά$, just as the sense organs are like the objects of sense. 'The mind passes over into the things which can be perceived.'

239 before they be: (*) This hath reference to the order of her utterance, exprest before.

248 notes: (*) So is thys lykewise referd to the order above-said, for the more perspicuitie.

261 men: mens 1595. em. G. Loane.

282 sensor: nose. Cf. *Hero and Leander* IV. 264.

328 encreast: (*) By this allusion drawne from the effects of sounds and Odors, hee imitates the eternitie of Vertue: saying, the vertues of good men live in them, because they stir up pure enclinations to the like, as if infusde in perfumes and sounds: Besides, he infers, that such as are neyther delighted with sounds (intending by sounds all utterance of knowledge, as well as musicall affections,) nor with Odors (which properly drye the braine and delight the instruments of the soule, making them the more capable of her faculties) such saith hee, perrish without memorie.

355 pregredience: a going before.

378 Dianas eye: (*) Allusion to the transformation of *Acteon* with the sight of *Diana*.

397 Forward, etc.: (*) A simile, expressing the manner of his minds contention in the desire of her sight, and feare of her displeasure.

445 prorected: ? projected at a right angle. Cf. Dyameter, *Hero and Leander* II. 123.

454 burning vapor: (*) This simile expresseth the cause and substance of those exhalations which vulgarly are called falling starres: so *Homer* and *Virgill* calls them, *Stellas cadentes*, *Homer* comparing the descent of *Pallas* among the Troyans to a falling Starre.

514 soule: (*) The amplification of this simile, is taken from the blisfull state of soules in *Elisium*, as *Virgill* faines: and expresseth a regenerate beauty in all life and perfection, not intimating any rest of death. But in place of that eternall spring, he poynteth to that life of life thys beauty-clad naked Lady.

place: peace 1595. em. Kermode.

525 fields of life: (*) He calls her body (as it were divided with her breasts,) the fields of Paradise, and her armes and legs the famous Rivers in it.

529 Spring-bird Lameate: ? as if protected by plates of golden armour. A lame is a plate of metal and lameate perhaps refers to 'bent of Gold curled into Nests'. bent: grass. The Spring-bird is probably the Halcyon and the passage is derived from *Met.* XI. 739–48.

535 Pelopian: see note to *Hero and Leander* I. 65.

541 These etc.: (*) Hee intends the office of her fingers in attyring her, touching thys of theyr courses, in theyr inflection following, theyr playing upon an Instrument.

of her: her 1595. em. Donno.

570 finde: minde 1595. em. Bush.

592 peculier: enjoy on one's own.

602 Cephalus: out hunting killed his wife Procris by mistake.

637 shaddow: (*) At the Sun going downe, shadowes grow longest, where-upon this Embleme is devised.

639 Decrescente nobilitate, crescunt obscuri: by the decline of excellence the ignoble become great.

642 Medio caret: (*) Sight is one of the three sences that hath his medium extrinsecally, which now (supposed wanting,) lets the sight by the close apposition of the Lawrell: the application wherof hath many construc-tions.

Medio caret: it lacks its own medium.

Aristotle *De Anima* III. 434b 28 refers to 'perceiving through a medium τὸ μεταξύ. 'Medio' may be a translation of μεταξύ.

644 Apollo: (*) The Sun hath as much time to compasse a Diall as the world, and therfore the world is placed in the Dyall, expressing the conceite of the Emprese morally which hath a far higher intention.

Emprese: motto or device.

646 Teipsum et orbem: you yourself and the world. Nosce = 'know' under-stood?

668 therein: (*) *Ovid* standing behind her, his face was seene in the Glasse.

672 Auriga: the constellation, The Waggoner.

The heavenly Goate: the star Capella.

675 Hacdy: Haedi, the kids. A small double star in the hand of The Waggoner.

724 action: (*) Actio cernendi in homine vel animali, vidente collocanda est. *Aristot.* 'The action of seeing must be assigned to a man or animal with the power of sight.' This is perhaps a reference to the problem raised by Aristotle in *De Anima* II. 413b 11, whether each of the faculties is a soul or only a part of one, and if it is only a part whether it can exist separately.

761 Prince of sence: (*) In Cerebro est principium sentiendi, et inde nervi, qui instrumenta sunt motus voluntarii oriuntur: The beginning of perception is in the brain and from there the nerves (or sinews), which are the means of voluntary motion, arise.

   P. Bartlett notes that this is a commonplace of physiology. It is, however, unlikely that it is a quotation from Aristotle.

764 my fate: (*) Natura est unius-cuiusque Fatum, ut *Theophr.* Nature is everyone's fate. A version of Heraclitus *Fragment* 119, ἦθος ἀνθρώπῳ δαίμων: Character is a man's destiny. Alexander of Aphrodisias *De Anima* quotes Theophrastus as saying that what is in accordance with fate is also in accordance with Nature.

789 perfect sence compact: (*) Alterationem pati est sentire: Perception is undergoing change. Cf. Arist. *De Anima* II. 416b 34, δοκεῖ γὰρ ἀλλοίωσίς τις εἶναι: 'For (perception) appears to be a kind of alteration.'

798 inward: (*) He intends the common sence which is *centrum sensibus et speciebus*, and cals it last because it dooth, *sapere in effectione sensuum*: Centre for the senses and appearances: To perceive in the production of sensation. Cf. W. D. Ross, *Aristotle*, pp. 139 ff. on *sensus communis*.

841 the superficiall: thy 1595. em. Bartlett.

901 sounds: (*) Qua ratione fiat Eccho: By which means an Echo is made.

952 Latonas Twinns: Apollo and Diana.

965 Engine: Engines 1595. em. Donno.

Intentio, animi actio: Intention, the action of the mind.

Salmacis and Hermaphroditus

Francis Beaumont (? 1584–1616), the son of a justice of common pleas, was educated at Oxford University and the Inns of Court. About 1607/8 he began collaborating with John Fletcher in writing plays, at first for boys' companies and later for the King's Men. *The Knight of the Burning Pestle*, *Philaster*, *The Maid's Tragedy* and *A King and No King* were the most successful results of their partnership. The poem *Salmacis and Hermaphroditus* was published anonymously in 1602 and was not attributed to Beaumont until reprinted by Lawrence Blaiklocke in 1640. (See C. M. Gayley, *Francis Beaumont, Dramatist*, New York 1914, pp. 39–42.)

The story of Salmacis and Hermaphroditus is told by Ovid in *Meta-morphoses* IV. 285–388. It is probable that the author of this poem had consulted Golding's translation. (See Bush, *Mythology*, pp. 180–3.)

Text. There are two editions of 1602 and 1640. This edition uses the Bodleian copy of 1602 as copy text.

The Author to the Reader.   3 Prodromus: runner before, harbinger.

99 foggy: marshy.

112 The golden shower in which Jupiter visited Danae. Cf. *Hero and Leander* I. 146.

145 Astræa: The goddess of Justice. In the golden age she lived on earth but was driven to heaven by man's impiety and can now be seen as the sign Virgo of the Zodiac. Ovid *Met.* I. 149.

225 uncouth: unusual, strange, grotesque.

303 collogues: conspire, coax, flatter.

472 catch-poles: a sheriff's officer who arrests for debt—hence a term of contempt, a bum-baillie.

501 Pithon: the great serpent sent by Juno to pursue Latona, mother of Apollo and Diana.

580 swarfie: dark, black, dusky. Donno emends to swartie. Cf swarty, l. 316.

596 glimsing: shine, gleam. Cf. *Hero and Leander* II. 320.

757 is: was 1602. em. Donno.

Willobie His Avisa

First published in 1594, the poem is ascribed to Henry Willoby in a prefatory letter written by Hadrian Dorrell, who claims to have been his 'chamber fellow' and to have found it among his papers. A Henry Willobie was at St John's College, Oxford, in 1591 and took his degree in 1595 after an absence. Since Thomas Darell from Brasenose College matriculated with him it has been suggested that they are probably the author and his friend. Certainly this Willoby had a brother, Thomas, and the 1635 edition has an added poem by 'Thomas Willoby Frater Henrici Willoby nuper defuncti'. However, the calling in of the poem by the Privy Council has caused some scholars to think that the author is, like his characters, a transparent allegory. Unfortunately the references do not now seem as clear and satirical as they did in 1599. G. B. Harrison identifies the author as Mathew Roydon and is confident that the initials H. W. and W. S. in the last section of the poem stand for Southampton and Shakespeare. If we could be sure of the identification of the poem's characters we might be more confident about its author. See G. B. Harrison, *Willobie His Avisa*, London 1926; E. K. Chambers, *William Shakespeare* I. 568; E. I. Fripp, *Shakespeare*, I. 372. For its literary importance see C. S. Lewis, *English Literature in the Sixteenth Century Excluding Drama*.

There are four editions extant: 1594, 1605, which says on the title-page
that it is the fourth time corrected and augmented (the other two editions are
believed to have been printed in 1596 and 1599), 1609 and 1635. This edition
uses the British Museum copy of 1594 as copy text. Only the first section of
the poem has been printed.

Canto I

43 Identified by G. B. Harrison as Cerne Abbas in Dorset.
55 reaching: artful, contriving.
60 filed: polished, smooth.
79 (1594 note in margin) Beautie without riches, is as a faire picture without
life.
85 (*) Jealosie breedes envy: Both together breed frenzie yet neither of them
both can prevaile against wandring fancie.
94 (*) A straunge bayte.
118 Identified by G. B. Harrison as the brothers Raleigh.
148 shout: shoot, offspring.
155 (*) A good gift.
189 linke: chain.
193 (*) 2 Chro. 15. 16.
199 (*) Numer. 25.6.
217 saies: attempts.

Canto IV

27 (*) Cornelius Agrippa. (Henricus Cornelius Agrippa, author of *De
Incertitudine et Vanitate Scientiarum et Artium*, 1530, translated into
English 1569, and *De Occulta Philosophia*, 1531.)

Canto VI

31 bane: brave 1594 ⎫ corrected in 1594 and inserted as 'faults escaped'.
33 wane: wave 1954 ⎭

Canto VII

15 feate: seate 1594.

Canto IX

14 can tame: Ev'n he that can mightie Kings tame 1594. corr. 1635.

Canto X

9 haggard Hauke: a wild female hawk caught when already in her adult
plumage—hence, wild, untamed.
10 checkes: a false stoop when the hawk forsakes its proper game.
lure: a bundle of feathers etc. used in training hawks.

44 cauls: a close-fitting cap worn by women.
59 markes: a mark was a coin worth perhaps 13s. 4d.

Canto XI

8 glosing: give a superficial shine to.

Canto XII

2 gill: a girl.

Canto XIII

10 linnes: ceases.

The Complaint of Rosamond

Samuel Daniel (1563?–1619). Born in Somerset, the son—according to Fuller—of a music master, Daniel is entered in the matriculation registers as being at Magdalen Hall, Oxford (now Hertford College), in 1581. In 1586 he was a servant to Lord Stafford the ambassador at Paris, and travelled in Italy with Sir Edward Dymoke. He became tutor to William Herbert, later third Earl of Pembroke, at the family seat of Wilton, near Salisbury, and was thus associated with the literary circle of Sidney's sister, the Countess of Pembroke. In 1591 a pirated edition of Sir Philip Sidney's *Astrophel and Stella* appeared containing twenty-eight of Daniel's sonnets. This piracy was the probable cause of his issue of the first edition of *Delia* in 1592—a volume which also contained *The Complaint of Rosamond*. In 1594 when he issued revised texts of both these works he added the text of his drama *Cleopatra*, which was designed as a companion to the Countess of Pembroke's *Antonius* which was a translation of Robert Garnier's *Marc-Antoine*. In 1595 he published *The First Fowre Bookes of the civile warres betweene the two houses of Lancaster and Yorke*. This work was corrected and continued in 1601 and 1609 but never finally completed. *Musophilus*, a defence of the poetic and contemplative life based on Castiglione's *Courtier*, appeared in 1599 and the verse *Epistles* and the famous treatise *A Defence of Ryme* in 1603. *Philotas*, his second tragedy, produced in 1604, caused some difficulty because of a supposed resemblance between its chief character and the Earl of Essex, and may have been the reason for Daniel's retirement to a farm in Wiltshire. During the years 1604–14, however, he was still writing pastoral plays and masques for the court and in 1612 published the first part of a prose *Historie of England* which was unfinished at his death in 1619.

Daniel's poem was extremely popular and was frequently revised and re-issued. For comparison with other poems published in the 1590's this edition follows the text of the earlier versions. There are two editions of *Delia* and *The Complaint of Rosamond* in 1592. The text of *Rosamond* printed for the *Poetical Essays* of 1599 is sometimes found bound with one of the editions of *Delia* 1592 and this was at one time considered a third edition.

The text of *Rosamond* was revised in all editions after 1592. This edition takes the Bodleian copy of 1592 A as its copy text.

See H. Sellers, *Bibliography of the works of Samuel Daniel*, Oxford Bibliographical Society 1927, and A. C. Sprague (ed.), *Poems and a Defence of Ryme*, Harvard 1930, for a full discussion of the text and variants.

The story of Henry and Rosamond occurs in the chronicles from the fourteenth century on. Robert Fabyan's *Chronicles* 1516 contains the first English account of Rosamond's murder by Eleanor. Holinshed and Stow have variants of the story and Daniel provides some details of his own such as the character of the matron and the elaborate mythological description of the casket. See Tillotson and Newdigate, Vol. V of J. W. Hebel's *Works of Michael Drayton*, Shakespeare Head Press 1961, pp. 102 ff., and J. Rees, *Samuel Daniel*, Liverpool 1964.

4 kinde: nature.
13 that: the 1592 B.
43 deygne: deynge 1592 A.
124 diapason: octave, or the whole range of an instrument.
154 that: which 1592 B.
161 hath: had 1592 B.
167 chastity: chastitiy 1592 A.
287 sees: see 1592 B.
298 when heate: when the heate 1592 A and B. 'the' omitted in all subsequent editions.
306 party: one side in a contest.
311 even in 1592 B: in 1592 A.
314 gan 1594 and subsequent editions: can 1592 A and B.
365 traind: drawn, dragged.
378 Amymone: one of the daughters of Danaus.
397 eyes: omitted 1592 A.
424 had I not: had I had not 1592 A.
441 to come: to co come 1592 A.
493 Argus: Argos 1592 A.
519 Witnes: Witnest 1592 A.
520 wondrous: wonrdous 1592 A.
542 She's: Sh's 1592 A.
595 The revision of 1594 adds three stanzas after this line.
602 The revision of 1594 adds twenty stanzas after this line.
606 th'ensigne: thc'nsigne 1592 A.
716 re-edified: reedified 1592 A.
720 renewd, my fame (1594 and subsequent editions): renewd by fame 1592 A and B.

Englands Heroicall Epistles

Michael Drayton (1563–1631), the son of a tanner, was born at Hartshill in Warwickshire. He became a page in the service of Sir Henry Goodere of Polesworth Hall and there, as he tells Henry Reynolds in a poem on *Poets and Poesie* (1627), he resolved, at the age of ten, to be a poet. On his death Sir Henry 'bequeathed' Drayton to Lucy Harington, Countess of Bedford. The sonnet sequence *Idea*, perhaps his first work as a poet, mirrors his love for Anne Goodere, younger daughter of Sir Henry, who married Sir Henry Rainsford of Clifford Chambers shortly after her father's death. Drayton's devotion lasted his life and its quality made him a welcome guest at Clifford Chambers. *Idea* and *Ideas Mirrour* were followed in 1595 by Drayton's Ovidian poem *Endymion and Phoebe*. But already, by 1594, Drayton had started to write a series of narrative tragedies on English history and was to remain deeply committed to this subject for the rest of his poetic career. *Peirs Gaveston, Matilda* (1594) and *Robert, Duke of Normandy* (1596) were followed by *Mortimeriados* (1596) which reappeared in 1603 revised and in a different metre as *The Barons' Wars*. *Englands Heroicall Epistles* were published in 1597 and the massive poem *Poly-Olbion* appeared in two sections in 1613 and 1622. At the end of his life he returned to, and developed, his earlier style of poetry in *Nymphidia* (1627) and *The Muses Elizium* (1631).

The form of his poem Drayton takes from Ovid's *Heroides* and his information on English history must have come from much the same sources as Daniel's in *The Complaint of Rosamond*. Giraldus Cambrensis is the first to mention Rosamond and later tellers add the details of the maze and the poisoning.

First published in 1597, this was much the most popular of Drayton's poems and other editions containing additions and revisions were published in 1598, 1599, 1600, 1602, 1603 (with *The Barons' Wars*) and in various collected editions of Drayton's poetry. Again, as in the case of Daniel, this edition follows the first edition for purposes of comparison with other poems of the 1590's. The copy text is the Bodleian copy of 1597. For a full account of later variants see Tillotson and Newdigate, Vol. V of J. W. Hebel's *Works of Michael Drayton*, Shakespeare Head Press 1961.

Drayton's own *Notes of the Chronicle historie* are given first.

Notes of the Chronicle historie:

> Well knewest thou what a monster I would bee,
> When thou didst builde this Labyrinth for mee.

In the *Cretean* Labyrinth a monster was inclosed, called a *Minotaur*, the history wherof is well knowne, but the Labyrinth was framed by *Daedalus*, with so many intricate waies, yt being entred, one could either hardly or never return, being in maner of a maze, save that it was larger, the waies being walld in on evry side, out of the which *Theseus* by *Ariadnes* help (lending him a clue of thred) escaped. Some report that it was a house, having one halfe beneath the ground, another above, the chamber doores therein so deceitfully enwrapped, and made to open so many sundry wayes, that it was held a matter almost impossible to returne.

Some have held it to have been an Allegorie of mans life, true it is, that the comparison will hold, for what liker to a Labyrinth then the maze of life? But it is affirmed by antiquitie that there was indeede such a building, though *Dædalus* beeing a name applied to the workmans excellencie, made it suspected; for *Dædalus* is nothing els but ingenious, or artificiall. Heereupon it is used among the auncient Poets for anything curiously wrought.

Rosamonds Labyrinth, whose ruins together with her well being paved with square stone in the bottom, and also her towre from which the Labyrinth did run, (are yet remaining,) was altogether under ground, being vaults arched and waled with brick and stone, almost inextricably wound one within another, by which if at any time her lodging were layd about by the Queene, she might easily avoyde perrill imminent, and if neede be, by secrete issues take the ayre abroad, many furlongs round about Wodstocke in Oxfordshire, wherein it was situated. Thus much for *Rosamonds* Labyrinth.

> Whose strange Mæanders turned every way.

Mæander is a river in *Lycia*, a Province of *Natolia* or *Asia minor*, famous for the sinuositie and often turning thereof, rising from certaine hills in *Mæonia*, heereupon are intricate turnings by a transsumptive and Metonimicall kind of speech, called *Mæanders*, for this river did so strangely path it selfe, that the foote seemed to touch the head.

> Rose of the world, so dooth import my name,
> Shame of the world my life hath made the same.

It might be reported, how at *Godstow* where this Rose of the world was sumptuously interred, a certaine Bishop in the visitation of his diocese, caused the monument which had been erected to her honour, utterly to be demolished, but be that severe chastisement of *Rosamond* then dead, at this time also overpassed, least she should seeme to be the *Shame of the world*.

> Am I at home pursued with private hate,
> And warre comes raging to my Pallace gate?

Robert Earle of Leicester, who tooke part with young king *Henry*, entred into England with an Army of 3. thousand Flemmings, and spoyled the Countryes of Norfolke and Suffolke, beeing succoured by many of the Kings **private** enemies.

> And am I branded with the curse of Roome?

King *Henry* the second, the first *Plantaginet*, accused for the death of *Thomas Becket*, Archbishop of Canterbury, slaine in the Cathedrall Church, was accursed by Pope *Alexander*, although he urgd sufficient proofe of his innocencie in the same, and offered to take upon him any pennance, so he might escape the curse and interdiction of the Realme.

> And by the pride of my rebellious sonne,
> Rich Normandie with Armies over-runne.

Henry the young King, whom King *Henry* had caused to bee crowned in his life, (as he hoped) both for his owne good and the good of his subjects, which indeede turned to his owne sorrowe, and the trouble of the whole Realme, for he rebelled against him, and raysing a power, by the meanes of *Lewes* King of Fraunce, and *William* King of Scots who tooke part with him, invaded Normandie.

> Unkind my children, most unkind my wife.

Never King more infortunate then King *Henry* in the disobedience of his chyldren; first *Henry*, then *Geffery*, then *Richard*, then *John*, all at one time or other, first or last, unnaturally rebelled against him; then the jealousie of *Ellinor* his Queene, who suspected his love to *Rosamond*: which greevous troubles, the devout of those times, attrybuted to happen unto him justly, for refusing to take upon him the government of Jerusalem, offered unto him by the Patriarck there, which Countrey was mightily afflicted by the Souldane.

> Which onely Vahan thou and I doe know.

This *Vahan* was a Knight whom the King exceedingly loved, who kept the Pallace at Woodstocke, and much of the Kinges jewels and treasure, to whom the King committed many of his secrets, and in whom hee reposed such trust, that hee durst commit his love into his charge.

Rosamond to Henry

111 distaine: staine.
115 slade: plain or valley.
121 gin: trap.

Henry to Rosamond

 88 simples: herbs.
134 date: end, termination.

Christs Victorie and Triumph

Giles Fletcher (? 1585–1623), the son of Giles Fletcher, Member of Parliament and diplomat, belonged to a poetic family. Phineas Fletcher, his eldcr brother, was also a poet and later the author of *Venus and Anchises* and *The Purple Island*, while the dramatist, John Fletcher, was their cousin. Giles was a scholar of Trinity College, Cambridge, and took his B.A. in 1606. He was made a fellow of the college and became successively reader in Greek grammar and Greek language before accepting a living from Bacon in 1617. He later exchanged this for another living in Bacon's gift, the rectory of Alderton in Suffolk, where he spent the rest of his life.

The Bible and Spenser are the chief sources for this poem, but Fletcher had clearly read widely in Ovidian poetry. See H. M. Belden, 'Alanus de Insulis, Giles Fletcher and the Mutabilitie Cantos', *S.P.* xxvi 1929.

The poem was first published in 1610 and reprinted for editions in 1632 and 1640. This edition uses the British Museum copy of 1610 as copy text. F. S. Boas, *Giles and Phineas Fletcher, Poetical Works*, Cambridge 1908, gives a full list of variants.

I.6.5 s'ed: said.

I.9.5 Eous: one of the horses of the Sun.

I.10.8 scoals: scales.

I.24.5 orizall: ? perhaps a form of o'er-risal, an uprising or rebellion against God. See *O.E.D.* over-risen.

I.28.7 wayne: waggon.

I.34.2 Dathan: one of the leaders of a revolt against Moses. Num. 16. 1.

I.34.6 the five proud Kings: the five Kings of the Amorites. Jos. 10. 5.

I.40.2 imbranded: to arm with brands or swords.

I.43.6 file: make smooth.

I.46.7 belgards: kind looks.

I.47.1 discolour'd: many-coloured.

I.47.7 Syrinx: a nymph pursued by Pan and metamorphosed into a reed from which he made his pipes.

I.52.6 vive: living.

I.61.6 mainc: strong.

I.69.4 Eirene: $\varepsilon\grave{\iota}\varrho\acute{\eta}\nu\eta$, peace.

I.78.6 earth: earrh 1610.

II.4.2 congies: bow, salutation.

II.19.1 mote: might.

II.24.2 elonging: to retard, delay.

II.28.5 craples: form of grapples.

II.32.2 Eüélpis: $\varepsilon\ddot{v}\varepsilon\lambda\pi\iota\varsigma$, good-hope.

II.34.1 seel'd: close up.

II.44.6 prim: privet.

II.50.6 Lyæus: a surname of Bacchus, from $\lambda\acute{v}\varepsilon\iota\nu$, to loose: wine loosens the tongue or frees the mind.

II.56.8 virges: a rod or wand of office.

II.59.3 rowe: roll.

III.1.1 Eridan: the river Po.

III.2.7 sallowie: sallow-withe, a willow.

III.9.3 asself: to take to onself, appropriate.

III.9.8 saine: said

III.12.1 punctualls: a minute point, a subtlety.

III.12.2 diss: abbreviation for Latin *disputabilis*, proper for disputation.

III.12.4 wiss: know.

III.19.1 incautelous: unwary.

III.21.3 Dires: Dire sisters, the Furies.

III.21.8 heyres: heirs.

III.28.3 virges: cf. II.56.8.

III.50.7 kixe: hemlock.

III.59.4 debellished: disfigure.

IV.3.5 Corylets: a hazel copse.

IV.11.8 heried: praised.

IV.20.7 discoasted: removed, distant.

IV.22 A compliment to James I for keeping England at peace.

IV.24.4 Harries: Prince Henry, who later died before James.

IV.28.3 Depur'd: cleansed, purified.

IV.41.1 lustre: a shining body.

IV.42.7 Beaw-peers: compeers, also used of a spiritual father in the church.

IV.48.1 Egliset: Eaglet.

IV.49 A reference to his brother Phineas and his poem *The Purple Island* where Thyrsil, a shepherd, praises *Eclecta* the daughter of will and reason and the chosen bride of Christ.